THE ESSENTIAL BRECHT

University of Southern California
Studies in Comparative Literature

VOLUME IV

THE ESSENTIAL BRECHT

by John Fuegi

HENNESSEY & INGALLS, INC.
LOS ANGELES   1972

For Penelope

CONTENTS

ILLUSTRATIONS

ACKNOWLEDGMENTS

With the material help of the Fulbright Commission in Germany and the Germanistic Society of America, I was able to spend two years in Berlin, studying the original materials upon which this book is based. My work at the Berliner Ensemble and at the Brecht-Archive in East Berlin was considerably helped by the cooperation of the late Helene Weigel (Brecht's widow), Fräulein Kiel at the Brecht-Archive, Elisabeth Hauptmann, Werner Hecht, and Benno Besson.

Upon my return from East Berlin, my work has been helped beyond measure by those who have been kind enough to read my manuscript at various stages of completion. Reinhold Grimm, Eric Bentley, Guy Stern, Edward Harris, Carl Baumann, Leroy Shaw, and John Spalek have all helped me avoid many errors both of fact and of interpretation. R.D. Peoples and Barbara Correll read, corrected, and copy-edited the final text. Needless to say, I alone am responsible for those errors which remain.

A more general debt is due to Charles Hoffmann of the Ohio State University. It was under his expert tutelage that I first became involved in the serious study of Brecht. With Professor Hoffmann, though in a somewhat different form, much of the matter with which I deal in chapter seven has been published separately in the *Festschrift für Detlev Schumann* (Munich, 1970).

My colleague Corliss Phillabaum's expertise in theater in general and the staging of Brecht in particular has been extraordinarily useful to me. He has also been kind enough to allow me to use his extensive slide collection in order to select the illustrations which buttress my interpretation of Brecht at crucial points. Further assistance with illustrations was provided by Helene Weigel and Percy Paukschta at the Berliner Ensemble; Brecht's former collaborator Gerda Goedhart; Dr. Frank Tornquist, attorney for the Caspar Neher estate; and Mr. T.V. Montgomery.

Dr. Siegfried Unseld of the Suhrkamp Verlag has kindly allowed me to quote extensively from Brecht's published work. I am also indebted to the *Modern Language Journal* and *Brecht Heute/Brecht Today*, where portions of chapter three and chapter eight, respectively, have previously appeared.

A rough-draft of all German translations in the text was done by Mr. Peter Brunner, but the final versions of the translations are my own. Mr. Douglass Peoples provided assistance with the index.

Finally, I would like to express my particular thanks to David Malone and John Spalek. Without their encouragement, this book would not have been written.

If the critics would view my theater as spectators do, without first emphasizing my theories, then what they would see would be simply theater, I hope, of imagination, fun, and intelligence.

Bertolt Brecht

INTRODUCTION

There were so many Bertolt Brechts that the student is hard-pressed to know where to begin and which Brecht to take seriously when. Should we listen to the young Brecht who damned virtually everyone except a few other iconoclasts such as G.B. Shaw and Frank Wedekind?[1] Or should we listen instead to the older man who saw much to be praised in even such men as the Greek playwrights, Shakespeare,[2] and those princes of the middle-class German aesthetic, Friedrich Schiller and Johann Wolfgang von Goethe?[3] In terms of dramatic theory, what credence should be given to the specifically anti-dramatic and rabidly anti-Aristotelian Brecht of the notes to the *Mahagonny* opera (1930)?[4] If we once decipher from the *Mahagonny* notes what "anti-Aristotelian" actually means to the young Brecht, what are we then to make of the Brecht of the *Short Organum for the Theatre* (1948),[5] who sheepishly returns to some of the central principles of the *Poetics*? In view of Brecht's bewildering changes in theory and practice, what, if anything, do crucial terms such as *Verfremdung* and "epic theater" mean?

When we turn to the plays of Brecht, the critical confusion engendered and fostered by his theories is immediately compounded. We have to ask ourselves, for instance, do the early theories in any way illuminate the later plays? Or conversely, do the later plays negate large sections of the early theory? Can one descriptive term (even one as protean as "epic") begin to describe the rich variety of constructs of Brecht's four major creative periods: the pre-Marxist or largely apolitical period (c. 1918-1928),[6] the staunchly pro-Marxist period (c. 1928-1938), the period of aesthetic and political complexity when Brecht "changed countries more often than his shoes" (c. 1938-1948), and finally, the last years of his life (1948-1956), years spent mainly in East Berlin and devoted more to the staging of the plays written while in exile than to the writing of new ones? Is there in fact very much in common among the asocial *Jungle of Cities, Drums in the Night, Baal,* Brecht's adaptation of Marlowe's *Edward the Second,* and the often austere, doctrinaire "didactic plays" of the pro-Marxist period? Or, going further, can we comfortably group the didactic plays with the richly ambiguous constructs of the exile period? Difficult as these problems are at a basic textual level (compounded further by the fact that we have reliable texts for almost none of Brecht's plays), we have seen very little of complexity and potential confusion until we allow Brecht the great producer-director to add his views. The resulting clash of opinions, as all these Brechts shout one another down, must strike the learned and the not-so-learned student as a deafening cacophony rather than the clear call for reason that we hear so often from at least one of these Brechts.

Yet beyond the confusion of often conflicting theories and varied theatrical practice, there remains the historical fact that, by some subtle alchemy, Brecht regularly fused in his plays and in his productions of those plays all the different facets of his being to create dramatic events of such searing intensity that they have some claim to be seen as the most important plays and productions of the twentieth-century stage. It would seem vital, therefore, despite the uproar, to simultaneously examine Bertolt Brecht as drama theorist, as playwright, and as producer-director. Perhaps, if we closely examine a number of his major plays in performance, we shall begin to see his creative work as aesthetic wholes. I propose that we follow Brecht into the labyrinth of his own creative imagination where production, play, and theory bewilderingly intertwine.

As Brecht wrote so many plays (over forty are given in the most recent edition of his collected works), I have chosen to examine only a representative collection of his best work. The eight play-productions I examine include both his first and last major efforts as playwright-director: the 1924 Munich production of his adaptation of Marlowe's *Edward the Second* and the 1956 Berliner Ensemble version of *Galileo* which was in rehearsal at the time of Brecht's death. Of the other six plays, only one, Brecht's adaptation of Gorki's *Mother*, is drawn from the period c. 1926-1936, although this is the period when Brecht's "epic" theory and practice came closest to conforming one to the other. My reasons for this are twofold. First, this period is distinguished more by Brecht's operas than by his plays, and because my own knowledge of the music of the period is slight, I feel that I cannot do them justice at this time. Second, I have tried to avoid overstating my anti-epic reading of Brecht.

As a comparatist, my choice of a number of Brecht's *Bearbeitungen* or adaptations of texts by earlier writers has considerable methodological significance. Brecht, like Shakespeare,[7] seems to have usually worked best when he could use an already existent text to be shaped by his own dramatic imagination. Such texts allow us to see with relative ease what it is about them that we can label specifically Brechtian and, further, how Brecht relates directly to the tradition upon which he so frequently draws. In making such examinations I have consistently tried to remember René Wellek and Austin Warren's dictum that "borrowed materials" in a new aesthetic construct may only distantly relate to their function in the original. In other words, to prove that Brecht borrowed this or that from here or there is not enough. As I shall try to show, a reading of Brecht's sources often accounts no more for the power and the beauty of his plays than a reading of Holinshed or of North accounts for the power and the poetry of Shakespeare's work.

Rather than attempting either a biography[8] of Brecht or a normative poetics in a book devoted primarily to an examination of some of the best drama the twentieth century has yet produced, I have introduced biography and genre theory only where they are directly germane to an understanding of what Brecht was *doing* and *saying* at different times in his life. As a help to the non-specialist, I have included in various appendices the main facts that we do know of Brecht's life, a short glossary of German and English literary and theatrical terms, and a selected bibliography for each play and production examined in my text. With these aids, plus concrete comparisons of major classical and modern examples of the epic and dramatic forms, it is my hope that we need not trip too often over terms that seem consistently to defy viable abstract definition. I shall therefore usually use the complicated and often self-contradictory term "epic" as Brecht defined it in the twenties and the early thirties.

Those English readers unfamiliar with the books that have been written in many languages on each of the Bertolt Brechts that I examine should be warned that what I say about Brecht in this book is rather different from much of what has been written on Brecht heretofore. Though a number of critics have questioned the general applicability of Brecht's theories to some of the plays, such criticism remains the exception rather than the rule. In the main, Brecht critics have contented themselves with showing the extent to which the plays do reflect "epic" theory. This is, I must stress, a valuable service and without it my own book would have been premature. The best argument for seeing the plays as examples of *episches Theater* and *Verfremdung* is that of Reinhold Grimm in his *Bertolt Brecht: die Struktur seines Werkes,* which is unfortunately unavailable in English translation. The German reader with a taste for dialectic might profit from a close reading of both my own argument and that of Professor Grimm. Our approaches are, I believe, more complementary than antithetical. Where Grimm examines primarily those elements that tend to fragment the action in Brecht's plays, my own concern is primarily with the devices he uses to tie his plays together. Out of the dialectic of the two approaches may come a deeper understanding of the plays themselves.

Before going on to the plays, I would like once again to direct the English reader's attention to the appended glossary and at least two crucial terms defined there. Of particular concern to any student of Brecht are the terms *Verfremdung* and *episches Theater*. According to my interpretation, and this must be stressed at once, the current English translation of *Verfremdung* as "alienation" is, at best, only half correct. In my view, depending on the context, the term can mean either "alienation" (or distancing) or "attraction" or "fascination." I have found no single English word that captures the fine duality of the German term. The closest we can come in English perhaps is to cumbersomely paraphrase Wordsworth's *Preface to the Lyrical Ballads* and say that what Brecht seems to have wanted to achieve was to "render the strange familiar and the familiar strange."[9] Except, therefore, where it is clear from the context that Brecht actually does mean "alienation" when he uses the term *Verfremdung*, I have kept the richly ambiguous German.

"Epic" poses, at least for the English reader, as many difficulties as *Verfremdung*. Probably we should discontinue usage of the term "epic" in English in reference to Brecht's plays. John Willett seems to suggest just this when he notes: "The high sounding term of the 1920s has been made to embrace any kind of play that Brecht wrote—taut or loose, realistic or fantastic, didactic or amusing—and some quite ephemeral mannerisms as well."[10] As John Willett hints here, we tend no longer to approach Brecht's plays as plays but to approach them only as objects to be fitted to the procrustean bed of the early theoretical writings. When we see or read a Brecht play now, whether it was written in 1920 or in 1950, we tend to outdo one another in finding the ways in which Brecht has (supposedly following his own "epic theory") fragmented the action of the play and has thwarted at every turn audience identification. Virtually nothing has been written on the question of whether fragmentation of action does in fact inhibit audience identification. Very little has been done to question Brecht's early hypothesis that the "epic" form necessarily produces cooler responses than material offered in "dramatic" form. The devices that tie Brecht's plays together and that arouse emotional responses have remained largely unnoticed and unstudied. Since these devices do not belong in "epic theater," we go to enormous lengths to avoid seeing them when they crop up.

As a radical expedient this book attempts an opposite approach. Instead of indiscriminately applying the "epic" theory of the late 1920s and early 1930s to all Brecht's plays, I suggest something very simple. When Brecht had no theory (his very earliest period) his plays fit no theory. When he later developed an explicit theory, his plays tended to fit his theoretical pronouncements of that period. For plays written after the mid-thirties I would suggest a reading of *The Messingkauf Dialogues*[11] (written c. 1939-1942) and the shorter version of the same, the semi-Aristotelian *Short Organum for the Theatre*[12] (written in Switzerland in 1948). By the time he wrote these later notes on theater he had completed all of his major plays and was attempting to formulate a theory that would describe them. Brecht recognized that to do this the troublesome and inappropriate term "epic theater" would have (albeit reluctantly) to be dropped.[13] I take this last theoretical testament of Brecht very seriously indeed. I suggest that we should begin to read the plays of Brecht as we read the work of Shakespeare or of Goethe. Brecht, like his great forerunners, wrote at different times of his life very differently shaped plays. Let us look closely at some of them.

CHAPTER ONE

THE RISE AND FALL OF THE EPIC THEATER

"Art is Shit."   *Piscator, 1918-1919*[1]

"The sooner everyone realizes that ART IS $HIT the better."
Jean-Jacques Lebel, 1968[2]

In 1920, the brash twenty-two-year-old student of drama and ostensibly of medicine, *Eugen* Berthold Friedrich Brecht (so reads his birth certificate), son of a middle-class father (the director of a local paper factory), wrote stridently of the typical middle-class theater of the typical southern German town of Augsburg, the town of his birth:

> Even the most indulgent opportunists would not have the gall to claim that the Augsburg City Theater contributes to culture—not even at Augsburg's level. Without a doubt it isn't

Author's Note: The title of this chapter is taken from the general thesis presented by Eduard Kopetzki in his Vienna dissertation of 1949, "Das dramatische Werk Bertolt Brechts nach seiner Theorie vom epischen Theater." According to Kopetzki, and I agree in the main with his observations, there is a visible rise and fall in Brecht's use of "epic" elements in his plays. The high point comes in the late twenties and the first half of the thirties and sinks steadily thereafter.

worth the money the city spends on it. This theater, directed
by a businessman, a former provincial actor on whom anything
of intellectual elevation is lost, with his miserable system of
dodging and hedging, his subterfuges, has proved the stupidity
of the local audience and in all these years has not even
managed to fulfill those duties of a city-supported theater
which are taken for granted.[3]

Two weeks later (his reference to kitsch and to Munich showing
that his strictures against theater in Augsburg could be applied
with equal force to much of the theater of the southern theater
capital, Munich), Brecht writes of another Augsburg production: "The staging of *Everyman,* even including the Bengal-
kitsch-style ending, leans heavily on the production of the
National Theater of Munich."[4] From these and other even more
vitriolic comments of the young reviewer, it is only possible to
draw a picture of German theater (and, by extension, of
international efforts), both provincial and big city, as being
rotten to the core. Plays, acting, directing, and even the
audience are all damned; all stand in need of the most drastic
reform.

An objective view of German, general European, and
American theater in the twenties bears out Brecht's contention
that much was wrong. But the objective viewer must also note
that much was also right and that the embattled and perhaps
deliberately non-objective young iconoclast was, in his cooler
moments, well aware of this latter fact. Had there not already
been people in prominent places in the international world of
the theater, people receptive to bright, highly innovational
young iconoclasts, sheer talent would not have been enough to
catapult this obnoxious, smelly, but brilliant young man to
national fame by the time he was but twenty-four and to
international fame shortly thereafter.[5] Brecht did not achieve
his success by attacking the whole of the contemporary theater
(though at times he did get carried away and indiscriminately
attack everyone); he made his career by exploiting an enormous
talent for self-publicity. On the one hand he publicly attacked
conservatives and "former provincial actors" who now essayed

to be producer-directors. On the other (as we know particularly from Arnolt Bronnen's diary notes from the early twenties), Brecht went to extraordinary lengths to meet and charm the leading members of the German theatrical avant-garde. He began at once to enlist the help of men such as the great Munich comic and cabaret artist, Valentin; the novelist and dramatist, Feuchtwanger; the great Berlin directors, Reinhardt and Piscator; and his greatest champion, the highly influential theater critic of a major Berlin newspaper, Herbert Ihering.

With too narrow a focus on Brecht, it is easy to see him as the one bright spot in utter darkness and to imagine him as he himself at times imagined himself—the Messiah come to save the modern theater. If Brecht was in fact a Messiah, we must in the interests of both fairness and historical accuracy remember that he had a host of John the Baptists preparing the way for him.[6] In the closing years of the nineteenth century and the early years of the twentieth many people (now almost forgotten) worked out theatrical innovations that later became associated with Brecht's name. The more we learn of this period, the clearer it becomes that many of the things we have previously assumed were originated by Brecht[7] are in fact either borrowings from other avant-garde artists of the period or are revivals of such musty forms as the medieval or the Jesuit theater or of exotic forms such as the various types of classical oriental theater. Seen in this light, Brecht's unbridled attacks on German theater in particular and international theater in general are simply an echo of something that the avant-garde had been shouting for decades. The crucial difference historically is one of manner rather than matter; when Brecht shouted, he shouted in such a way that he could not be ignored. There can be little doubt that Brecht's magnificent poetry and plays would be far less known than they now are (and deservedly) had their author not possessed an almost infinite capacity for shocking the bourgeoisie and demanding thereby the attention of the bourgeois press. Brecht, unshaven and unwashed, with his leather jacket, silk shirt, proletarian cap, and his cigar, caused headlines with his deliberately provocative stance. One simply could not ignore Brecht's presence. Then, as now, you either loved him or you hated him. Either way, with his flair for the dramatic, he made headlines.

When Brecht came to Berlin to work "permanently" in 1924, his first job was with Max Reinhardt, the internationally famous producer of mammoth spectacles. As a dramaturg at Reinhardt's theater, Brecht must have seen Reinhardt's 1924 staging of Pirandello's *Six Characters in Search of an Author.* This production lasted through two seasons and may (as Willett notes[8]) have given Brecht his first view of a play in which characters, in a certain sense, step out of their roles and view them critically. The importance of Pirandello's innovation to Brecht's later theory of *Verfremdung* cannot be overlooked.

While Brecht was ostensibly working for Reinhardt, we know that he actually spent most of his time elsewhere. Part of his time was spent studying the work of the second of the triumvirate of great directors who dominated Berlin theater life in this era, Leopold Jessner. It is more likely than not that Brecht, who visited Berlin for a long period in late 1921 and early 1922, took back to Munich with him something of Jessner's deliberately anti-heroic approach to the classics and applied this lesson to his own provocatively "shabby" 1924 production of *Eduard II.* Brecht himself acknowledges his indebtedness to Jessner's use of three-dimensional lighting effects, but there was another side to Jessner's work that was more important to Brecht than this specific technical detail. Jessner's productions of German and English classics (particularly Shakespeare) were distinguished not only by the famous Jessner staircases (a prominent feature of almost all of his productions of this period) but by his deliberate stripping of his texts of the "monumental grandeur" with which the classics were usually produced at this time in Germany. According to the Berlin theater manager, Ernst Josef Aufricht (later to become famous for opening the Theater am Schiffbauerdamm with Brecht's *Threepenny Opera*), it was Jessner with his contemporary productions of the classics who, after 1918, got rid of the "plaster monument style" beloved by the Kaiser Wilhelm and the old German court theaters.

From Brecht's own writings and from Piscator's enormously important *The Political Theater,*[9] we know that Brecht learned most from the third great Berlin director of this period, the pre-eminently political Erwin Piscator. Brecht himself notes: "I took part in all of his [Piscator's] experiments."[10] At another point Brecht adds: "More than anything else, the involvement of the theater in politics was Piscator's contribution. Without this involvement the theater of the playwright [Brecht] is scarcely imaginable."[11] This particular "innovation" of Piscator (probably derived from both Shaw[12] in England and post-revolutionary experiments in Russia[13]) is, however, but one side of Piscator's activity. There is another side to the early Piscator that the early Brecht might have found very attractive indeed. Like Brecht, before becoming involved in exerting an influence on politics through the medium of theater, Piscator was himself an aesthetic nihilist.

After Piscator's return from the trenches of World War I with a first-hand view of the stupidity of that cataclysm, he turned away from "establishment" politics and from politics' subservient handmaiden, Art. He rejected, as did most of the intellectual, aesthetic elite, including, of course, Brecht, everything connected with the old and discredited Establishment. Art (with a capital "A"), in all its forms, had clearly been a part of that establishment and went into intellectual exile as surely as the Kaiser Wilhelm with his withered arm and withered hopes. The political nihilism of the last war years and the bitter, cold, and hungry years immediately following had direct aesthetic repercussions. An enormous wave of "anti-artists," labelling themselves Dadaists, Futurists, etc., ridiculed and denounced any art form that did not permit, indeed demand, "unlimited artistic anarchy." The theorists of the new movement, subsumed under many different names and spreading from Vladivostok to London,[14] wondered aloud with Brecht's friend the

artist, George Grosz: "Perhaps art is completely finished."[15]
Piscator commanded: "Away from art, an end to it!"[16]
Gradually, as the years passed, instead of "Art," "Loftiness,"
and "Emotion," the key words were to become "freezing,"
"cooling off," "logic."[17] As they moved from nihilism to
"logic," some of the erstwhile Dadaists began to place their
new, cool, documentary, epic, objective, anti-bourgeois, anti-
Art "art" "in the service of politics."[18] All the watchwords of
this broad movement of the arts, as they move toward putting
their art at the service of the "new left," anticipate the young
Brecht. It is absolutely clear that when Brecht (in 1927) asks
the standard rhetorical question of the aesthetic nihilists,
"Should we not destroy aesthetics?"[19] and buries his nose
instead in the communist classics, he reveals an across-the-board
affinity with what had for several years been the dominant
interests of the pan-European avant-garde. Sociology and
economics á la Marx are now the watchwords, and the slogan
"Art is Shit" might be given as the suitably provocative
watchword of the whole movement.

Within the anti-Art world of the Dadaists certain "new"
terms, terms borrowed in fact from the old aesthetics and given
a new twist by their new context, begin to appear. One such
"new" term that was to become important in Brecht's theory
and practice was "episches Theater"[20] (epic theater). Piscator,
perhaps working from memory rather than checking the
published text, speaks of the subtitle of Alfons Paquet's play,
Fahnen (produced by Piscator in 1924), as "Ein episches
Drama" (an epic drama). The actual subtitle used by Paquet (as
Reinhold Grimm has pointed out to me), though closely related
to Brecht's term, was in fact: "Ein dramatischer Roman" (a
dramatic novel), a term used several years earlier by Lion
Feuchtwanger. Helge Hultberg writes of Piscator's use of the
term "episches Drama" in this period: "We are not dealing here
with genre description; 'epic' merely indicates the political-
documentary, the tendentious, the anti-artistic."[21] Hultberg's
view is backed up by a comment of Piscator's and Brecht's

co-worker, Leo Lania, on Piscator's production of the Paquet play. Ignoring completely the selection process that enabled Paquet to reduce the Chicago anarchist show trial to manageable and stageable proportions, Lania claims that Paquet "intentionally did without every artistic form, and limited himself to letting naked truth speak for itself."[22] Alfred Döblin, another friend of Brecht's and a man who often referred to himself as an *Epiker,* more accurately sums up Paquet's achievement when he writes: "Paquet intentionally dramatized the anarchist's rebellion in Chicago in such a manner that the resulting product stood at a point between drama and reporting."[23] With this remark, Döblin summarizes two key features of "Epik" theory and practice in Germany in the 1920s; "The naked facts" that Lania saw in *Fahnen (Flags)* are to be dramatized only to the point of making them mountable on a stage. During this process the "raw" materials should remain as raw as possible; they should not smack at all of Art, of selection and organization, but should retain the power and (hopefully) the force of the revolutionary Russian "documentaries" such as *Potemkin,* then being shown in Germany.[24] In this new theater, the facts of the world out there were to remain more important than the aesthetic organization of those facts. It is surely significant that in this early, formative period of the "new" aesthetic vocabulary, Piscator employs the term "epic" as a synonym for "political."[25] Fighting one of the perennial battles of art and art criticism, Piscator demands in essence that the "lies" of "Art" be replaced by the "true" world of facts. The world out there will be brought into the theater in all its "epic breadth and fullness" and will be allowed to tell its own story; this story, rather obviously, will have profound political implications.

Brecht's own use of the term "epic theater" and, occasionally, "epic drama," shares in the 1920s and the very early 1930s[26] Piscator's concern with rawness, with facts, with bringing the whole world into the theater in order to give the public lessons on political and economic questions of the day.

For Brecht also, facts are not to be "dramatized" or "theatrical-ized," they are to be allowed to speak for themselves, to address the audience directly, to narrate their own complex history and fate without an artist standing between them and the public and polishing these "raw" materials beyond recognition. As Brecht was himself fully aware, this concern of his and of his generation linked him closely with the torrent of facts of the realists and Naturalists[2][7] of the previous century. Brecht notes: "The Naturalists (Ibsen, Hauptmann) tried to bring the new material of the novel to the stage but found no other form than specifically that used by the novel: the epic."[2][8] After con-ceding apparently that the dramatic form of the Naturalist works of Ibsen and Hauptmann was in fact "epic," Brecht goes on: "When they [Ibsen, Hauptmann] were accused of being undramatic, they immediately dropped both this form and these materials. The advance came to a standstill. Seemingly it was an advance into new areas of material; in reality it was an advance toward the epic form."[2][9] What Brecht seems to yearn for here is essentially a return to the *Form* and to the content (*Stoff*) that critics of Naturalist drama had insisted could be more properly handled in the nineteenth- and twentieth-century epic form, the novel. Instead, therefore, of either inventing a new form, or using an available new epic form, the film, Brecht would seem here to openly acknowledge and clearly advocate a return to an old form that had improperly fallen into disuse.

Brecht's frequent use of the term "Form" points up a crucial difference between his own theater practice and that of Piscator. Gradually, for Brecht, the formless world out there that he theoretically welcomed to the theater, begins to take shape and form through the pressures of the dramatic medium itself. Gradually, and perhaps unbeknownst to himself, the late artist shifts away from the earlier theorist and comes eventually to write and mount those highly organized aesthetic forms that are the plays of his major creative period. At the same time, Piscator, consciously true to his raw, formless notions of *Stoff* (content of material) continues to mount mammoth spectacles having considerable value as political spectacles or happenings but having no viable aesthetic form beyond the productions themselves. Meanwhile Brecht, forced in part by exile and lack of proper staging facilities, concentrates more and more on a search for aesthetic forms that would give meaning to the raw and formless "world out there."

Again and again the word "Form" crops up in Brecht's statements of those early years. Always it is linked to the "real world," the world of facts and figures and the problems of presenting that world of facts and figures on the stage. Always the word "Form" is linked with the word "epic." In 1929, at the height of the economic crisis, Brecht asks rhetorically: "What then must our great form be like? Epic. It must report. It must neither believe that one can identify [emotionally] with things in our world, nor must it even want to. The materials are enormous and terrifying and our dramaturgy must reflect this."[30] The year before, as the stock market collapsed, Brecht had written: "The old form of the drama does not permit us to present the world as we see it today. The typical fate of a man of our time cannot be presented within the framework of present day dramatic form."[31] Lamenting then the narrowness of the scope of plays and productions of the period (and ignoring, incidentally, Piscator in Germany and Meyerhold and Tretiakov in the Soviet Union) Brecht notes: "The battles over wheat etc., are not to be found on our stage."[32] At another point in the same period he observes that "petroleum struggles against the five act form," and then goes on: "Once we have to some extent orientated ourselves towards these materials, then we can go over to the inter-relationships of them, which today are horribly complicated and which can only be simplified through *form* [Brecht's italics]."[33] Failing to define this new *form*, Brecht then shifts his ground to a discussion of purpose to be served by it and concludes: "This new form can only be reached by completely changing the purpose of art. The new purpose creates the new art. This new purpose is called: pedagogy."[34] Ignoring for the moment that Brecht's "new purpose" had been proposed earlier by Piscator and is as old as art itself, we can now summarize the principal tenets and objectives of Brecht's "episches Theater" as he himself saw it in the 1920s and early 1930s.

The "epic theater" Brecht envisioned was to rest on three pillars: new dramaturgical constructs embracing different raw materials; a new style of production that would de-emphasize emotion; and a new spectator who would coolly and scientifically appreciate this new theater concept. As was usual for Brecht in the twenties and the early thirties, he deliberately stressed how different his approach was from that of "former provincial actors." In Brecht's view, the standard theater of his day, the theater he railed against in provincial Augsburg and later in Munich, Berlin, and every city and hamlet he visited in exile, was what he loosely termed an "Aristotelian" theater of a high emotional and low political content. In a word, this theater was deliberately reactionary; it deliberately excluded topical and pressing social-political problems; it amused people in a mindless way; it was in fact an opiate of the people and a barrier on the highway leading to revolution. In his view, the standard spectator came to such a theater to be mesmerized, to escape from an ever more intolerable reality, and to creep into the skins of the reactionary heroes he saw on the stage. As long as Brecht continues to describe what he is against, he remains on fairly firm ground; the real difficulties begin when he attempts to spell out exactly what he is for in the theater. It was simplest, of course, initially to say that his theater was what the standard theater was not. Thus, if emotion and Aristotelian dramaturgy held sway in the boulevard theater, then reason and specifically anti-Aristotelian dramaturgy would rule in his new "smoking theater." In this new theater the coolly smoking spectators would not be allowed to become emotional or to fall into a trance. They would instead be forced rationally to consider the most basic and the most complex problems of capitalism, communism, technology, and the megalopolis. Film strips, graphs, statistics and projected photographs would all involve the mind rather than the emotions of the new audience. Very confusingly, Brecht chooses as his model spectator the observer of sporting events. Taken with the fact that smoking was allowed at boxing and soccer matches and at the six-day bicycle races then popular in Berlin, Brecht wanted the theater to emulate the arena. He wanted, he said, the kind of expert attention to his plays that was given by sports fans to athletic events. He conveniently ignores here, of course, the fact that few things are more dramatic than a closely fought athletic contest. Also, though it is perhaps true that the average spectator at a sporting event has enough knowledge of the sport to genuinely appreciate the skill of the performers, it is plainly ridiculous (as Esslin notes in the 1970 German edition of his book) to see such a spectator as a model of calmness, rationality, and objectivity of judgment. The average spectator at a Berlin sporting event in the 1920s was at least as emotionally aroused by that event as his counterpart sitting in a theater.

It is more helpful to an understanding of what Brecht was justly railing against in those days to ignore Brecht's model spectator (yelling for blood) and to listen instead to recordings of some of the mesmeric, aria-like performances of Adolf Hitler or of some of the great stage artists of the period. It is helpful also to see the emotional effect that many a play of the period frankly called for. However, we can now be fairer than Brecht and see that though the dominant theater style of the day, Expressionism, did in fact often stress hair-raising emotional effects (certain plays of Wedekind, *The Deluge* by Ernst Barlach, Bronnen's *Vatermord,* and Georg Kaiser's *Gas I* and *II* come immediately to mind), it was frequently "progressive" in at least three ways. In terms of content, the Expressionist playwright frequently concerned himself with pressing social and political problems. Brecht's idol, Frank Wedekind, for instance, was passionately concerned with attacking the hypocrisy of bourgeois society. Likewise, both Georg Kaiser and Ernst Toller attacked in play after play the mechanized and brutalized world in which they found themselves. Further, in terms of dramatic form, these men had little interest in tightly linked or "Aristotelian" dramaturgical constructs. A typical Expressionist play falls into a long series of separate scenes that often have only a tenuous link between them. Finally, the Expressionist set designers did much to undermine the kind of detailed realism in sets which we associate with the Moscow Art Theater in Russia and with David Belasco in America. Though we may note the aptness, therefore, of Brecht's response to some Expressionist drama as being overly emotional, we must also note that he could and did learn much from the content, the form, and the staging of the Expressionist period. Years later he would be able to acknowledge this himself, but at the time he formulated his "epic" theory he needed easily grasped slogans that could be used to bludgeon his considerable opposition. He needed to stress the contrast between his own work and that of his rivals; it would not have helped his cause at all to point out similarities. Only in the thirties, in exile, does he really begin to be able to acknowledge his many and varied theatrical debts. Even as late as 1935, however, he was not above telling his friend the American designer Mordecai (Max) Gorelik that he (Brecht) was the "Einstein of the new stage form."[3 5]

A few years after the above immodest declaration, Brecht wrote another essay in which he frankly acknowledged that his own work in theater was not really very new at all. In an essay written in 1939 he notes: "For at least two generations now, the serious European theater has found itself in an era of experimentation."[3 6] Among the people, periods, nations, and movements he then mentions and deems important to his own development are: Diderot and Lessing, Antoine, Brahm, Stanislavsky, Gordon Craig, Reinhardt, Leopold Jessner, Piscator, Meyerhold, Vakhtangov, Okhlopkov, experiments with oriental theater, experiments with mask, experiments in buskin, mime, and pantomime; the breakdown of the distinctions between "revue" and "Theater"; Expressionism, which, "enormously enriched the means of expression of the theater"; the use of

"V-effects" in the Chinese theater and in "the classical Spanish theater, the folk theater of Breughel's period, and the Elizabethan theater." Inasmuch as Brecht himself acknowledges that he has been anticipated by this host of innovators, it is difficult to object in the main to Professor Weisstein's conclusion: "Daring experimentalist and thinker that he was, Brecht merely succeeded in fusing the many overt and latent trends in the German and European theater of the twenties into a whole."[37]

What is true for innovations in the physical theater is also true of innovations in dramaturgy. In the essay in which he lists theatrical influences upon him, Brecht also notes a number of writers whose innovations in dramaturgy preceded his own. He reiterates, for instance, his awareness of the importance to his own style of the work of playwrights such as Büchner, Ibsen, Tolstoy, Strindberg, Chekhov, Hauptmann, Shaw, Kaiser, and O'Neill. In another "essay," "Song of the Playwright," he acknowledges whole schools of dramaturgy which were important to his own development. He writes:

> In order to show what I see
> I read about the representation of other nations and other
>   times.
> I've imitated a few plays, examining precisely
> Their respective structures and impressing upon myself that
>   which could prove useful to me.
> I studied the portrayals of the great feudal figures
> Through the English, rich figures
> By whom the world is used to develop their greatness.
> I studied the moralizing Spaniards,
> The Indians, masters of beautiful sensations,
> And the Chinese, who portray the family
> And colorful fates in the cities.[38]

The bag that Brecht presents here is obviously a very mixed one, but there are two important strands that link the various items together and provide insights into Brecht's development as a dramatist. The playwrights and schools of dramaturgy cited show either a great deal of social concern (Shaw, Hauptmann, Ibsen, Tolstoy, etc.) and/or an interest in anti-naturalistic (or, as Brecht would say, anti-Aristotelian) modes of dramatic construction. Where the anti-Aristotelian and the social overlap (as in Shaw, Hauptmann, and occasionally Shakespeare), Brecht is particularly charmed. Where only one of these elements is to be found in a playwright or school of dramaturgy, Brecht's reactions become confused. If, for instance, he sees a dramatic form he likes being used to express content that he dislikes, he tends to dismiss both form and content in a fit of critical pique. The best example of this kind of overkill, one which has given rise to endless discussion, is Brecht's reaction to Shakespeare.[39]

From Brecht's post-World War II comments it is quite clear that by then he had the highest possible regard for Shakespeare. In the 1920s, however, he could not heap enough scorn on Shakespeare. In 1929, for example, the newly converted communist Brecht, in a conversation with Ihering (the leftwing critic and his great admirer) says with an air of finality: "I have given up even bothering to do productions of the classics."[40] Asked why (and the context makes clear that the principal "classic" referred to is Shakespeare), Brecht replied: "The classics catered to their contemporaries. The usefulness of the classics is too limited; they do not show the world [itself], rather, simply themselves. Showcase personalities. Words used as jewels or ornaments. Small horizons, bourgeois. Everything with measure and according to measure."[41] When asked by Ihering: "OK, fine, even if in the final analysis the content of the classics is not useable, why couldn't you retain classical forms?"[42] Brecht replied: "The form of our classics is not classical. Stabilization comes too soon [and is predicated on], the principle of everything being both clear and explained."[43] What Brecht may have meant by this oracular statement is more clearly put in another essay of the same period, "Concerning a New Dramaturgy." There Brecht says flatly: "The old form of the drama [presumably the reference here is to Greek or "Aristotelian" drama] does not permit us to present the world as we today see it."[44] The later Brecht (and was he perhaps by this time aware that his own mode of dramaturgy had an enormous amount in common with his great Elizabethan predecessor?) cautions those who treated Shakespeare with disrespect to beware. In total opposition to his own earlier remarks he says in 1955: "In order to treat of great actions we need to study the structure of the classics, particularly that of Shakespeare. Shakespeare often used the entire substance of a newer piece in a single scene, and nothing significant was left out."[45] At another point in this essay he combines censure of "crude readings" of the "classics" (and one wonders if his earlier remarks to Ihering would qualify as such) with praise of Elizabethan play construction. His description of this technique sounds suspiciously like a description of his own plays. He writes:

> In primitive critiques it is often described as the picturebook technique. One picture appears after the other, without the plot being pulled together or the suspense being directed. Naturally this is a stupid lack of appreciation of the great dramaturgical constructs of our classical authors and the art of the Elizabethan playwrights. The plot (story line) of these plays is rich, but the individual situations and incidents, as picturesque as they may be, are in no way simply loosely linked together, but each demands the other. Every scene, long or short, pushes the plot along. There is atmosphere in this, but it is not that of milieu; there is also suspense here, but it is not that of a cat and mouse game with the audience.[46]

By the time Brecht writes these highly complimentary remarks about Elizabethan drama, Brecht the playwright had most of his career behind him. Is it too far-fetched to wonder if Brecht, himself by this time a classic, is not telling us here (in his usual elliptical way) that an understanding of his own plays is best begun by looking at such classic authors as Marlowe and Shakespeare and ignoring, in large measure, the crude pronouncements of the angry young man of the twenties? If we are to give any credence to the carefully considered aesthetic pronouncements of Brecht in the last years of his life, we might find ourselves well served in heeding his advice, in putting aside the early theory for awhile, and looking at his plays as plays. They are, so he intimates, full of "fun, imagination, and intelligence."

CHAPTER TWO

THE ELIZABETHAN BRECHT:
EDUARD II

> ". . . all in all it is a good play modelled on Aristotelian dramaturgy."
> *Bernhard Reich*[1]

> "The seed of 'epic theater' is already present in *Eduard.*"
> *Bernhard Reich*[2]

Students of Brecht's plays usually divide his work into four major periods. The first, the period of Brecht the virtually apolitical iconoclast,[3] ends about 1926-28 with his conversion to Marxism. Then, for almost a decade, his "didactic plays" present a vision of Communism often most narrowly conceived. He returns to a wider view of humanity and its foibles with the great plays of the exile period, the works upon which his major international reputation rests. With Brecht's return from exile in 1947, his plays again, until his death in 1956, tend to be narrow in scope and dogmatic in political message. The subject of this chapter, Brecht's adaptation of Christopher Marlowe's chronicle play, *Edward the Second,* is eminently representative of Brecht's first major period. The play, and even more significantly, the production of it under Brecht's direction, marks the first major way station on the road to what the critics and Brecht would later refer to as "epic theater."

Helped by his numerous friends in the Munich theater and by his having won the prestigious Kleist Prize for dramatic literature the year before,[4] Brecht was hired by the Munich Kammerspiele in 1923 to direct a production of *Macbeth*. For reasons not entirely clear, Brecht began instead to prepare a revised German version of Marlowe's *Edward the Second*. The adaptation was worked on jointly by Brecht and his friend, the established novelist and dramatist, Lion Feuchtwanger. The choice of this particular play was probably dictated, at least in part, by its homosexual subject matter, a subject sure to antagonize a Munich audience at that time. We know also (Herbert Ihering's contemporary opinion[5] notwithstanding) that Brecht was very much concerned with several different kinds of "aberrant" sexuality at this time. *Eduard the Second* is preceded chronologically by two plays concerned overtly with homosexual relationships: *Baal* (with its clear echoes of the Rimbaud-Verlaine relationship) and *The Jungle of Cities* (with the extraordinary "friendship" of Garga and Shlink). Brecht's use of *Edward the Second* is also interesting from a purely formal point of view. Had Brecht's primary concern been, at this time, "epic" elements such as breadth and fullness of subject matter and very loosely knit constructs, surely he would have been better served by the two parts of *Tamburlaine* or the rambling and episodic *Faustus. Edward the Second* is Marlowe's most tightly constructed, least episodic play.

Before proceeding to an examination of what happened to Marlowe's play in the audacious and immensely skilled adaptation that Brecht and Feuchtwanger put together, it is necessary to have some clear idea of the original and its theatrical milieu. Those familiar with the work of Marlowe and the tradition from which he sprang will know how close Marlowe often is to the form of many great exemplars of late medieval dramaturgy in England. Concerned not at all with the pseudo-Aristotelian limitations that Italian critics such as Minturno, Scaliger, and

Castelvetro had popularized a generation earlier in Italy and France, Marlowe drew instead on the open, episodic, basically narrative forms native to the British Isles: the medieval morality and miracle plays and crude farces still popular in the sixteenth century. If epic drama is non-Aristotelian drama, then Marlowe certainly qualifies as an "epic" dramatist working in a strictly non-Aristotelian tradition. Clearly anticipating Brecht's later, formally expounded theory of epic theater are elements in Marlowe such as extensive use of strictly narrative prologues and epilogues; use of a chorus; use of direct audience address and frequent asides; and finally, frequent interruptions of the play's serious action in order either to insert moral commentary (the illustrated lecture on the seven deadly sins in *Faustus* is perhaps the best known example of this) or to insert immoral or deliberately farcical commentary and thus to lighten the mood of the piece. Castelvetro would clearly have been appalled by the loose sequence of scenes in both *Faustus* and *Tamburlaine.*

Just as the structure of Marlowe's (and many another Elizabethan's) plays formally anticipate many elements that will later become keys to the structure of Brecht's epic theater, so do the Elizabethan physical theater and modes of production. The early Brecht who preached the superiority of sporting contests over the legitimate theater later was to relish the fact that the early public theater in England had to compete directly with contests staged in bearpit and cockpit. Attempts to describe the London theaters of this period bring forcefully to our attention the crude, brawling framework in which Elizabethan plays were staged. It is clear from contemporary accounts such as those of Dekker[6] that an Elizabethan audience came to the theater to see and to be seen. What is perhaps even worse for our modern sensibilities, this audience made itself rather clearly heard. It was not at all unknown for a dandy who had bought himself a stool on the stage itself to seek to upstage the actors. We can imagine a member of this sporting audience at some dramatic moment in the performance getting up from his stool on the stage and striding out, clad more brightly than the players, tripping as he went over the feet of other spectators or of the actors themselves, and upsetting in his lordly and deliberate passage from the stage whatever little dramatic illusion the actors might have been able to conjure up on their bare boards. Remember also, that beyond the tight circle of the dandies on the stage were the infamous "groundlings." Finally, "In all parts of the house people amused themselves by cracking and eating nuts, and munching apples and pears, often throwing the cores at any actor who displeased them."[7]

The actors themselves had, of course, precious little to work with. Working with no "set" as we understand the term, with no curtain, with no changes of lighting possible in midafternoon on an open-air stage, with all parts to be played by men, with no microphone to permit nuances of speech to be rendered clearly, the Elizabethan playwright and actor were clearly aware of the limitations on the degree of imitation of action possible in this theater (fig. 1). Shakespeare himself, adept at creating theatrical mood under even such adverse conditions, has the chorus apologize in the prologue to the highly episodic *Henry the Fifth:*

> But pardon, gentles all,
> The flat unraised spirits that have dared
> On this unworthy scaffold to bring forth
> So great an object: can this cockpit hold
> The vasty fields of France? or may we cram
> Within this wooden O the very casques
> That did afright the air at Agincourt?

Fully aware that mimesis in any full and direct sense is quite impossible under such conditions, Shakespeare has the chorus tell the audience that it will have "to piece out the perform-ance's imperfections with their own thoughts"[8] (fig. 2).

It is quite clear that for an actor in such a presentational theater, the "fourth-wall" representational techniques of Stanislavsky would be quite useless. An actor had to be prepared at all times to be interrupted by hecklers, to ward off thrown objects, to improvise comic inserts, or to cut, on the spur of the moment, overly long speeches. Beyond all these elements, however, another feature of the Elizabethan theater surely prevented too close an identification (on the part of either audience or actor) of an actor with his part. As Parker[9] has pointed out, the "cool acting" that Hamlet demands of the players may well have been demanded simply by the formidable size of the repertoire a typical Elizabethan actor had to have at his command. Though other critics such as Bernard Beckermann[10] and Sir Edmund Chambers anticipate Parker in noting the size of the Elizabethan repertoire, Parker is the first critic to link the specific requirements of the Elizabethan theater to Brecht's own production style. As Parker notes: "The Elizabethan actor would perforce see most of his parts as *roles,* not extensions of himself, and the sheer turnover would make him systematize his methods of portrayal. Elizabethan theatre economics, therefore, would impose very much the same approach of actor to character as Brecht devised theoretically."[11]

Before leaving the Elizabethan playhouse, one final element of *Verfremdung* in Elizabethan performance deserves brief mention. We know that very successful companies made up entirely of boys played fully adult plays. We know also that the adult companies would employ boys in the women's parts. To draw an example from Marlowe and remembering Marlowe's own love of boys, what must have been the effect of the long kiss that "draws out" Faustus' soul in Act V, scene i of the play? Would a non-homosexual actor be able to fully identify the boy playing the part of Helen with Helen and react to him-her with the passion the play seems to call for? Likewise, how complete (for audience or actor) would identification be in those plays calling for a double reversal of the boy-girl role, plays that abound in the Elizabethan repertoire?[12] What of Viola in *Twelfth Night* or Portia in *The Merchant of Venice,* plays in which a boy actor playing a woman's role is then called upon to disguise him(her)self and "play" a male role?

The man who boldly rewrote Marlowe's play may not have been fully aware of the extent to which the Elizabethan theater had practiced many of the things he himself was to call for. The later Brecht (now thoroughly versed in theater history) could note, in 1939-1940, of the Elizabethan theater, played and rehearsed as it was in the open air in full daylight: "How down to earth, profane, and lacking in magic was this production style."[13] In the same essay (written, incidentally, in dialogue form and extraordinarily reminiscent of Dryden's "Essay on Dramatic Poetry") one of Brecht's spokesmen says of Elizabethan theater as a whole:

> Women were already admitted to this theater but the women's roles were still played by boys. Inasmuch as there were no sets, the poet took upon himself the task of painting in the landscape. The stage itself completely lacked specificity and could represent an entire heath. In *Richard III* (V, 3) a ghost enters between the two army camps of Richard and Richmond as they dream in their tents. Within earshot and in sight of both, the ghost addresses each of them alternately.

With this brief introduction to the non-Aristotelian dramaturgy of the Elizabethan theater and to the Elizabethan theater itself, full as it was of "V-effects,"[14] we are ready to go on to compare the Brecht and Marlowe versions of the life of Edward II and to evaluate Brecht's contributions as "epic" theater. In examining the changes that he introduces, I shall deliberately oversimplify the history of the genesis of the German text. It is quite clear, as Brecht himself acknowledges in his critical commentaries on the play, that he was considerably indebted to his friend Lion Feuchtwanger in composing it. Rather than involve myself, however, in the extra-literary problem of which writer contributed most, I refer the reader to the considerable bibliography[15] on this topic and return to the literary text. For the sake of brevity I shall refer to *Eduard II* as Brecht's play.

Though the role of Feuchtwanger in the creation of *Eduard II* can no longer be established with any degree of certainty, one other literary debt is traceable and measureable. It is clear, as Eduard Kopetzki first showed,[16] that the adapters, though using the original English text in part, also used many words and phrases from an existing German translation by Walter Heymel. Heymel's workmanlike translation is mined for about one line in six of Brecht's play.[17] Even where Brecht takes lines directly from Heymel, however, we must beware of simplicistic conclusions because they appear in a wholly new context and bear an unmistakably Brechtian stamp. With remarkably little change of Marlowe's work or Heymel's translation, Brecht has created a play only distantly resembling its English cousin.[18]

Turning first to changes in the plot or fable, we find that Young and Old Mortimer, two characters in Marlowe, are reduced to one in Brecht. Likewise, the several clerics of Marlowe have been reduced to one in Brecht. In Brecht, nine years elapse between the outbreak of civil war and the death of the king's favorite, Gaveston, whereas in Marlowe this time span is unclear and could be either longer or shorter than Brecht's historical inaccuracy. These deceptively few changes in the main line of the dramatic action give no hint of the fundamental changes in character of individuals and in the metaphysical character of the whole that Brecht has achieved. A major clue to the tone changes made by Brecht is provided when he states: "We wanted to make possible a production that would break with the traditional stylistic treatment of Shakespeare on the German stage, that plaster monument style that is so dear to the petty-bourgeois."[19] In order to smash the plaster monument style, Brecht, as one reviewer complained, placed "a royal play in a garbage dump."[20] Brecht's change of the locale from court to "garbage dump" is helped by his view of the king in Marlowe's play as "completely unspecific." In Brecht's view (one which I do not share), the king "could as easily be seen as strong and evil as weak and good."[21] From Brecht's reworking, it is clear that he wants his king to be basically strong. From Marlowe, however, it only seems possible to draw a weak, fickle, vacillating man.

Brecht works his change in Marlowe with subtle economy. His basic means is simply to drastically narrow the gap between the mightly lines and puny deeds of Marlowe's king. As an illustration of this gap, the following scene does as well as any. On the battlefield, when the king is urged to fly, he replies:

> What! was I born to fly and run away,
> And leave the Mortimers conquerors behind?
> Give me my horse, and let's reinforce our troops:
> And in this bed of honour die with fame.

To which his companion, Baldwin, responds:

> O no, my lord, this princely resolution
> Fits not the time; away! we are pursued.[22]

at which point the resolute prince flees ignominiously. What Marlowe has done here is the equivalent of wedding Hotspur's lines to Falstaff's deeds. The mighty line serves, by its inappropriateness in the king's mouth, to reveal his basic weakness, for he is consistently persuaded to change his mind. Another important weakness of Marlowe's king is revealed when, having just heard of the death of Gaveston, he instantly switches his affection to Young Spencer. By so doing, he is revealed as not even strong in love, though it must be granted he is strong in homosexual desire, regardless, apparently, of the object of this desire.

When we turn to Brecht's king and his environment, we turn quite literally to another world. Marlowe's king may be unmanly, fickle, even possibly stupid, but he moves among the outer trappings of kingliness. In Brecht, the king, though still a homosexual, is definitely manly, usually firm in resolve, clearly careless of honor, and he moves (after the opening few scenes of the play) in an atmosphere of incredible squalor. Gone completely are the physical and linguistic trappings of the court. Rejecting all notions of honor, Eduard beats the peers by breaking his word (fig. 3). His sordid world of the army camp, totally lacking in royal pomp, is described thus by his wife immediately after his departure: "All that is left of him is half-eaten kitchen scraps and a hammock full of holes."[23]

It is no wonder that a man who prefers such a camp to the sumptuous court of Marlowe's foppish king should react differently in scene after scene of the new play. In the famous dungeon scene, for instance, we read in Marlowe:

> This dungeon where they keep me is the sink
> Wherein the filth of all the castle falls
>
> . . . .
>
> And there in mire and puddle have I stood
> This ten days' space; and, lest that I should sleep,
> One plays continually upon a drum.
>
> . . . .
>
> My mind's distempered, and my body's numbed,
> And whether I have limbs or no I know not.[24]

Whereas in Brecht, the passage, set in the same basic physical situation, runs:

> The pit in which they keep me is the cesspool
> And for seven hours now the shit of London has fallen
> On me. Nevertheless, the sewage strengthens my limbs.
> They are already as hard as cedar. The stink of sewage
> Raises me to unmeasurable greatness. Good
> Noise of drums, wakening the weakened
> So that his death comes to him as he
> Wakes rather than when he is unconscious.[25]

Changing one detail of the situation itself (Brecht substitutes seven hours for ten days as the time spent in the dungeon), Brecht then makes every detail of the punishment serve a diametrically opposed psychological function. Brecht's garbage dump king is hardened, not softened, by the sewage falling upon him, and even the dreadful smell elevates him. The drums he welcomes, for he wishes to be aware of his own death. The character change from Marlowe's suffering fop to Brecht's usually determined monarch could hardly be greater, and yet this is in a scene in which the changes in actual physical situation could hardly be fewer.

Precisely the same kind of change is made in the passage where the king makes his final comment on the metaphysical Gestalt of his world. Marlowe's king says:

> Come, Spencer; come, Baldock, come, sit down by me,
> Make trial now of that philosophy,
> That in our famous nurseries of arts
> Thou suck'dst from Plato and from Aristotle.
> Father, this life contemplative is Heaven.
> O that I might this life in quiet lead."[26]

Contrast this passage with Brecht's version, which begins:

> Come Spencer; Baldock come, sit down by me
> Test now that philosophy drawn from
> Aristotle and Plato at the breast
> Of most famous wisdom.

The passage ends:

> Ah, Spencer
> Because words are rough and only separate
> Heart from heart and understanding has not
> Been given to us, within our deafness
> All that remains for men is the touch
> Of Bodies. But even this is very little and
> Everything is vain.[27]

The better conclusion sours the entire passage, makes what were Marlowe's words no longer Marlowe's but wholly Brecht's. Gone is the hopeful wish for peace and quiet of Marlowe's king; in its place is utter metaphysical despair, reminiscent of Garga and Shlink in another of Brecht's plays of this same period, *In the Jungle of Cities.*

As radical and economical as the changes made in the part of Edward, are those made in Edward's chief opponent, Mortimer. By combining Marlowe's Young and Old Mortimers, Brecht creates neither an Old Mortimer as circumspect and almost as windy as Polonius, nor a Young Mortimer as hotheaded as Hotspur, but rather gives us a young-old scholar, a man capable of action only after failing to achieve his ends by debate. Robbing him of the fire and action of youth, Brecht makes him world-weary, bitter, disillusioned. This is in direct contrast to Marlowe, who has Young Mortimer blaze gloriously for a moment and declare this moment of glory, though short, worthwhile. Marlowe's Young Mortimer exclaims:

> Base Fortune, now I see, that in the wheel
> There is a point, to which when men aspire,
> They tumble headlong down: that point I touched,
> And, seeing there was no place to mount up higher,
> Why should I grieve at my declining fall?[28]

As then, head high, he strides out of the play and life to "discover countries yet unknown," he is, to use Harry Levin's apt term, the very prototype of the Elizabethan "over-reacher."

In Brecht, the "same" speech, as Reinhold Grimm[29] has correctly observed, serves a totally different tonal function. Brecht's Mortimer, who, unlike Marlowe's, has been pushed against his will into the world of politics and who, from the first moment of Brecht's play, is contemptuous of greatness and power, first begs for his life (something Young Mortimer would not dream of doing), then bitterly cries:

> There is, my boy, a wheel that the
> Slut Fortune turns. It forces you with it upwards.
> Upwards and upwards. You hold on tight. Upwards.
> There comes a point, the highest. From there you see
> There is no ladder. It forces you downwards.
> Because it's round. He who has seen this, is he forced
> To fall, my boy, Or does he let himself fall? The question's
> A joke. Relish it![30]

Where Young Mortimer "aspires," Brecht's Mortimer is passive, is dragged along by the wheel. Where Young Mortimer saw the highest point as a point of glory, Brecht's Mortimer views this elevation as bitter and macabre, as a metaphysical practical joke. His whole unwilling rise yielded no triumphs, no joy, only the metaphysical perplexity of his ultimate rhetorical question. The question implies a world view as bleak as the king's conclusion that "All is vain." Again, Marlowe's basic scene, situation, and fable has been twisted to reflect a view of the world having almost nothing in common with the heroic "Elizabethan world picture." Again, the change has been wrought with the utmost economy of means.

A comparison of the Queen (Isabella in Marlowe, Anna in Brecht) yields a very similar conclusion. Again the movement of the character is from bad in Marlowe to worse in Brecht. At least, in Marlowe, the queen loves Young Mortimer and her love is in some measure returned by the young and highly desirable Mortimer. In Brecht, in sheer desperation, the queen seeks at least sexual solace with the no longer young, no longer desirable Mortimer who observes: "With knees spread wide and eyes closed you snap at everything and cannot be satisified, Anna."[31] It is no wonder that the queen, rejected by her husband and treated thus by Mortimer, should seek refuge in alcoholism and that we finally find her laughing "at the emptiness of the world."[32] In this laugh, the main metaphysical theme of the play is again sounded.

Whereas the other three major characters of the play (the king, Mortimer, and the queen), in their passage from Marlowe's play to Brecht's, change from bad to worse, Gaveston changes from bad to slightly better. Marlowe's minion is nothing but a totally asocial adventurer; his aim is, as he says at the beginning of the play, to "draw the pliant king which way I please." Never does Marlowe's Gaveston do anything but relish a position which enables him to scoff at the earls of England, to "wear a lord's revenue on his back," and to "riot it with the treasure of the realm."[33] In contrast, Brecht's Gaveston is well aware of the havoc his aggrandizement has caused. Writing his will, he speaks of being "wrung out by too much good fortune," and concludes, playing for the fourth time the guiding metaphysical motif of the piece, that he is "very much grieved" that he "does not simply turn to dust."[34]

For Gaveston, as for the other characters in Brecht's play, this is the worst of all possible worlds. The king, because of his uncontrollable and logically inexplicable passion, and all the others, as a result of this passion and with a high degree of unwillingness, are crushed by "the slut Fortune." Locked aesthetically, physically, and linguistically in the close embrace of lovers and enemies, the king, Gaveston, the queen, and Mortimer move swiftly, knowingly, but unwillingly to their violent end. Marlowe's Renaissance metaphysic has been displaced by Brecht's: "All is vain."

If we try to find in the text of Brecht's version of *Eduard
II* more epic elements than we find in Marlowe, we immediately
run into problems. For the English reader, if he uses the term
"epic" in its dominant English sense and looks for "lofty
characters in a long narrative poem," he must see Marlowe's
lengthier and more elevated (both linguistically and metaphysically) poem as the more "epic" of the two. Brecht,
however, seems to mean by the expression "episches Theater"
something having very little to do indeed with what is
understood by "epic" in English criticism. In German genre
theory less is made of loftiness and length than of narration as
the key to epic composition. It is probable that the early Brecht
followed the dominant trend (then and now) in German genre
theory and saw the division between the "dramatic" and the
"epic" modes as the difference between "erzählende Kunst"[35]
(third person or narrative exposition), i.e., "Epik"; and first
person, mimetic, representational, or "darstellende Kunst," i.e.,
the drama. For Brecht, it would seem the movement from the
dramatic to the epic mode might be effected at the simplest
level by a translation of as many lines as possible from the first
into the third person. The "episches Theater" *tells* a story
rather than having actors *become* the story. Both Brecht's view
of his theater as being similar to an eyewitness of a traffic
accident narrating what he has seen[36] and his admonitions to
his actors (in rehearsal) to translate their lines into the third
person support the idea that the key element is that epic is
primarily a "narrative" as distinct from a "mimetic or representational art."[37]

Even if we ignore for a moment the obvious fact that
classical epic is not strictly narrative and that classical drama
often has long narrative sections, and apply the notion of epic
as "narrative art" to Brecht's reworking of the Edward theme, it
is difficult to show how the text of Brecht's play can be
considered more epic than Marlowe's. Except for the "narrative" placard that prefaces each scene in Brecht's version, only
one other supposedly "narrative" element has been inserted by
Brecht. A ballad seller appears once early in the play and sings

of Eduard's love for Gaveston. Instead, however, of interrupting the action (as the songs are supposed consciously to do in *The Threepenny Opera,* for instance), the ballad peddler appears as himself (i.e., in the first person) and is extraordinarily fully integrated in the dramatic action as his singing is reinforced by full chorus (see below). It is by his deliberate and demonstrative denunciation of this seller of "treasonous" songs that Spencer first worms his way into the good graces of Eduard and Gaveston. A cursory glance at the Elizabethan drama shows that songs punctuate the action of these plays quite frequently and often are but distantly related to the basic story line of the play.[38] Viewed historically, Brecht's insertion of the ballad seller in *Eduard II* is an extremely conservative use of a classic dramatic device. In fact, the same might be argued for his use of placards. It is possible that "narrative" placards were used in the performance of Elizabethan plays[39] to reinforce whatever vague notion of time and place of action the playwright might already have given in the spoken lines of the play.[40]

Even if we restrict ourselves to Brecht's early and naive view of "Epik" as being quite simply "narrative art," however, we see that the text of his play is no more "epic" than any number of examples that can be drawn from our knowledge of the Elizabethan repertory and of Elizabethan dramaturgy. We can extend the notion of "epic" to include the raw, formless, episodic, and large or panoramic stage productions that Brecht (heavily under the influence of Piscator, Meyerhold, and Döblin) speaks of the following year (1925) as being "epic"; Brecht's play with its reduced cast, shorter lines, tighter structure, and less involved, less episodic story line than Marlowe's play then qualifies even less as an exemplar of "epic" dramaturgy. And Marlowe's *Edward II,* let us repeat, is the most tightly organized, least episodic, least "narrative" play that he wrote. We are forced to conclude that, totally original, brilliantly forceful in language and structure, and specifically Brechtian in its bleak metaphysics as Brecht's adaptation is, it hardly qualifies (either as to form or as to content) in Brecht's own terms as an even moderately "original" contribution to epic, open, or panoramic dramaturgy. Whether one looks backward to the Greeks or the Elizabethans, or forward to Piscator, Weiss, Hochhuth, O'Neill, Miller, and Anouilh, Brecht's *Eduard II* must be viewed as a piece of tight and conventional dramaturgy. We might see the play as a piece of dramaturgy considerably less open, less panoramic, less narrative, in a word less "epic" than a host of plays written before and after Brecht began using the expression "episches Theater," to describe his work.

Gradually we have tended to shift (as Brecht himself so often did) from literary text to the physical theater. Brecht speaks mainly, though not exclusively, in the years when he is formulating his theater theory, of "epic *theater*" rather than "epic *drama.*"[41] It is quite clear that for Brecht as director *and* playwright, the line between text and staged play is an extremely difficult if not impossible one to draw. With play after play, his arguments slide bewilderingly from text to stage and back again. Difficult and often arbitrary though such a distinction may be, it is methodologically useful to attempt to distinguish between the term "epic" as Brecht the playwright and theorist applied it to texts, and the term as Brecht the director-producer applied it to performance. Even if the text of *Eduard* was not "epic," we can still ask: Was *Eduard II* an "epic" production in Brecht's own staging of it? To establish this, we must both look at his 1924 production of *Eduard II* and try to reconstruct his idea of what constituted at that time an "epic" production of the play.

For Herbert Ihering, who presumably knew the host of other innovators in German and foreign theater at that time, it was Brecht and perhaps Brecht alone who broke down the "monumental plaster" and ecstatic or hymnic style that dominated German theater in the 1920s. In 1928 in a recorded interview with Brecht, Ihering deplores the false grandeur of the plaster monument style, a style that in his and in Brecht's view ruined the classics, and says categorically: "A new concept had to be substituted for greatness. You substituted for greatness: distance. That is your achievement in theater history. The turning point was your production of *The Life of Edward II of England* in Munich."[42] Basically, continues Ihering, this was achieved by a new acting style: "You [Brecht] demanded a reckoning of the events. You demanded simple gestures, you forced the use of clear and cool speech. You tolerated no cheating by the use of emotions. This resulted in the objective, the epic style."[43] From these comments of Ihering, who probably saw only the finished production, and those of Brecht's friend and collaborator of those days, Bernhard Reich, who saw the rehearsals also, there emerges a fairly complete picture of what it was about this production that made it, in the view of knowledgable contemporaries, "episch."

To the key words, "distance," "objectivity," and "coolness," used by Ihering in this interview, Reich adds the observation that above all, Brecht's play was cast with extraordinary care, was rehearsed longer than was normal in those days, and that this care permitted the working out of the story line with extraordinary exactitude. In this production, every word, every action, every stage requisite, every detail of the sets and lighting was submitted to microscopic and rational examination. One example of this detailed precision in the production is recalled by Reich, when he describes Brecht's rehearsal of the hanging scene:

> Those playing the soldiers who were to hang the king's favorite, made, initially, a few gestures that might have indicated a hanging for those with a willing imagination. Every other German director would simply have gone on. Brecht interrupted [the scene] and demanded that the actors do it properly: tie the hangman's knot and fasten the rope to the beam above. Shrugging their shoulders, the actors tried to follow the unexpected instructions of the director. Brecht stopped them again and demanded grimly and unswervingly that they repeat the hanging. He then set them the task of hanging Gaveston as virtuosos of the gallows. The public should enjoy [he said] watching how they actually hanged the young man. Brecht then repeated the scene patiently and seriously.[44]

From this and other remarks, it is clear that in Reich's view when *Eduard II* was actually performed, the actors (with the exception of Oskar Homolka—Mortimer—who was thoroughly drunk during the second half of the play) knew exactly what they were doing and why they were doing it. Instead of simply casting themselves emotionally into their roles, and thus letting emotion carry themselves and their audience through the play, they remained, in a sense, outside their roles and coolly and methodically presented their highly rational interpretation of what the characters would do in each specific situation. Quite gratuitously one other "epic" element was added. H.O. Münsterer reports that the stage hands must have been poorly drilled, for the scene changes took so long that the public became restless and the first performance ended after midnight. Except for this particular "epic" element, every detail of the directorial approach that Brecht was much later to employ with his beloved Berliner Ensemble is present here in a remarkably clear form. It is no wonder that Reich, many years later, should recall with some astonishment that much of Brecht's later theory was but a gloss on his practice in 1923-24.[45]

If we may grant with Reich and Ihering and other such contemporaries as Lion Feuchtwanger and Marieluise Fleisser that Brecht's 1924 production of *Eduard II* was a clear model of "epic theater" style, we might expect that the response to the production would have been primarily cool and rational. Let us look, however, at some general criticism of Brecht's use of language (particularly verse and songs) in this period, and some specific commentary on the kind of response elicited by the *Eduard* production in particular.

In 1922 when he sought to justify giving the Kleist Prize to an almost totally unknown playwright, Herbert Ihering wrote of the use of language in Brecht's early plays: "One feels this language on one's tongue, on the palate, in the ear, and in the spine. Lacking conjunctions it rips open perspectives. It is brutally sensual, melancholically tender. There is coarseness in it and abysmal sadness. Grim humor and the lyricism of pity."[46] One felt all this best, he added, when one heard the playwright sing his own songs: "From the first word of his plays on, one knows: a tragedy has begun."[47] Finally, Ihering draws attention to "the whipping rhythms that lash one into a fury"[48] that distinguished the verse of his protégé, Bertolt Brecht.

The playwright, Carl Zuckmayer, who, like Peter Suhrkamp (Brecht's publisher) and Arnolt Bronnen, first met Brecht while he was singing, notes: "His singing was raw and cutting, often as crude as that of a street singer, with the unmistakable accent of Augsburg, often almost lovely, floating without emotional vibration, and in every syllable and every half note completely clear and well articulated."[49] Of the effect of this model of "epic" performance, Zuckmayer notes: "When he picked up the guitar, the hum of conversation ceased," while around Brecht people sat "as though caught up in a magic spell."[50] And of his own response, Zuckmayer (who also sang professionally at this time) stated that he was "completely captivated, moved, charmed." Virtually every contemporary account of Brecht's singing speaks of an almost uncanny fascination with this man as he sang his own works—set, usually, to his own tunes. This is the man who prepared the music for *Eduard II.* There is no ground for supposing that the Brecht of the café and the beer hall did not carry over into the production that Brecht was then directing.

Marieluise Fleisser, herself a dramatist of considerable skill, tries in her account of some fifty years of the Munich Kammerspiele to reconstruct her impressions of Brecht's production of *Eduard II.* "This was," she notes, "street-singer-like theater. Brecht directed the play himself; he used disconcertingly simple and at the same time easily perceptible means that quietly sawed on one's nerves."[51] One of the most striking features of the production for her was the various sound and other effects used to grate on the nerves of the spectator. She notes, for instance, that the "Song of the Ballad Seller" in which the refrain, "Intercede for us, intercede for us, intercede for us!" makes up every second line, was rendered quite extraordinary in a brilliant and sustained piece of stage business (figs. 4 and 5). Fleisser writes:

> Ghostlike before my eyes stand the tall stage flats of the London houses with [their] many small window shutters; suddenly all the shutters fly open, and out of every window pops the head of someone speaking, and all of these heads together recite a kind of a prayer that is more an indictment than a complaint, interrupted, as in a litany, by the oft-repeated, "Intercede for us." This "Intercede for us," however, is not a request for mercy, but much more a hasty, hostile whisper that gets on one's nerves with its ice-cold threat, and everyone recognizes that this is nothing less than revolution. And after the last ghostly "Intercede for us," the shutters fly closed again with one dry crash.[52]

Equally unnerving for Mrs. Fleisser was the dungeon scene where Eduard grated metal on metal as he scraped out his empty food pan with a lead spoon, filling as he did so the small space of the chamber theater with his half demented shaking of the metal net that separated the stage from the audience (fig. 6). To further help the general mood of calmness and rationality thereby established, high up above the stage was strung a plank which was crossed at breakneck speed in the battle scenes. The device is one that Brecht would use again with Grusche and her baby in the escape scene in the *Caucasian Chalk Circle.*[53] Another contemporary observer of the battle scenes in *Eduard* has written: "In this English army, with their filth encrusted helmets, were not only the terrible times of 1550 but every army of the European World War."[54] The tone of all these remarks hardly suggests a performance distinguished by its calm and rationality. Yet we must remember that this very production established Brecht in the view of contemporaries such as Reich and Ihering as an "epic dramatist" and an "epic director." In view of the effect of performances of *Eduard II* in that memorable 1924 production, it is all but impossible for us now to understand why the term "epic" should, albeit retroactively, have been applied to it. It is significant to note, however, that no one (including Brecht) actually spoke in 1924 of either the play or the production as being in any way "epic." Ihering, climbing aboard the fashionable bandwagon, first applies the term to the production in the late twenties in the radio broadcast with Brecht, "Conversations About the Classics."[55] Reich's application of the term to *Eduard II* is made some thirty years after the original production.[56] It would seem, therefore, that when "epic theater" entered Brecht's and the general German theater vocabulary in the mid-twenties,[57] attempts were immediately made to fit Brecht's earlier plays and productions to it. The attempt was as confusing then as it is now.

This insistence on the term "epic" by Brecht and his contemporaries in the late twenties would seem to be based on both the accident of the overly emotional style of the period and either ignorance or deliberate oversimplification of the epic genre. Most confusingly (and Goethe was probably at least in part to blame for this), Brecht seems to have identified at this time the drama with emotion and the epic with coolness or distance. However much Brecht himself may have complained in later years that he had been misunderstood and that the emphasis on Reason and Coolness in his early theory was but half of the story, it is obvious that the main thrust of this theory, as he had attempted to define it in 1927 in the essay, "Observation on the Difficulties of the Epic Theater," was in fact "Reason." He writes: "The most important thing perhaps about the epic theater is that it appeals less to the emotions than to the rational intellect of the spectator. Instead of [emotionally] sharing the experience, the spectator should set himself [rationally] at odds with it."[58] Though Brecht may have carefully added in the same essay that it was not his intention "to deny emotion in this kind of theater," Ihering's impression (quoted above and, incidentally, uncorrected by Brecht) that Brecht's theater was cool and objective remains the dominant one in most critical writing on Brecht to this day.

This early use of the term "episch" is confusing on two counts. First, as I have tried to show with *Eduard II*, there is remarkably little evidence to support the contention that either "cool" acting in general or Brecht's productions in particular actually produced basically cool responses. One confuses intention with simple fact if one assumes as the early Brecht seems to have done that a cool performance will produce a cool audience response. Second, there is no general historical basis for the contention that the drama is a "hot" and the epic a "cool" medium. As to the first point, we shall see with play after play of Brecht's, in his own productions, that audience and critical response was not in fact cool despite the most heroic attempts of the post-war Berliner Ensemble to act (in Eric Bentley's sensitive formulation) as a "fire-brigade,"[59] pouring cold water on any incipient emotion in the "epic" texts. The second point, Brecht's view of "epic" as a cool medium, can be shown to be an oversimplification.

A cool look at the history of the epic mode reveals that the standard German formulation of "Epik" as quite simply "narrative art" contributes to what Emil Staiger calls "a critical tower of Babel."[60] Unless we are willing to ignore Homer completely in our definition of "Epik," it is manifestly unsuitable to speak, as most German criticism does, of "Epik" as that form characterized by a "story" or "action" set in the past and narrated in the third person. Equally faulty is the concurrent view of drama as a form distinguished by action happening (as distinct from being narrated) in the present and in the first person. The most cursory glance at classic examples of the epic (Homer) and the work of the major tragedians reveals (as Goethe and Schiller sometimes recognized) that such a formulation is an oversimplified one. Great sections of major plays are narrations of happenings in the past. *Oedipus Rex, Prometheus Bound,* and the *Agamemnon* (to name but three prominent examples) would be unintelligible and unplayable if one were to cut out those enormously long passages that are not in the first person and the present tense. Likewise, when one removes all the first person, present tense speeches from the *Iliad,* it is virtually impossible to make sense of what remains. If a normative poetics is possible (and the work of Emil Staiger, Julius Petersen,[61] Wolfgang Kayser,[62] and Peter Szondi[63] does not make this seem likely) then surely such a poetics must be so formulated that it provides adequate housing not only for the descendants of Homer, Aeschylus, Sophocles, and Euripides but for the original grand masters themselves. Except in the crudest and most confusing manner, the description of "Epik" as "narrative art" and "Drama" as "mimetic or representational art" fails to grant the complexity of the classic examples of the major genres. When Brecht naively took up the term "episch" as used in German criticism then (the 1920s), he took up also the welter of confusion that this term, as "defined" above, still produces.

At least as inadequate and just as confusing as this definition of "Epik" is the fact that "Epik" thus defined tends to produce somewhat mistaken ideas as to performance of major classical examples of the two poetic modes: the drama and the epic. Brecht is surely mistaken when he assumes that drama is emotional and epic rational. This simply does not square with what we know from the classical period of epic and dramatic performance. It is quite clear that Greek rhapsodes, as W.H.D. Rouse notes in the preface to his translation of Plato's *Ion,* "held large audiences spellbound and moved them to amazement, laughter or tears."[64] From Ion's own description of his performance it is quite clear that he both does and does not maintain "epic distance" from the material he is narrating. He says: "Why, whenever I speak of sad and touching scenes, my eyes are full of tears." When Socrates asks if his performance does not in turn bring his audience to tears, the hot-cold narrator Ion replies: "Oh yes, indeed I do! I always look down from my platform, and there they are crying and glaring and amazed, according to what I say." Apparently, even in the midst of a passionate rendition of the poem, however, Ion does not get completely carried away, for he adds immediately that while the audience is crying and glaring and he is crying and glaring he is *at the same time* paying very careful attention to the audience's reaction. He notes: "Indeed, I'm bound to pay careful attention to them. If I leave them crying in their seats, I shall laugh at my pockets full of money; if I leave them laughing, I myself shall cry over the money lost."[65] One wonders if the response to a specifically dramatic performance in Athens at the time of Plato involved any less spectator response than did Ion's brilliant "narrative" performance of the *Iliad* or the *Odyssey*. As far as the classic epic is concerned it is quite clear that rhapsodes of Ion's stature could quite literally not afford to appear unmoved during a performance. There would seem no ancient ground for distinguishing the effect of an Ion "decked out in gorgeous raiment" and "wearing a golden crown," as he performed rather than recited an epic poem, from that of his counterpart in the drama, the actor in mask, elevator shoes, and long robes as he intoned, with gestures broad enough to be intelligible in the bleachers, the dramatist's account of this or that segment of Greek mythology. A careful look at classical drama and epic reveals that one should not expect too much difference between epic and dramatic effect. The plays of the period have far too many narrative sections, too little action per se for us to be able to define the classical mode of drama as non-narrative.[66] Likewise, the epic form as Homer shaped it gives ample opportunity for the narrator to abandon the third person or narrative mode and assume instead the first person that long sections of the *Iliad* are couched in. Whether one takes the classical forms and their respective modes of production as one's guide, as I have done, or one looks at as simple an "epic" situation as a grandmother telling a group of spellbound children a story, as Willi Flemming has done in *Epik und Dramatik*,[67] one has little ground to distinguish between the *effect* of epic or dramatic performance. Brecht's attempt to define "episches Theater" in terms of its cool acting or cool spectators often fails when applied to either classical examples of the two major genres or when applied to his own experience in directing his own supposedly "epic" plays.

The conclusion is inescapable, therefore, that the *Eduard II*, either as a play or in Brecht's production of the play, is only marginally, in any classical or even contemporary sense, "episch." The application of the term to Brecht's production can only produce, as he himself was later to discover, considerable confusion. The basic play is certainly no more narrative than most Elizabethan or Greek drama; the action of the play is tighter than that of Brecht's model; paradoxically, as we have seen from contemporary responses, the performance of the play, with its lack of unrestrained emotion on the part of the actors, was perhaps more gripping than any emotional or plaster monument production might have been in 1924. Deadened by too much empty emotion, deafened by the empty shouts of some of the wilder Expressionists, the theater was ready to be awakened, to be shocked alert by considerably subtler productions that worked on the emotions of the spectator in a somewhat different way. To paraphrase Herbert Ihering, "*Eduard II* showed the way; this was Brecht's contribution to theater history." Altering with sovereign freedom the work of his great forerunner in open dramaturgy, Christopher Marlowe, Brecht achieves a radical renaissance of some of the earliest and most powerful forms of theatrical expression: poetry, song, and dance will once again be welcome in a twentieth-century theater. Henceforth, the man who was also one of Germany's greatest lyric poets of this or any other century would range freely through the lyric, epic, and dramatic modes to create dramas that combine the earthy and contemporary with the most lofty and timeless.

CHAPTER THREE

BERLIN 1932, FROM EPIC NOVEL TO
EPIC PLAY: *THE MOTHER*

"Unlike very few new works, the form of this play rests upon
the structure and style of the German national theater (from
Goethe's *Götz* to Büchner's *Woyzeck*)."

Bertolt Brecht, 1951[1]

"The play *The Mother,* written in the style of the didactic
plays but requiring professional players, is a piece of
anti-metaphysical, materialistic, *non-Aristotelian* dramaturgy.
In no way does it use as thoughtlessly as the Aristotelian
[drama] the *emotional surrender* of the spectator, and it
takes a very different stance towards certain psychic effects
such as catharsis."

Bertolt Brecht, 1936-37[2]

It is difficult to imagine a greater political and philosophical
change than that which obtains between the 1923-24 Munich
production of *Eduard II* and Brecht's 1932 Berlin production of
his own consciously "epic" stage version of Gorki's novel,
Mother.[3] From homosexuality as a theme he turns to mother-
hood; from the "meaningless metaphysical struggles" of early
characters such as Garga, Shlink, Eduard, and Mortimer, he
turns to unabashed support of Communism at its most
dynamic, concrete, and anti-metaphysical; from the incompre-
hensible rampages of the "slut Fortune" he turns to the thesis
that the "destiny of man is man." Finally, whereas in Munich
theater had played primarily against the backdrop of Hitler's
gross and almost comic-opera beer hall putsch, in Berlin with
Hitler's star very much in the ascendancy, theater had become

for Brecht a naked political weapon. The young man who had written *Baal, In the Jungle of Cities, Drums in the Night,* and *Eduard II,* out of a sense of disillusionment with politics, and had scored a smashing popular success in the late twenties with the anti-political *Threepenny Opera,* had with plays like *The Mother* (and others written "in the style of the didactic plays") decided to light a candle rather than curse the darkness. Matches and candle came courtesy of the Communist party, and lighting that candle with those matches in Berlin in 1932 (while Hitler's rowdies roamed the streets, beating to a pulp any suspected Jew or Communist) was tantamount to searching for a large gas-leak with a flamethrower.

During those very years when Brecht was undergoing this change from Saul to Paul, he was beginning to formulate the anti-aesthetic of the "epic theater." Like the theory and the theater of Piscator (who, it will be remembered, consistently used the term "epic" as a synonym for "political"),[4] Brecht's own early theory and practice is inconceivable without its specifically political orientation. Out of Brecht's concern with the obviously imminent collapse of the Weimar Republic, grows an interest in the machinations of the stock exchange, the international money market, economic theory, and viable political alternatives to Fascism. Elisabeth Hauptmann tells us in her diary entries that he began in 1926 to investigate the workings of the Berlin and Vienna stock exchanges and to study the "Communist classics."[5] Attempting then to deal with complex political-economic-historical problems on the stage, Brecht reached the conclusion: "These things are not dramatic in our sense, and when one adapts them they are no longer true and the drama no longer has anything to do with them. When one sees that the present-day world can no longer be fitted into the drama, then [one sees that] the drama no longer has a place in the world."[6] A lesser man or a more dedicated politician might then have abandoned the drama forthwith, but this was not Brecht's way. He attempted instead to formulate a theory of the stage that would justify the theater's existence. Miss

Hauptmann notes: "In the course of these studies Brecht constructed his theory of 'epic drama.' "[7] In the epic theater, or so the diary note implies, the modern world will be treated in all its complexity, without losing anything of its "truth," though it might possibly be lacking in a quality of the "dramatic," "in a technical sense." Like *Das Kapital* the new theater would be neither sprightly nor "culinary" in style. The epic theater would have as its cardinal trait political teaching rather than simple (in a dual sense) entertainment. The plays that Brecht writes several years after he first proposes "epic theater" as a distinct theatrical species are the plays of a newly converted Marxist; they are, to use his own term, *Lehrstücke,* "didactic plays," to be played largely by amateurs, and what they seek to teach is the gospel according to Marx and Engels.[8] One of these new "epic" or "teaching" plays, though Brecht himself never called it formally a *Lehrstück,* is his 1930-32 adaptation of the Gorki novel, *Mother.*[9] In form and content, the various versions of Brecht's *The Mother,* are representative of the austere years that preceded Brecht's being forced into exile. *The Mother* (like the "didactic plays") represents, as Kopetzki[10] has observed, perhaps the closest marriage of epic theater theory and epic theater practice that Brecht in his long career as dramatist and theorist ever managed. We would expect to find, therefore, in the austerely stylized dramaturgy of *The Mother*, a play that would, if any play of Brecht would, prevent emotional identification on the part of the spectator and force the spectator to respond in a cool and "scientific" manner. There is grave doubt that even this play achieved this effect.[11]

A major difficulty in discussing *The Mother* is the fact that there really is no single definitive text. Besides the *major* published version (the essentially theatrical *Stücke* and *Werkausgabe* texts based largely on the 1933 *Versuche* version[12]) there is now a published Berliner Ensemble playing version[13] that has as much claim to manuscript authority as the other published version(s). The major difference between the *Versuche-Stücke-Werkausgabe* version and the Berliner

Ensemble text is the creation of a new major character. In the Ensemble version a worker by the name of Semjon Lapkin is given a substantial role.[14] From the Ensemble records and information given to me by Elisabeth Hauptmann,[15] I know that this role was created specifically for Brecht's friend, Ernst Busch, when Busch consented to play in the Ensemble production of the play. Brecht created this new role in a rather curious way. He took away a number of lines from other characters, most particularly from Pawel Wlassow[16] (son of Pelegea Wlassowa) and gave them to Lapkin. Technically, this yields some important results. Literally and figuratively the role of Pawel is reduced to a bit part in the play. At the same time, Lapkin is not developed far enough as a character to challenge seriously the supremacy of the role of the mother herself. As a result, the mother becomes virtually the whole play. The importance of the reduction of the epic cast of the Gorki novel to the one focused character of the Ensemble play tells us a great deal about the pressure of the stage form itself and the formal demands that stage production tended to make on Bertolt Brecht.

Of enormous importance to Brecht in reducing Gorki's sprawling novel for the stage form is an intermediary German dramatization of the novel by G. Stark and G. Weisenborn. A comparison of the seventy-nine typewritten pages of the Stark-Weisenborn dramatization[17] with Brecht's version(s) of *The Mother* shows that his work is not so much a dramatization of the original novel as an adaptation of the Stark-Weisenborn play. With only one important exception, the continuation of the play up until the 1917 revolution,[18] Brecht uses the same scenes or raw materials that Stark-Weisenborn had selected from the Gorki novel. Brecht himself inserted in the first edition of his version the admission that he had used a "Dramatization by G. Stark and G. Weisenborn."[19] We do not know why Brecht left this comment out in the later *Stücke* and *Werkausgabe* editions of the text. Despite this omission, it is quite clear that any proper consideration of Brecht's dramatization of Gorki's novel must take into consideration both the novel itself and the Stark-Weisenborn adaptation.

Dealing first with Brecht's treatment of material borrowed from the earlier dramatization, we find that he has applied a number of the principles he now calls "epic" to his own version. For instance, where Stark-Weisenborn present the opening scene of their version in standard, "fourth wall theater" dramatic form (Pelegea Wlassowa discusses the cutback in her son's wages with her next door neighbor), Brecht introduces what he sees as an "epic" change, when he has the mother (played by Helene Weigel) address the audience directly: "I'm almost ashamed to serve soup like this to my son. But I don't have any more fat to put into it, not even half a spoonful."[20] Theoretically, the use of direct address is supposed to make audience and actor see a role as a role. In fact, however, it would seem possible that the Berlin working class audiences of 1932 were drawn closer to the actress by her taking them directly into her confidence than they would have been had Brecht kept the "Naturalistic" beginning of the Stark-Weisenborn version. Likewise, if one goes on from the use of direct audience address to the songs that Brecht wrote specially for the production, is it possible that these songs drew the audience closer to the action than is healthy for "children of the scientific age"? Might we share perhaps the doubts of Plato and Thomas Mann about using music (particularly when there is no hint of parody in the music used) to further rational thought? When I hear Helene Weigel and Ernst Busch (perhaps the greatest singer of propaganda songs in Germany in his day) in the Berliner Ensemble recording of the play, my own sense of reason and distance is, I must confess, sorely tried. Though I agree with these critics in but little else, I must concur with Alfred Polgar, who speaks of an "obstinate tattoo" in the songs that is almost hypnotic in its power,[21] and with Bjørn Ekmann, who dwells at length on the emotional effect of the play's propaganda and states flatly that the play's primary appeal is not to reason but emotion.

If such responses are possible even today, without Hitler to threaten us and with only the sound to guide us, what must have been the punch of these performances before highly sympathetic audiences of Communist workers in Berlin in those dark days immediately preceding Hitler's rise to supreme power in the German state? [22] Was this performance, given at the time that Brecht's theory and practice of epic theater were most closely joined, one that set the audience at ease, that separated them from "the brainwashed, believing, magically mesmerized mass,"[23] the people who nightly packed the boulevard theaters? Or was Brecht perhaps playing to another "brainwashed, believing, magically mesmerized mass," a mass itching to sing along with songs like the one titled: "In Praise of Communism" (fig. 7), or the untitled song beginning, "Arise, the Party is in danger!'"? There is no evidence whatsoever that supports the idea that these working class audiences who knew that indeed the party was in the most deadly danger felt that the songs and direct audience address produced a feeling of distance or coolness.[24] The translation of Stark-Weisenborn's first person, present tense action into the third person, past tense narrative and/or choral forms which dominate Brecht's text may well have heightened rather than lessened the audience's emotional response to the basic material that is used in both plays. The replacement of first person action by choral odes (one of the very oldest dramatic devices there is) is no guarantee of the transformation of a "mesmerized mass" into cool, objective, independent observers. If one measure of "epic theater" be in fact the largely non-emotional audience response that the early theoretician Brecht seems to call for, then *The Mother* as produced by Brecht in the early thirties is not a particularly good exemplar of the "new and cool play form."

From the above discussion of Brecht's early use of the term "epic theater," it will be remembered that he felt that not only must the epic play allow the audience to remain "cool" and "scientific," it must also embrace more "raw material" than traditional dramatic forms (particularly "Aristotelian") permitted. The theoretical writings of the years immediately surrounding his first production of *The Mother* present a view of epic theater that is remarkable for its call for the kind of "epic breadth and fullness" that distinguished the theater of Tretiakov and Meyerhold in the Soviet Union and Piscator in Berlin. If there was doubt that Brecht's *The Mother* achieved the rational response that the epic theory stresses, there seems even more reason to doubt whether *The Mother* has the kind of breadth and fullness that "epic theater" is supposed to have. To demonstrate this, one need only turn to two other treatments of the "same raw material" that Brecht presents on the stage: the original sprawling treatment of the theme by Gorki (based, incidentally, on historical fact), and the Russian director, Pudovkin's, film treatment of the Gorki novel. We should expect, at least in theory, that the new stage form will permit the treatment of epic materials on the kind of epic scale that Piscator consistently employed. Is this in fact so?

When we turn to the opening pages of Gorki's novel we enter the kind of broad and circumstantial world of the *Epiker*, whether he be called Homer, Dickens, or Balzac. We are introduced to an entire city set in the expanses of pre-revolutionary Russia. After a "long-shot" of the city we are given a medium shot of its industry and the problems of its workers. Only then does the "Epiker" bring us closer to the Wlassow family and their particular problems. We are introduced first to the father and his brutal mode of life. We are introduced to the huge, vicious, mongrel dog that is the father's pride and joy. We are told how the father has been reduced almost to the brute status of his dog by hard working conditions and hard liquor. We are then introduced to his wife, the meek Christian, Pelegea, and his son Pawel who shows promise of becoming as much a brute as his father. After the death of the father, the scene again widens as we are introduced to the revolutionaries who gradually win Pawel over to their side. Gradually the novelist shows us how the Christian sentiment of Pelegea becomes invested in the "good and Christian" goals of the revolutionaries with whom her son has sided. Throughout his narrative (which abounds, incidentally, in first person, present tense dialogue) Gorki allows himself to wander freely in time and space. The pace is slow, the realistic details pile up until they create an impression of the vast panorama that was pre-revolutionary Russia.

When Pudovkin translates the novel into the medium of the film, he retains the epic breadth of the original. He too has a long shot of the whole city before closing in on the Wlassow family in all its circumstantial detail. We see too in Pudovkin's abstractions of moods (after showing a laughing face, he cuts in scenes of a bubbling brook, a happy child, and of birds playing in a farm pond) something startlingly akin to the introduction by Homer of similes of peace into a narrative of war. Turn then from the Pudovkin film, from the world in all its multiplicity of detail, with its streaming and gigantic crowds, vast distances, and the sweep of its history; turn now to Brecht's play.

What has happened to Russia in all its "epic breadth and fullness"? It is reduced to a flat in Tver (fig. 8), another in Rostov (fig. 9), one factory yard (figs. 10 and 11), four street scenes (one of these in "the country"), one prison visit (fig. 12), an estate kitchen, a "national copper collecting booth," and a number of projected photographs of grimy factory towns. Of further interest to the technically minded, over two-thirds of the lines in the play are spoken or sung in interior scenes, either in Pelegea's room or in the flat of the teacher who befriends her.[25] What has happened to the great outdoors of Gorki and Pudovkin? What has happened to the whole town and its host of inhabitants? What has happened to Pelegea's husband? What has happened to the family dog? When one stops to ask these questions, one becomes aware at once that Brecht has reduced the sprawling, circumstantial, epic material to its bare dramatic bones. In either major version (with or without Semjon Lapkin), we are given only that which is germane to the central dramatic conflict: in Brecht this is the direct opposition of Pelegea to the Tsarist authorities. Nothing that cannot be presented with ease on a fairly conventional stage is allowed to appear. In a series of tightly knit scenes (scenes that could only be presented coherently in the order in which Brecht presents them) the figure of the mother develops rapidly. The ignorant woman who first addresses the audience on the theme of her own helplessness, becomes by the end of the work a tower of strength, virtually a personification of the revolution.

Whereas in Gorki the mother is only gradually drawn into the revolutionary movement and is led there by her son's example, in Brecht's play (particularly in the Ensemble version), the mother takes over the lead very early. The play begins and ends with her complaints against Tsarist oppression. Gone completely is Gorki's meek Christian who invests her Christian feelings in a movement that she sees dimly as a form of Ur-Christianity, a movement seeking to unburden the heavy-laden, seeking to give bread to the hungry, and giving the poor somewhere to lay their heads. In contrast, Brecht's Pelegea is violently anti-Christian (in a formal sense) and subscribes completely and immediately to the party-line atheistic ethos. Pelegea takes up the banner the church had dropped. Finally, as an old woman she is brutalized by the Tsarist secret police and robbed of her only son (fig. 13), and uses her last ounce of energy to talk of the promised land to those who will follow her. The play closes with her teaching address to the audience:

> He who is struck down, rise up!
> He who is lost, fight!
> He who has recognized his position, how can he be stopped?
> For the conquered of today are the conquerers of tomorrow
> And out of never, shall come: today[26] (figs. 14 and 15).

There is no indication in the text or in the music itself that we are supposed to be alienated here. Are we then supposed to "surrender emotionally" (not thoughtlessly as we would with Aristotelian dramaturgy, of course!) to her theses? This woman is all leader. She no longer has to be convinced herself; she convinces. She does not persuade; she does not appeal to cool reason; she demands. The figure (for all its supposed underplaying) has been invested with enormous dramatic magnitude. She has become both figurehead and diesel engine of the proud vessel of revolution. The "epic" figure and the "epic" situation have been sharpened to their maximum dramatic potentiality. Pelegea is, using the term in its old-fashioned sense, one of Brecht's very few genuine heroes. The grand master of dialectic might have justified the scale and the effect of the figure of the mother by the following note: "The usefulness of Aristotelian effects should not be denied; one confirms them simply by showing their limits. If a certain social situation is ripe a practical solution can be arrived at by the above means. Such a work is the spark which sets off the powder barrel."[2][7] Had Brecht not gone to such lengths as even to italicize his contention that *The Mother* is non-Aristotelian, he could have spoken of the play as being just such an Aristotelian spark. Certainly the time was ripe for one, and indeed most rightwing reviewers were terrified of the play precisely because they saw it as an attempt to ignite a powder barrel in the tensest possible political situation.

In an essay published a year before Brecht's death, his old enemy, Georg Lukács, sought to define the "Bases for Distinction between the Epic and Dramatic Modes."[2][8] When one applies the traditional concepts developed by Lukács to a play like *The Mother,* one sees at once that Brecht's play is far closer to traditional notions of what constitutes drama than to those defining the epic mode.

Lukács asks what Shakespeare has done with the Lear "material" in order to sharpen its specifically dramatic quality. After noting that "Both tragedy and the epic demand a representation of the totality of the life process,"[2][9] he goes on to show in his neo-Aristotelian way that the tragedy is traditionally more condensed, less circumstantial than the epic. Using *King Lear* as an example of a panoramic play that creates the impression of encompassing much of "the world out there," Lukács writes:

Missing are the relationships between parents and children, missing are the material roots of the family, its growth, its fall etc. One can only compare this type of drama with those great panoramas of the family which pose the problem of a family; with *Buddenbrooks* of Thomas Mann and *Werk der Artamonows* of Gorki. What breadth and fullness of the real circumstances of the family are included here! What generalizing on the purely human and moral, the will-determined, which is in conflict with the changeable characteristics of mankind! Yes, one needs must admire the extraordinary dramatic universality of Shakespeare, in that he manages to portray the older generation of the family through Lear and Gloster alone. Had he—which an epic poet implicitly would have had to have done—given either, or both, Lear and Gloster, a wife, he would have had to either weaken the emphasis on the conflict (as the conflict with the children would have brought about a conflict among the parents), or the presentation of the wife would have been a dramatic tautology as the wife could only have served as a weakened echo of the man. It is characteristic of the rarified atmosphere of dramatic generalization that this tragedy necessarily works upon the audience as an unnerving experience, and therefore the question of the missing woman never arises.[30]

Might we not ask with reference to Brecht's play: what happened to the husband and the family dog? Would it be fair to conclude that the playwright Brecht has very sensibly removed them as they are not directly germane to his central dramatic conflict? Is the specifically dramatic conflict not strengthened and concentrated when the playwright shifts almost the total weight of Tsarist oppression from a wide group of carefully delineated, fully three-dimensional individuals to the figure of Pelegea (particularly as played by the diminutive Helene Weigel), his only fully developed character? To generalize from the two specific instances, *King Lear* and *The Mother,* might we not argue with Lukács, Hegel, and Aristotle[31] that the dramatic medium is, in large part, distinguished by the fact that it is more concentrated and/or focused than the epic? The drama,[32] whether ancient, Shakespearean, or modern, tends to seize only upon those portions of epic "material" that are directly germane to some central collision. The drama often succeeds as drama to the extent that it is willing to abandon the "breadth and fullness" of the epic mode. Viewed thus, might we not ask whether Brecht's play is not perhaps more closely related to Elizabethan or even to Greek dramaturgy than it is to the classical epic mode? Has Brecht not created in his portrait of Pelegea Wlassowa a focused portrait closer to Euripides' Medea or Ibsen's Nora or Goethe's Margaret than the early theorist Brecht could comfortably have admitted? It is possible that the master playwright who was also a master teacher, faced with the spectre of Hitler's rise to power, created in Pelegea Wlassowa a character that could sweep an audience along, alert this audience to the Fascist threat, and involve them in resistance?[33]

Both the pressure of his own urgent political convictions and the pressures of the dramatic mode itself seem to have forced Brecht to retreat from the epic presentation of a Gorki or a Pudovkin. In terms of usage of narrative (actually a chorus) Brecht returns to a standard and most ancient device used by dramatists, East and West, since drama first was. *The Mother* relies less on "narrative" than *Prometheus Bound, Vasantesena, Peter Squentz,* the various productions of Meyerhold, Tretiakov, and others in the Soviet Union, or Piscator's production of Alexey Tolstoy's *Rasputin. The Mother* (in both of Brecht's major versions and in the 1932 and 1951 productions), viewed within the broad compass of the dramatic medium, is a largely traditional, highly conservative, rigidly selective example of the dramatic mode. Using traditional procedures, Brecht has reduced or condensed an epic work to dramatic proportions and has made it eminently suitable for stage presentation.

If we carefully consider all the constituent parts of Brecht's play in his two major productions of it, we see that everything about both play and production works in a focused or implosive manner. Choral odes, projected photographs, and the music are concentrated, in the main, on the mother herself.

If we can make ourselves use the theory of *Verfremdung* against the theory of *Verfremdung* itself (and what, theoretically, could be more Brechtian?), we can begin to see the dialectical importance of *The Mother* and several of Brecht's other plays of this same period. Working, in theory, against Aristotle, Brecht returns us in some of the great teaching plays to that austere and focused playing area that Aristotle most warmly recommends. The fable, or story rather than the trappings of spectacle, resumes its Aristotelian primacy. Again following Aristotle, this primary emphasis on fable leads Brecht directly to placing his secondary emphasis on character.

Brecht's characters, whether we look at the early, middle, or late plays, have extraordinary magnitude and dramatic salience. Over and over again, as with Shakespeare, Marlowe, the French neoclassicists, and the Greeks, Brecht's plays bear the name of a central character who then carries the whole play. Then, instead of having these major figures become virtually indistinguishable from their environment (physical and psychological), Brecht keeps our attention riveted firmly on them and on virtually nothing else. To illustrate this, we need only compare Brecht's austere but beautiful, highly functional sets (the one Neher designed for *The Mother* is an excellent example) with, on the one hand, what we know of "sets" in the Elizabethan and Greek theater, and, on the other, typical sets of the Naturalist and Expressionist periods. In seeing plays like Gorki's *The Lower Depths* and Hauptmann's *The Weavers* our primary memories are of situation rather than of individual character. Character, in a technical sense, has become a function of environment. The success or failure of these plays depends, as Stanislavsky well knew, at least as much on the talents of the casting director (will he be able to find tubercular, hunchbacked dwarfs?), the set designer, and the designer of the costumes as upon the playwright. Words and "character" are not enough to carry most such plays. The obverse of the same argument can be used to describe such examples of Expressionist playwriting as George Kaiser's *Gas I* and *II* and Elmer Rice's *The Adding*

Machine. Environment is, quite literally, an expression of character. It is really not at all surprising that plays which emphasize the physical and psychological milieu rather than character have left us so few memorable characters. In contrast, Brecht, like the Elizabethans and the Greeks (and, incidentally, following Aristotle to the letter), concentrates his attention on fable and character. These characters then play in an environmental space that is often curiously unspecific as to both its when and its where.[34] We are asked, as the Greeks, the Elizabethans, and Oriental theater ask us, "to piece out the setting with our thoughts."

The abstract argument that Brecht's emphasis at each stage of his career is on plot and character rather than on what Aristotle understood under the heading of "spectacle," is factually supported by Brecht's experiences in staging *The Mother* in 1932. The Berlin authorities, openly cowed by Hitler's henchmen, and terrified of the frank call for revolution in the play, refused to give permission for the play to be done as a full-scale production and then taken on tour to working class neighborhoods. Instead, "readings" of the play were done in bare union halls. Martin Esslin notes: "The effect of mere reading was as great if not greater than a fully acted performance."[35] As with the very best tragedies (so argues Aristotle), a "mere reading" was enough to move an audience profoundly. Cutting through the non-Aristotelian trappings of the Naturalists and the Expressionists, Brecht returns us in *The Mother* to a theater world in which fable and character bear the main burden of the play. The playwright-dialectician has come full circle. Seeking to avoid what he felt was "the Aristotelian mode of theater," he groped his circuitous way back to a style of dramaturgy closer to Aristotle in all essential particulars than the "Aristotelian" Expressionists he had so scornfully left behind.

CHAPTER FOUR

THE METAMORPHOSIS OF AN ARISTOTELIAN
CLASSIC: *ANTIGONE*

"... The major concern here is a new playing method rather
than a new dramaturgical construct ..."

Bertolt Brecht[1]

The tide which Brecht had tried to turn in 1932 with his
production of *The Mother* reached full flood within a year. The
day after the Reichstag fire and Hitler's final seizure of
dictatorial power, Brecht, high on the Nazi liquidation list
precisely because of such overtly Communistic plays as *The
Mother,* was forced into exile. For a man whose very life was
the stage, the exile years, full as they were of every kind of
deprivation and many kinds of indignity, were made far worse
for him and for his wife, Helene Weigel, by the fact that they
were cut off from regular working contact with the physical
theater.[2] During the next fifteen years Helene Weigel would
play very few professional roles and Brecht would have little
opportunity to produce his plays in his own way. Cut off from
the stage and forced to watch from afar the events leading to

World War II and the early advances of Hitler's seemingly unbeatable armies, Brecht now wrote mainly "for the desk drawer." Only with his return to Europe in late 1947 (hounded out of the United States by the House Unamerican Activities Committee[3]) do its contents (plays, poems, and major theoretical works) begin to reach an international audience. Only after Brecht begins once again to direct his own plays do they radically alter the theatrical map of both Europe and America.

Any discussion of Brecht as both a great playwright and as a highly inventive director is complicated by the very fact of his magnificent versatility. If we try to treat the plays in the order in which they were placed in the desk drawer, then what do we do when Brecht, over a decade later, makes significant changes in the text when he comes to stage them himself? Should we then pay more attention to the published versions of the plays (versions dictated often by the exigencies of time, health, or a changeable political climate in East Berlin), or should we ferret out the directing copy with Brecht's marginalia from the Brecht Archive in East Berlin and then supplement this version with photos of the production itself and the personal reminiscences of those who were directly involved?[4] Confusing though this latter course may be, I do feel that this is the more reasonable course to take if one is in search of that which was essential to Brecht's working methodology. As Brecht observed a year after finishing a version of his *Good Person of Sezuan* and still, somehow, not entirely satisfied with it, "Without trying it out in production, no play can be completed."[5]

If we wish to consider primarily "completed plays" and the development of Brecht as stage theoretician, playwright, and director, perhaps the most important production between the end of the "didactic period" and his return to his native language and the physical theater is the 1947-48 production of his *Antigone.* With Caspar Neher (figs. 16 and 17) as co-director and scene designer, this production in the small Swiss town of Chur marks an important way station as Brecht, Neher, and Weigel prepare for what they hope will be a triumphal return to

Berlin.[6] In this production the great actress will begin the long process of reestablishing herself on the German-speaking stage (figs. 18 and 19). The great director will begin to grope his way to showing on a stage the substantial changes that his own view of theater has undergone in his fifteen years of exile. I believe it to be of considerable significance that Brecht at this time not only publishes *A Short Organum for the Theater* with its many, many hints of a return to the classical *Poetics* of Aristotle, but also that he should choose at this vitally important point in his career to stage a specifically "Aristotelian" text. The work in Chur represents on the practical plane the rapproachement between Brecht and Aristotle that is worked out (albeit very deviously) in Brecht's post-1947 theoretical pronouncements. Clearly, the fighting pronouncement, "I have given up doing productions of the classics" because their usefulness is "too limited," has undergone some modification in the years of exile.[7]

Brecht's diary notes on why he selected *Antigone*[8] are confusing. He does not mention in the notes that the play was among Hegel's two or three best-loved works in dramatic literature. This might, however, have been in the back of his mind when he made the choice. In practical terms, however, the role was not perhaps perfect for a forty-eight year old actress. Further, the whole notion of having a royal figure become a heroine of the resistance was not, we know, very appealing to Brecht. Despite such impediments, the play seems to have been selected because Caspar Neher had highly recommended the Sophoclean text in Hölderlin's very fine early nineteenth-century translation. Neher, working with another director, had designed a production of the Sophocles-Hölderlin *Antigone* in Hamburg the year before.[9] Though willing to take the unsatisfactory text, Brecht went to work on it at once to try to shape it to his own ends. One of these ends, the theme of the victory that eluded the "great man," Hitler, would be grafted onto the Greek text as Thebes became a metaphor for Berlin, the tide-turning Battle of Stalingrad is refought at Argos, and

Antigone calls forth echoes of Count von Stauffenburg's plot against Hitler. As usual, misreading (either by accident or design) an "original" text, Brecht provides himself with the point of view which serves to turn his revision entirely to his own ends, making it almost a counter play to the original and giving it an unmistakably Brechtian stamp. All this is again (as we have seen with *Eduard II* and we shall see with *Schweyk*) achieved with a maximum borrowing of lines and entire scenes from the "original," combined with radically altered readings of these lines and scenes by the new context.

It is important, however, to note at the outset that Brecht's changes in the text are overwhelmingly ones of content rather than of structure. He changes characters, single words, entire speeches, motivation, etc., but he retains the old (presumably Aristotelian) framework of Sophocles' play. Brecht's "epic" version is somewhat shorter than the Sophocles-Hölderlin text and cuts out one of the limited cast of characters of the original.[10] In fact, it is clear that in this play Brecht is at least as Aristotelian as his Greek model. He has returned to the very model of drama that he so roundly and soundly denounced in his early fulminations on dramatic form. It is clear that Brecht was himself aware of his own backsliding, for he notes of his reworking of Hölderlin:

> Inasmuch as the major concern here is a new playing method rather than a new dramaturgical construct, the new play cannot simply be given in the usual way to theaters, to have them stage it as they may want. Therefore, an obligatory staging model has been put together, a model that can be followed by means of a collection of photographs to be used jointly with notes to clarify meaning.[11]

Brecht plainly admits here that his play does not qualify as an example of epic *dramaturgy*, but tells us that epic elements should be sought instead in the staging. Nevertheless, enough important changes have been made in the plot to make a consideration of performance alone insufficient; we must consider Brecht's textual changes as well.

Most importantly, instead of having Eteocles and Polynices fighting on opposite sides (as Greek legend and Sophocles have it), Brecht places them on the same side. Also, instead of bitterly fighting each other for their father's kingdom as they do in Sophocles-Hölderlin, Brecht has them reluctantly fighting a war of aggression at the behest of the tyrant and usurper, Kreon. In Brecht also, Kreon does not simply assume power after the death of the direct heirs to the throne (Polynices and Eteocles) but seizes it before the play begins. Kreon is therefore, in Brecht, a usurper and "tyrant" in the narrowest and most pejorative modern sense of the Greek term. Brecht would seem to seek to draw this view of Kreon from the Greek text itself when he writes:

> In Sophocles, the Antigone-Kreon situation is in the aftermath of a successful war; the tyrant (that is to say, the ruler) is in the process of getting even with those personal enemies who had hindered victory. The actions of the tyrant bring him in conflict with a human custom and, as a result, he suffers the destruction of his own family.[12]

Brecht would seem to imply here that Kreon planned and directed the war that has just been won. Though this is true of Brecht's Kreon, it is not true of Sophocles' character. It is also questionable that the Sophoclean Kreon is dealing after the war with personal enemies. One might in fact interpret his reason for not burying the one brother as primarily a reason of state rather than one of personal enmity. Brecht has obviously read into the text that possibility which he wished to find there.[13]

The clearest way to illustrate the radical changes Brecht makes in the Sophocles-Hölderlin text is to note carefully how distant Brecht's characters are in language, psychology, and point of view from the characters in the Greek and in Hölderlin's translation. The character that best illustrates the scope of Brecht's changes is Kreon himself. Again and again, as both text and the *Model Book* make plain, plot, language, and staging style point away from a basically mild monarch who makes one moral error, toward a dyed-in-the-wool villain, to the bad man of the twentieth century—Adolf Hitler. Not only do the pictures of the 1948 production of the play clearly show the actor playing Kreon made up as Hitler, the prologue[14] and numerous other textual changes indicate that this interpretation was intentional. Whereas in Hölderlin a guard addresses Kreon as "Mein König" ("my king"),[15] Brecht's guard says "Mein Führer" ("my fuehrer").[16]

Though Brecht subsequently tried to deny the specific connection of his Kreon with Hitler and wrote a different prologue for later productions, it remains questionable whether his play makes very much sense without these references. I would suggest that unless we see Kreon as Hitler and understand the historical reasons for his attacking the Soviet Union, we have no valid reason in Brecht's play for Kreon to lust after the ore deposits of his neighbors. Though Brecht claims that "The war of Thebes with Argos is realistically presented,"[17] and goes on to note of the war, "Its goal is the mines of Argos,"[18] he fails to provide adequate motivation for Kreon to want the ore. He has neither a real nor a compelling reason within the play to launch an unpopular war against his strongly defended neighbor; his actions are therefore, within the context of the play, simply demonic. Brecht is clearly trying in this play to present Kreon as a thorough villain and to eliminate anything whatsoever that might tend to draw our sympathy. In Brecht's radically shortened ending, for instance, Eurydice is omitted. Perhaps she is simply superfluous (i.e., does not directly contribute to the central story line) as the East German critic Witzmann[19] has suggested, but it is also likely that the death of Eurydice, serving as it does in Sophocles to direct our pity or compassion toward Kreon, would be out of place in a play that consistently seeks to blacken Kreon's character.

Further evidence of Brecht's reduction of Kreon almost to a melodramatic villain is his character's treatment of the two sons of the exiled Oedipus. Not only does Kreon seize power from them and arrive on stage with announcements of deaths and of booty, but it soon becomes clear that he has driven one of Oedipus' sons to his death and has killed the other with his own hands. Antigone herself reports:

> The galloping fugitive had
> Crossed the Dirzain brooks; recovering his breath
> He sees Thebes, the seven-gated, standing, when
> There seizes him Kreon, covered with his [the fugitive's]
>   brother's blood, Kreon, busy in
> The rear whipping everyone into battle, seizes
> Him and chops him in pieces.[20]

Our final view of Kreon, seen before as booty hunter and blood-spattered killer of his own kin, is one of a man who, having learned nothing in the course of the play, exits, consigning his own city to the vultures.[21] It is clear that Kreon in Brecht's play is not so much a man as scapegoat on whom Brecht has loaded all the sins of that class he deemed responsible for war in Europe in the twentieth and other centuries. These crimes are perhaps a little too much for one man to bear.

The radical changes Brecht introduces in the character of Kreon change the whole relationship of Kreon to Antigone. In Brecht's play it takes superhuman courage for Antigone to oppose the superhuman villainy of her uncle, the killer of her brother or brothers. In this context, Antigone becomes a one-woman resistance movement, and again the parallels with those few Germans who did openly oppose Hitler are made abundantly clear.[22] Aware of the crying need for moral action in a world run by a mad killer, Antigone must resist the tyrant.[23] Dismissing the cowardice of the middle-class chorus and deeming their scruples against opposing the tyrant short-sighted, she bursts out:

> I cry for you, the living
> For what you will see
> When my eyes are already filled with dust.[24]

As she exits, almost in triumph, the Elders comment:

> She turns and goes, long stride, as though
> She was leading her guards.[25]

Her abrupt turn, long stride, and the chorus' comments on her actions all make Antigone an almost classical heroine. She reminds us most of Marlowe's Young Mortimer as he strides out to "discover countries yet unknown."[26]

It is worth noting however that the Marxist Brecht who seemed content to make Kreon a thoroughgoing villain was not happy with Antigone as an unadulterated heroine. Her upper-class origins surely had something to do with this. Soon after the chorus remarks on the manner of Antigone's exit, they also observe of her:

> But even she once
> Ate from bread baked in
> Dark caves.[27]

Clarifying this remark, the chorus continues:

> In the shadow of the towers
> Sheltering misfortune: she sat calmly, until
> Something deadly emerged from the House of Labdacus
> And returned; deadly.[28]

Though she is the only one providing resistance to Kreon (and the parallels to Count von Stauffenberg are striking), she apparently did not act soon enough to distance herself from the position of "the ruling class" and when she did act it was only because she was personally affected by Kreon's decree.

In seeking to present Antigone ambiguously, Brecht is forced into a rather curious structural expedient. He had to find someone or some group within the play to comment darkly on her motivation. He decides to give these comments to the chorus, but one wonders how apt these words really are in the chorus as Brecht characterizes them. If we remember Brecht's oft-repeated definition of the bourgeoisie ("that class which converts all human relationships to economic gain"), it is impossible to view the Elders of Thebes as anything but typical members of this hated class. Note for instance how Brecht introduces the chorus and how this introduction differs from that of Hölderlin. In Hölderlin (buried in a long choral ode) we find the following verse:

> Great named victory has come,
> Rich in wagons, good. And now for the Thebans,
> The war is over and forgetfulness makes all smooth.[29]

Brecht makes this the very first verse spoken by the chorus and makes only one small but significant change: where Hölderlin speaks of "der grossnamige Sieg" ("great named victory") Brecht has the unequivocal "der grossbeutige Sieg" ("victory, rich in booty"). Later in the same choral ode, he underlines the importance of this substitution by changing Hölderlin's line, "Kreon. . ./ Kommt wohl, um einen Rat/ Zu sagen"[30] ("Kreon comes to bring us news"), to "Kreon, Meneokeus' Sohn, hastete wohl/ Her vom Schlachtfeld, Beute zu künden. . ."[31] ("Kreon, son of Mendeceus, hurries here from the battlefield to announce the booty."). After Kreon declares, "Argos no longer exists," the ancients again respond in purely mercenary terms:

> Lord, you paint a lovely and moving picture.
> And, when we tell the story to the city it will be sure to
>   please,
> If mixed with another: One of wagons
> Rolling up the lanes, filled with possessions.[32]

This "capitalistic" stress is only barely hinted at in Sophocles and Hölderlin; the purpose of Brecht's stress change is obvious.

So grasping are Brecht's Elders in the opening scene that it is aesthetically jarring that they should be used almost immediately thereafter, in some of the finest verse passages in the play, to muse on man's inhumanity to man and to berate Antigone. Neither the ode to Bacchus (with its haunting memories of *Baal*) nor the second choral ode make much sense in the mouths of people first presented as grasping fools.[33] In fact, though much of the second choral ode is borrowed word-for-word from Sophocles-Hölderlin, it is the changes that make it particularly unsuited to the character of the Theban Elders. These subtle but profound changes warrant closer examination. Again, as with his adaptation of Marlowe, Brecht has changed enormously much by changing surprisingly little. In Greek the second choral ode begins:

πολλὰ τὰ δεινὰ χοὐδὲν ἀν-
θρώπου δεινότερον πέλει·

H.D.F. Kitto renders the text in English as:

Wonders are many, yet of all
Things is Man the most wonderful.[34]

Now it is not possible in English, as Kitto's rendering shows, to capture the full ambiguity of the Greek text, with its primary sense of the positive "wonderful" but with dark undertones of potential terror. German, in contrast to English, does permit a similar ambiguity and Hölderlin comes very close to the dual nature of the original with his choice of the German word, "Ungeheuer." The German word carries the double burden of something "great" or "something of wonder" (either positive or neutral qualities) and the clearly negative meanings: "monstrous, atrocious, frightful." In modern usage the negative connotations of the word have almost entirely squeezed out its earlier neutral or positive potentialities. It is possible that when Hölderlin completed his translation in 1803 that "Ungeheuer" still retained some residual traces of its ancient duality. By 1948 all positive traces had disappeared. Yet we know from the rest of the Sophoclean ode and from Sophocles' work in general that he intended the first line of the ode to carry, primarily, a positive burden. The notoriously "dark" translation of Hölderlin which, though often quite accurate, does include the more pessimistic rendering whenever a choice is offered, has shifted the balance in the direction of a "dark" reading of the opening two lines of the ode. This shift of balance is then largely corrected by the general positive nature of the ode as a whole. Brecht, however, shifts the balance of the whole ode immeasurably further by keeping the word "Ungeheuer" and then inserting into the ode additions that underline the negative qualities of man. Brecht's version of the ode begins:

Ungeheuer ist viel. Doch nichts
Ungeheuerer als der Mensch.[35]

This would then have to be rendered in English as:

> Much is monstrous. But nothing is more
> Monstrous than Man.

The tone of this line, rather obviously, is a little different from that of Kitto's English rendering of the original Greek:

> Wonders are many, yet of all
> Things is Man the most wonderful.

The reversal of meaning of the Greek sentiment is then underscored in Brecht when we are told that not only does man force the bull to bend its neck (this is in agreement with Sophocles), but he also "bends the neck of his fellows." Further, man also "tears out the guts" of his fellows and "builds walls around them."[36] But at this point in the ode Brecht the poet, having perhaps forgotten that these words are then to be placed in the mouths of the odious Elders, representatives of the hated bourgeoisie, can contain himself no longer and adds: "and these walls must be torn down!"[37] One can understand these words in Brecht's mouth; we can understand this cry particularly well if we think of Berlin today;[38] but what is more difficult to understand is why such "capitalist swine" as the Elders of Thebes should suddenly gratuitously offer a sensitive and richly poetic ode on the theme of man's inhumanity to man. Why should they, of all people, demand such progressive change as the tearing down of walls? It would seem that Brecht, full to bursting with poems on this theme and working in great haste on the adaptation, simply could not resist giving his own thoughts expression, even though they are so obviously irreconcilable with the fundamental immorality of the bourgeois chorus as he first presents them.

In Sophocles-Hölderlin, in contrast, the age of the Elders gives them a certain claim to wisdom, experience, and insight. As Kreon's decision regarding the corpse is seen (partly because of Antigone's vigorous opposition) to be incorrect, they attempt (and in their attempt morality and expedience are inextricably intertwined) to get Kreon to change his mind. In the mouths of Sophocles' Elders, the lovely philosophical odes couched in complex rhythms, the commentaries on the history of the House of Labdacus, and the moral growth of the chorus which culminates in their finally being asked by Kreon to give their advice (and in Kreon's acceptance of this advice) hardly seem at all out of place. They are, from the beginning, venerable and thoughtful men whose advice, when they are allowed to tender it, is practical and morally sound. In view of this, surely it should not surprise us that the mantle of the bourgeoisie that Brecht had cut to fit Mackie Messer, Jonathan Peachum, Thiers in *The Days of the Commune,* and the barber in *The Good Person of Sezuan,* should not exactly have a "made to measure" look on the shoulders of Thebes' venerables. Working in haste (he completed the adaptation between November 30 and December 12, 1948), Brecht seems simply to have reworked the opening speeches of the chorus to fit his own vision of the Elders as unscrupulous members of an unscrupulous class, but to have left other speeches (which clearly contradict this view) in a form very close to that found in Sophocles-Hölderlin. The result, in my opinion, is a complete break in character between the different parts of the chorus' role.

Brecht's work in Chur on the text of *Antigone* makes clear how much his interest has shifted as he returns to work in the physical theater, to use once again his own native lanugage, with Weigel once again as his leading actress, and with Neher again doing his stage designs. Whereas the exile years, because of his enforced absence from continued contact with the physical theater, had been so enormously productive of texts for the theater, the returned exile was naturally primarily concerned with getting these great plays staged. In this new phase, it is the physical theater that has become primary, and "the mere literary text" secondary. It is perhaps for this reason that he produces in that last decade of his life some of the world's finest theater and but few first-rate literary texts. Of significance therefore to our final examination of *Antigone* as it was staged in Switzerland is the manner of the staging. With this play we see how careless Brecht had become as to text per se, and how careful he had become as to actual staging detail. Whatever "epic" elements we are able to find in his last years should be sought primarily in his staging methods.

Brecht's staging of *Antigone* largely followed the sketches of his lifelong friend, Caspar Neher, the designer of *Eduard II* and most of his major productions. Sitting in a semicircle on simple benches before an almost colorless backdrop, the actors in Chur simply arose and came forward to act their roles in a square playing area that was marked by four posts on which were hung the skulls of horses (figs. 20 and 21). The only other items on stage were, on one side, a large square gong and on the other a rack containing masks set on long poles (figs. 22 and 23). The chorus held these masks in front of them during long choral odes (fig. 24) and then replaced them in the rack. The tempo of the production was extremely fast and no curtain was used at all. Scene followed scene with extraordinary rapidity. The acting, partly because of and partly in spite of the pace of the production was deliberately stylized and no attempt was made at "realistic" portraiture in the manner of Stanislavsky. The role of Kreon was deliberately the most stylized, with his makeup suggesting Hitler and his movements (frequently going over into exaggerated dance steps) suggesting the kind of bloody clown that Brecht presents in his *Schweyk* adaptation and in *Arturo Ui* (fig. 25). It is certain that Brecht was completely successful in this case in preventing identification with such a clearly identified villain.[39] As Frank Jones has suggested, this treatment of Kreon characterizes the play as something very close to melodrama, "with all the black on one side and all the white on the other"[40] (fig. 26).

It is perhaps unfair to link the partially melodramatic style of this new production (with all the pejorative connotations of melodrama) with the "new playing style"[41] that Brecht claims to be presenting in his production.[42] Despite the claim that he is presenting a new playing style, it is virtually certain that Brecht was fully aware in 1947-48 that the style was not so much new as a renaissance (with some modifications) of many aspects of the stage style of fifth-century Athens—the stage style that Aristotle knew and praised. By 1948, with the staging of *Antigone* and the composition of the *Short Organum*, Brecht has beaten a skilled retreat from much of his earlier iconoclasm. The author of the 1927 essay, "Should we not Destroy Aesthetics?" now consciously attempts to generate a consistent aesthetic, and says specifically that his earlier attacks on many aesthetic criteria had been determined by the heat of battle and the fact that his opponents had preempted much of the necessary vocabulary for their own reactionary purposes.[43] "We," announces the now regal Brecht in the preface to the *Short Organum,* "despite general dismay, therefore revoke our [earlier] intention to emigrate from the realm of the pleasurable, and we hereby announce, to even greater dismay, our intention of taking up residence there."[44] In Section Four he comes perilously close to praising "the catharsis of which Aristotle writes."[45] In Section Nine he speaks of improbability on the stage as being perfectly admissible as long as it "remains of a constant kind."[46] By the time he reaches Section Twelve Brecht has mellowed enough to speak of the "great Shakespeare" and to state further: "And according to Aristotle—and we agree there—the plot is the soul of the drama."[47] The *Short Organum* then closes (and we are reminded of Aristotle's preference of "poetry" to "history") with the observation: "If art does mirror life, it does it with special mirrors."[48] It is clear both from the production of a classic text and from the new tone of the *Short Organum* that Brecht in 1948, on the brink of becoming a classic himself, has begun to treat his great forerunners in dramaturgy and stage theory (particularly Aristotle and Shakespeare) with considerable respect. Nevertheless, it must be granted that Brecht is still very reluctant to grant the similarity of his own work to that of other classical writers. On the one hand (considering his earlier iconoclastic statements), it would have hurt his pride to retreat too openly, and on the other, the classical writers had served other masters than the proletariat that Brecht was hoping to serve upon his return to

East Berlin. Yet however reluctant he may be, and however devious he is in granting his similarities to other writers, he does now seek consistently to point out in what ways other dramatists and theorists have anticipated him.

Perfectly aware by 1948 that not only were there narrative, epic, and lyric elements in the Greek drama,[49] and that the use of choral odes to interrupt the action was a definite anticipation of key elements in his epic theater, Brecht was also surely aware that both Goethe and Schiller had anticipated him in noting and commenting favorably upon these facets of Greek drama. Yet Brecht writes: "Hellenic dramaturgy sought, through a certain amount of usage of *Verfremdung*, and particularly through the segments devoted to the chorus, to save some freedom of [rational] calculation, freedom that Schiller did not know how to secure."[50] One may be permitted to wonder here why there is any reference to Schiller at all, if, as a footnote of Brecht's seeks to establish, the Schiller of the Goethe-Schiller *Correspondence* is really inept. Surely Brecht knew by 1948 that, important though the *Correspondence* is to the history of German criticism, it is of less importance to the history of thought on the epic than essays such as Schiller's on naive and sentimental poetry and the one on the role of the chorus in Greek tragedy, and Goethe's essay on the dramatic and the epic modes. Viewed in the larger context of the theoretical writings of Goethe and Schiller, Brecht's citation from the *Correspondence* reveals either a general ignorance of their other writings or a deliberate piece of tendentious citation to prove both their ignorance and his own originality. The similarities to his "own theory" are so striking that it is difficult to believe Brecht was so ignorant of the German classics in 1948 that he was unaware, to give but one instance (from the famous introduction to his *Bride of Messina*), of the following very "Brechtian" hypothesis of the ignoramus, Schiller:

> Just as the chorus brings life to the language, it brings calm to the action—but it is the lovely and lofty calm that is essential to a pure work of art. For the soul of the spectator should

retain its freedom even in the midst of the most violent passion; this does not mean that it should be robbed of impressions, but rather that it should always clearly and serenely distinguish between itself and the emotions which it suffers. Thus, the common judgment against the chorus (that it destroys illusion and disrupts the emotive hold of the play on its audience), can be used as the chorus' highest recommendation. This is because the genuine artist wishes to avoid the blind power of emotion and deliberately spurns the creation of illusion. Should the blows which tragedy strikes our hearts strike uninterruptedly, then suffering would win the victory over action. We would become one with the tragic material rather than rise above it. The chorus holds the individual parts of the tragedy apart and enters between passionate outbursts with soothing contemplation, and it is because of this that our freedom is restored to us, freedom that would otherwise be lost in a storm of emotions.[51]

Schiller, it would seem, was not as ignorant as Brecht's one tendentious citation from the *Correspondence* makes him out to be. Schiller knew a thing or two about *Verfremdung,* about "a feeling of distance," about pacing of a drama, about deliberate episodic fragmentation; in a word, Schiller knew something about what Brecht seems to have been talking about. It is clear from Brecht's own copious production notes that his use of the chorus in Chur was a return in some particulars to the theoretical function assigned to it by Schiller, and a return in practice to the oldest of Western dramatic modes, the drama Aristotle was talking about when he formulated his *Poetics.*

As surely as Brecht must have known by 1948 that the German classics had anticipated many of his theoretical points, he must have known also that his earlier view of a theatrical audience sitting hypnotized in a darkened auditorium and creeping into the skins of the characters on the stage described only a very narrow segment of the history of the physical theater. Certainly he knew by this time that neither the Greek nor the Elizabethan theater (to cite but two prominent examples) fitted this general description. Despite Brecht's claim to be presenting "a new playing style," I see no major differences in probable effect between the style of his Chur presentation and well-known classical Greek theatrical practice. One does not need a profound scholarly knowledge of Greek theater to know that Brecht has come perilously close to returning to the very theatrical mode that he most despised in the 1920s. If anything, Brecht's production in the small Swiss theater may have been considerably less epic than *Antigone* in its original setting. How hypnotized, we might wonder, was a member of the Greek audience of some 14,000, a person knowing the mythological background of the tale inside out? Did the actors with their broad gestures, elevator shoes, masks, and loud voices hypnotize this huge assembly sitting there in daylight? Did the long choral odes, backed by as many as fifty strong voices, break the action or did they intensify it? We know only that these elements are all "epic" as Brecht defines the term; we do not know with any certainty whether they succeeded any more in the Greek world in achieving a *Verfremdungseffekt* than they did in Brecht's theater. We might assume that despite the considerably larger number of "epic" elements in Greek dramaturgy and performance, the audiences were as profoundly moved as Brecht's audiences, twenty-five centuries later, tended to be.

From what we can reconstruct of Brecht's 1948 production of his version of *Antigone,* we know that he was able to recapture beautifully many powerful and essential features of the original Greek play in its original setting. Freeing himself, as had the Greeks, from the burdensome limitations of strict naturalism in acting and in settings, getting rid of the curtain between the actors and the audience, using a unit set that required absolutely no changes that would interrupt the action, Brecht used mime and mask, choral ode and dance for broad and specifically theatrical effects. The result was, as even many fairly hostile reviewers granted,[52] magnificent theater. Whatever the drawbacks of the clumsily reworked text (hidden, in all probability, by the sheer pace of the performance), the staging of the text not only recalled the 1924 production of *Eduard II* and the 1932 production of *The Mother* but pointed ahead to Berlin and to the great productions of the exile plays that would make Brecht, as playwright and as director, world famous. We underestimate Brecht's humor if we overlook the conscious irony of the grandmaster of anti-Aristotelian "epic theater," as he prepares himself for his last major period of work in the physical theater by adapting and indeed intensifying an Aristotelian text, and presenting that text in a largely traditional style.

CHAPTER FIVE

THE EXILE'S RETURN: THE BERLIN
MOTHER COURAGE AND HER CHILDREN

> "Of all Brecht's plays *Mother Courage,* by its structure, comes closest to the traditional pattern of European tragedy."
>
> *Walter H. Sokel*[1]

> "Brecht's best-known and most successful play and the classic example of epic theater [is] *Mother Courage."*
>
> *F.N. Mennemeier*[2]

From Switzerland, hampered in his movements by the Western Allies and harassed by the Swiss authorities, Brecht finally reached Berlin at the end of October 1948. In the Eastern sector of the shattered city, he began work at once on rehearsing *Mother Courage and Her Children,* a chronicle of the Thirty Years War. With his old friend Erich Engel as co-director, using as a stage model the sets and stage requisites that Teo Otto had designed for the wartime world premiere in Zürich,[3] and with Helene Weigel playing the lead, the play was ready to open on January 11, 1949 (fig. 27). As he had hoped, the play was an instant success. At one stroke, the Brecht who had won the hearts (if not the heads) of the Berliners almost exactly twenty years before with his *Threepenny Opera,* reestablished himself in what still remained the capital of German language theater. From now on, the plays of Brecht and Brecht's productions of them would receive the exceedingly liberal financial support of the East German government.[4] By means of this support, Brecht and Helene Weigel were able to gather the greatest assemblage of theater talent in the world, to form the nucleus of the Berliner Ensemble. From 1949 until his death in 1956 he was able to use the Ensemble to create the kind of theater of which he had hardly dared dream during the long years of exile.

The fame that had seeped away during the exile years was now to be won back again through the talents of Brecht's theater group as a whole. Touring the major cities of Eastern and Western Europe,[5] the Ensemble would make famous the various stage devices we now associate with Brecht's name: the half-curtain that allowed the audience to see part of the scene changes, stage lights almost always at full,[6] sets that merely suggested playing locales rather than making any attempt to reproduce a "realistic" setting, raucous music and highly traditional music combined in such a way that it both soothed the nerves and sawed on them, and, above all, an exceedingly well-trained group of actors, playing with extraordinary intensity Brecht's best plays, which they had often rehearsed for up to a year before presenting them to the public. Everywhere the company went it became a theatrical event of the first magnitude. Henceforth, directors, designers, playwrights, and actors would make an obligatory pilgrimage to East Berlin to study Brecht's working methods with the Ensemble. Within three years of his return to Berlin, Brecht was acknowledged as the leader of the international theatrical avant-garde. All this had been made possible by that epochal 1949 production of *Mother Courage.*[7] Let us look at the play in Brecht's production and try to establish why the reverberations of the play and the production spread so wide.

The play itself had been written in exile in Sweden in 1939. The year is significant; the play was to warn against the participation of "the little person" in the catastrophe that everyone then saw on the horizon. For his morality play, Brecht freely mined Grimmelshausen's bloody and sordid tale of the adventures of one Simplicissimus during the Thirty Years War.[8] Instead of going to the whole disjointed novel cycle of Grimmelshausen, Brecht condenses his material and chiefly mines a single section of it: the independent part entitled "A Narrative Description of the Arch-Rogue and Camp-Follower Courasche." In the *Courasche* novel each chapter begins with a descriptive heading, telling what the following chapter will contain. These headings are similar in form and even in script to the placards Brecht uses in his production to introduce each scene. In the novel, Courasche, now old and poor and diseased, reduced to a shadow of her former luscious and wealthy self, undertakes to tell the story of her life. She begins her tale with the usual invocations of virtue that precede most tales of extraordinary vice. Her simple narration of her wild life, will, or so she says, induce her listeners to stick to the straight and narrow path. She was, she says, brought up by decent, god-fearing, foster parents. As a teenager she goes off to war disguised as a page, falls in love with her soldier master, and loses, with gusto, her "virtue" after a promise of marriage which is not kept. She then leaps from one bed or barn to another. Finally, she does marry, five times or so in fact; engages with great joy in considerable commercial sex on the side; becomes for a brief while a sutler woman; and has, in all, some twenty-eight chapters of the most diverse adventures connected only by the threads of her own shrewdness and nymphomania. The tale is highlighted by her contracting "an obscene disease," and finally simply peters out with a description of a thieving adventure with some gypsies. Though shorter and simpler than the *Simplicissimus* novel as a whole, *Courasche* has two important hallmarks of the epic mode, as the early Brecht himself understood the genre. The exposition of the tale is entirely narrative, and the various loosely linked adventures could easily be shuffled without making the tale any less understandable.

In Brecht, a small number of Courasche's adventures (and her disease) are given to Yvette, the prostitute, and Courage herself is presented as primarily a businesswoman-mother. Her own sexual adventures are largely a matter of the past (all of her children have different fathers) and she has, within the play, a specifically sexual relationship only with the cook from Utrecht. We are not told in Brecht why Mother Courage got involved in the war in the first place; we learn, in fact, next to nothing about her early life. For all we know, she may have been forced into the trade of camp-follower in a world that had destroyed all other means of livelihood. In contrast with Grimmelshausen's detailed description of some seventy years, Brecht has twelve years of war. The tale told by Brecht is a relatively simple one. A businesswoman-mother enters the scene with three grown children and a loaded wagon. In the course of the play she loses all three of her children (though she only learns of the death of two) and most of her goods through the fortunes of war. She leaves the stage, with almost no goods to sell, with no children to help her pull the wagon, and having learned nothing from the chain of tragic circumstances that have befallen her. So much for the basic fable or plot. Now let us turn to Brecht's shaping of the plot in his production of the play.

The play opens with a conversation between a sergeant-major and a recruiting officer about the relative merits of peace and war. Standing on the front edge of the revolving stage against an indiscriminate grey backdrop,[9] they conduct a conversation distinguished mainly by its frank inversion of what we suppose to be traditional values. Their sentiments are couched in a language that is terse to an extreme but at the same time, vivid, coarse, apt. All the characters in the play will speak this same language, language described by Hans Mayer as being "naked, stripped of all conventions and previously accepted moral principles."[10]

Beneath the surface of the complaints and banter of the soldiers are layers of meaning that amply reward intense formal analysis. In the world to which Brecht introduces us here, man, when distinguishable from other beasts at all, distinguishes himself by the ingenuity of his cruelty. The brutal world of Brecht's plays, lyrics, novels, and short stories—a world in which the shark is preferred to man[11]—appears again with all its usual ferocity in *Mother Courage.* To return to the soldiers, we find the recruiter complaining that after he has talked a man into signing up and has even bought him a drink, the man, more likely than not, will be lacking in "loyalty and faith" and will escape at the first opportunity. The recruiter says specifically: "He runs, like a louse from scratching."[12] Man, in the image of the metaphor, is a louse. No wonder, says the recruiter, "I've lost my confidence in mankind here."[13] This "non-heroic" vision of "God's creature" man and his relation to the "lower orders" is then reinforced when the sergeant-major observes: "In peace man lets the cabbages run to seed. People mess around with men and cattle as though they were nothing."[14] The deliberate confusion of man and the other animals is given greater specificity in the Feldwebel's next line: "No one knows how many young people and good nags there are in this town up ahead; nobody's ever bothered to count."[15] It becomes clear that for these men, as for Courage herself a little later in the play, the feeders of the war machine only distinguish between men and cattle, sacks of corn and bundles of shoes, as an organizational device. It is easier to supply the machine, and the machine will use its fodder more efficiently, if a proper filing system is kept.

After the opening interchange between the two soldiers (these scenes are reversed in the Ensemble production) there appears at once an extraordinary vision, one of the most powerful symbolic requisites of the twentieth-century stage, the wagon of Mother Courage[16] (fig. 28). The wagon, hung inside and out with tradeable items, is not drawn by a horse but by the two sons of Mother Courage, Schweizerkäs and Eilif (fig. 29). On the wagon sit or lounge the boys' mother and their sister, the dumb Kattrin[17] (fig. 30). Mother Courage brightens at the sight of two potential customers; the soldiers glow at the sight of the two husky lads drawing the wagon. It is clear that each group eyes the other not as human beings but as instruments of barter and sale. Immediately upon being stopped by the soldiers, Mother Courage sings the moving song that formally opens, links, and closes the play:

> Captains, let the drums be stilled
> And let your infantry stop awhile.
> Mother Courage has boots
> That are easier on the feet.
> When marching into battle,
> With lice and vermin,
> Baggage, guns, and gear,
> They'll want good boots.
> > *Refrain:*
> > The spring is coming. Christians awake!
> > The snows melt. The dead rest.
> > And what hasn't died yet
> > Had better get out of bed.
> Captains, don't let your men march to their death
> Without at least some sausage.
> Let Courage cure them first, with wine,
> Of that which ails body and soul.
> Cannon on an empty stomach,
> You captains, that's not healthy.
> When they are fed, then with my blessing
> Lead them into the maw of hell.
> > *Refrain:*[18]

It is Mother Courage herself who brings the sausages without which men would not be prepared to die. It is she who, in the imagery of her own song, is the handmaiden of war and of death itself. Again the language of the play is vivid, "naked, stripped of all normal conventions and moral concepts," again lice, men, dray animals and beasts for slaughter are heaped indiscriminately together. Death lowers over this wagon; death dominates the song; the song of death is repeated again and again throughout and finally closes the play, as Courage, all her strong and much loved children now themselves dead, grinds the meaningless mill of the turntable stage beneath her staggering feet.

After her opening song, Courage is asked to state her name (received, she says, because of her fearless pursuit of profit at the siege of Riga) and to produce her papers. While the recruiter eyes the boys, Courage produces her papers theatrically and with considerable humor (fig. 31). Beneath the surface of her humor, however, lurks the shark of Brecht's imagery, a shark that bites, however humorous the scene may seem superficially. One extraordinary document produced by Courage illustrates the duality of her humor. She produces a piece of parchment that "proves" that the *Schimmel* (a word that means both mildew and a white or greyish horse) that she does *not* have, does *not* have foot and mouth disease. Again man and beast have been confused, as her own sons have now replaced the horse. This same confusion is then deepened by the actions of the recruiter. In the Ensemble production[19] he walked around the boys like a farmer contemplating the purchase of a pair of horses or oxen; he felt their muscles; and then remarked with barely concealed admiration: "I see these lads have grown up like birch trees, deep chested, strong legs: why does something like *that* [my italics] try to avoid the draft?"[20] (fig. 32). He then addressed the boys contemptuously, trying to shame them into abandoning their "animal" condition and joining the "human" race of soldiers. After asking them for their names the recruiter says: "You'd be better named Jacob Ox and Esau Ox; after all, you do pull the wagon." He then concludes, with fake resignation, "I guess you'll never get out of harness."[21] The recruiter is literally and figuratively correct. The young men will live and meet their violent end with no more ability to avoid their fate than the brute ox and horse with which they have been justly compared.

This interpretation of the surface and sub-surface of Brecht's treatment of Schweizerkäs and Eilif can be carried over to the other characters. The recruiting officer, the sergeant, Kattrin and her mother, and all the other characters yet to be introduced will draw the wagon of war, will confuse in their own persons, men made in "God's image" and the hyenas of the war. All, even when they show a "human" trait, such as Eilif's smartness and daring, Schweizerkäs' honesty, and Kattrin's love of children, will be shot down like dogs precisely because of these human traits. As beast or as man all will die. Honor and bravery are only necessary in a bad world, observes Courage sententiously. Her own courage is questionable. Even her mother instinct is surely not an unmixed blessing; perhaps she is stupid in *not* always putting herself first.

As poignantly as the animal/man confusion sounds the depths of "man's" misery while laying the foundations of Brecht's tightly knit play, so does another layer of language and action generalize toward the timeless theme of "man's in-humanity to man" while economically tracing another basic pattern in the complex weave of the play. *Mother Courage* is a play as littered with images of the cross as the corpse- and grave-littered landscape through which the wagon of this "war of the cross" (Crusade) passes. The power of the image of the cross, the image of the sufferings of the man-god Christ,[22] suffuses the play with its own mixture of barbarity, human sacrifice and suffering, and dynamically links beginning, middle, and end in that fusion we look for in examples of high and enduring art.

The opening scene, for instance, is deepened and extended by means of the image of the cross. After pulling a knife on the soldiers in defense of her young, Courage resorts to fortune-telling, a favorite device of Brecht's,[23] in order to frighten her children into staying with her and not risking their lives in the fortunes of war. She turns demonstratively to her children, in full view of the soldiers, and tears up a sheet of parchment.[24] She announces as she does this: "Eilif, Schweizerkäs and Kattrin, may we all be thus torn if we involve ourselves too deeply in war."[25] The "demonstration" turns out to have the significance of Oedipus announcing the terrible fate that will befall the murderer of Laius if and when he be found. Having torn the parchment, Mother Courage makes crosses on all the pieces and drops them into a helmet provided by the recruiting officer. She then has the soldiers and all three of her children draw a fatal cross (fig. 33). Brecht extends the cross imagery by having her complain of Kattrin's "good heart," adding, "you are yourself a cross."[26]

The image of the cross is then further underlined by the use of an extremely prominent stage requisite, the cross-shaped tongue of the wagon. Is it pure accident that this requisite reenforces throughout the play the linguistic and gestic use of the cross in the opening scene? Is it an accident that the tongue of the wagon juts out center stage as the soldiers interrogate the family and examine the boys (fig. 33)? Why too, in the Berliner Ensemble *Model Book* photos, do the characters pulling crosses from the helmet group themselves around the tongue of the wagon? Why does the bowed stance of the pullers, after Eilif has been seduced away by the soldiers (fig. 34), recall so forcefully the stumbling figure of Christ toiling toward Golgotha? Why, when Mother Courage contemplates and rejects the idea of abandoning Kattrin (her cross) for the friendly haven of the inn at Utrecht, does an actual shabby, battered crucifix happen to dominate the background (fig. 35), while in the foreground the tongue of the wagon again stands demonstratively upright, directly confronting the audience (fig. 36)? Finally, when Mother Courage reluctantly acknowledges that Kattrin is dead, that she did indeed *draw* a cross, that Kattrin's good heart has killed her, why does the wagon again stand in the same position as she sings her profoundly moving lullaby to the dead Kattrin?[27] As the play closes, Mother Courage takes up the tongue of the wagon, and draws her now empty and tattered wagon from the stage (figs. 37 and 38). As she leaves, the armies of Christ sing a song we have heard once before:

> Spring is coming. Christians awake!
> The snows melt. The dead rest.
> And what hasn't died yet
> Had better get out of bed.[28]

Is all this nexus of symbology an accident? If it is, it is a magnificent accident. If it is not, must we interpret it all ironically? Not irony but pure aesthetic power sweeps the audience as Courage staggers from the stage. All the themes sounded in the opening scene are sounded once again. All the prophecies are fulfilled. The full wagon is now empty. The family is reduced to one, the only one who did not draw a cross. The wheel has come full circle (fig. 39). Thus closes a play that for harmony, wholeness, balance, stage effectiveness, and aesthetic impact (even of the bare literary text) has but few rivals in the long history of the drama.

Given the complex unity of language and imagery, the fortune-telling scene that forewarns of death, and the numerous songs[29] that both recapitulate and forewarn, it does not come as a surprise that the individual scenes in this play are closely and carefully linked in a firm dramatic construct. Only scenes five (four pages long), seven (one page), and ten (one page) could either be left out of the play without harming the basic fable or be shifted and placed somewhere else in the play.[30] Every other scene belongs exactly where Brecht has placed it. Dramatic economy rather than epic breadth mark the play from the first line and scene to the last. Again the overall economy of the playwright is best illustrated by returning to that master-piece of dramaturgy, the opening scene of the play.

To ask again some of the questions we asked of Brecht's reworking of *The Mother,* we shall see that Brecht's choices are primarily dramatic rather than epic. Where, for instance, does Courage come from? Grimmelshausen gives us a detailed account of his Courasche and tells us exactly how she got involved with the war. Brecht gives us precisely nothing.[31] We are presented with a Mother Courage who already has three grown children and are told only the names of the fathers and how she herself received her name. The opening scene tells us only the facts we need to know if we are to understand the story about to be enacted. Nothing else.[32]

To continue this line of questioning we might ask: Why are we introduced to the soldiers just before the wagon heaves into sight? Why is it that no real horse pulls the wagon? Why are

Courage's boys grown up enough to be ready for service but not yet in the army at the time the play opens? In an area packed with recruiters from both the Protestant and the Catholic sides, why has Mother Courage never had to resort before to the trick with the crosses to frighten her children away from soldiers? Why does a soldier interrogate the family in the very first scene of the play and thus permit a "natural" exposition (within the play) of the shady history of Courage and her family? The epic does not need any of this highly artificial arrangement for its exposition. The very questions that reveal how "artificial" the opening scene of Brecht's play is, and how lacking in epic relaxation and breadth, reveal also how much art has gone into the specifically dramatic relationship of the constituent parts. Had Brecht written but this one play, he would be remembered as one of the great masters of the dramatic medium.[33]

Though I have argued in an earlier chapter that an epic well read can have an enormous emotional impact, I added that according to Brecht's own theory a specifically "epic" quality of his own plays and productions was the "narrative coolness" he supposed the medium to possess. For most critics, both Communist and non-Communist, *Mother Courage and Her Children* is singularly lacking in this "cool" quality. The best test case for critical response is obviously Brecht's own production of the play with the Berliner Ensemble. In this production we might suppose that the grandmaster of epic theater, using the sets of Neher, and the acting talents of Angelika Hurwicz[34] (as Kattrin), Helene Weigel[35] (as Courage herself), and Ernst Busch[36] (as the cook), would present the epic theater's very essence. In fact, the play has been compared to the harrowing tragedies of the Greeks and Elizabethans.

The Soviet critic Sachawa, well versed in what Brecht wanted to achieve with the capitalist Courage, the hyena of the battlefield,[37] writes of the final scene of Brecht's production: "The heart of the viewer is unwillingly seized when he sees how hopelessly the wagon has aged, how run down it is, and into what a frightful ruin a formerly energetic, active, and level-headed woman has been changed, who, in spite of her frightful condition, still does not understand its cause: the scene is a terrifying symbol of the tragic fate of an entire people."[38] Echoing the communist judgment, the Western critic George Steiner observes of the play as a whole: "She [Mother Courage] is so enormously alive in each leathery sinew, so rapacious and unconquerable. She is the salt of the earth, destructive yet zestful. We cannot detach ourselves from the play and merely pass cool judgment on her faults. We too are hitched to the wagon, and it is beneath our feet that the stage turns."[39]

When one turns from the play as a whole to individual scenes, the response to them is even more intense. Albrecht Schöne writes: "Scene Eleven of *Mother Courage* is one of Brecht's best scenes in terms of its effectiveness on the stage. On the roof of a peasant hut dumb Kattrin beats a drum in order to save the children of the city of Halle from a night attack. She is struck by a bullet and the sound of her last drumbeats is echoed by the cannon of the wakening defenders. If anywhere, it is here that Brecht's theory of alienation is in itself alienated; here the critical distance of the [calmly] smoking audience is destroyed"[40] (fig. 40). Brecht's principal interpreter in America, Eric Bentley, says flatly of Scene Eleven: "The 'drum' scene is possibly the most powerful scene, emotionally, in twentieth-century drama."[41] Overwhelmed by the response to Kattrin, Brecht—the man who had argued for years for the dominance of reason over emotion in the theater—said rather lamely: "Spectators are permitted to identify with Kattrin in this scene. They may identify with this being and note with pleasure that they have such powers even within themselves."[42] So much for the "permitted" emotional response to the "good" Kattrin, but what about the "bad" mother herself and the responses she elicited?

For many critics, however aware they may be of the words of a traveling companion of Courage that she is to be seen as a "hyena of the battlefield," the final scene of the play (already discussed in this chapter) and the scene where she must fail to recognize the body of her son Schweizerkäs, run the "drum" scene a close race in emotion. Surely Brecht overestimates his own directorial, or, if you will, dictatorial powers when he maintains, to paraphrase the Brecht of the later years, "Emotions are permitted when I say that they are permitted." His overestimation of his own powers is concretely illustrated by the reaction of George Steiner who says in his *Death of Tragedy:*

> There comes a moment in *Mother Courage* when the soldiers carry in the dead body of Schweizerkäs. They suspect that he is the son of Courage but are not quite certain. She must be forced to identify him. I saw Helene Weigel act the scene with the East Berlin ensemble, though acting is a paltry word for the marvel of her incarnation. As the body of her son was laid before her, she merely shook her head in mute denial. The soldiers compelled her to look again. Again she gave no sign of recognition, only a dead stare. As the body was carried off, Weigel looked the other way and tore her mouth wide open. The shape of the gesture was that of the screaming horse in Picasso's *Guernica.* The sound that came out was raw and terrible beyond any description I could give of it. But, in fact, there was no sound. Nothing. The sound was total silence. It was silence which screamed and screamed through the whole theater so that the audience lowered its head as before a gust of wind. And that scream inside the silence seemed to me to be the same as Cassandra's when she divines the reek of blood in the house of Atreus. It was the same wild cry with which the tragic imagination first marked our sense of life[43] (fig. 41).

We are back, as Steiner himself divines, with the terror and the pity of the ancient tragic mode.

The play *Mother Courage and Her Children,* either as text or as staged play, totally transcends Brecht's crudely anti-Aristotelian theory of the twenties. He had become increasingly aware that he could not, despite the most stringent efforts of his "fire brigade," dampen the emotions his plays and productions called forth. He notes with pride and bewilderment of the numerous productions of *Mother Courage* that he either served as an advisor on or directed: "The success of the play, that is to say the impression it made, was, without doubt, enormous. People pointed to Weigel on the street and said: 'There's Courage!' But I don't believe now and did not believe then, that Berlin and all the other cities that saw it, understood the play."[44] Faced with the fact of rampant emotion, with identification, with misunderstanding, Brecht reacts as though he had not really expected such a response to his troupe of stars of the epic theater. There is reason to doubt, however, that this was all such a mistake. Brecht the master of dialectic gives us, in other notes from the same period as the above complaint, a clear idea that all this emotionalism was highly intentional, that he the director had deliberately built it into the production. He claims, for instance, to have sought to plumb extraordinary depths of *Schrecken* (fear or horror—shades of Aristotle) in the scene immediately preceding Kattrin's mounting the ladder to beat the drum. Brecht writes: "It is advantageous [in perform-ance] to avoid the direct or 'immediate impression' of the apparently singular [non-recurrent] terrible event, *in order to reach a deeper strata of fear* [my italics], where frequent, ever-recurring misfortune has forced mankind into ceremoni-alization of his defense mechanisms, which of course can never save him from actual fear itself. We must break, in performance, through this ceremonialization of defense."[45] Perhaps simply being wise after the event, the man who staged the farm scene, "to reach the deeper strata of fear," said (in 1952) of his East Berlin production of *Mother Courage* in particular and his theater theory in general:

> It is not the case—even though it is an integral part of it—that epic theater—and this is also an integral part of it—is simply undramatic theater. Its fighting slogan has been spread abroad as: "This way Reason! Out of the door with Emotion (feeling)!" Yet it [Epic theater] does not in any way reject emotions. Certainly it does not reject either the feeling for justice, or for freedom, or justified anger. In fact, not only does it not reject these feelings, it does not even simply rely on their presence; it actively seeks either to strengthen them or to

create them. The "critical stance" it seeks to induce in its
audience cannot be passionate enough for this theater.[46]

This statement is surely a far cry from the 1927 essay, "The
Epic Theater and its Difficulties," where Brecht had noted:
"The most important point to be made about the epic theater
perhaps is that it appeals not so much to the spectators' feelings
(emotions) as to his reason. The spectator should not identify
with [characters or action] but set himself at odds with it."[47]
Though Brecht adds very carefully in the "Difficulties" essay,
"However, it would, at the same time, be wholly incorrect to
deny emotions [altogether] in this theater,"[48] the damage is
already done; the primary focus is still very obviously on
Reason. The only exit from the earlier cul-de-sac is, as Brecht
well knows, a complete reversal. He does not hesitate to invest
the words "critical stance" in 1952 with a diametrically
opposed meaning from that which they had possessed in 1927.
With this reversal[49] (and however deviously Brecht tries to
disguise it, it is a reversal) he returns in theory as he long since
had in fact to the fold of the traditional drama and to the
effects of that drama upon the spectator.

When we speak of *Mother Courage* and of the Western
dramatic tradition, there is another major concern that con-
fronts the sensitive reader of Brecht's "Chronicle Drawn From
the Thirty Years War."[50] It is quite obvious that the play is
closely related in form to Shakespeare and to Shakespeare's
open or panoramic dramaturgy. Though one can hear in this
play the echoes of the host of German playwrights who
themselves learned much from Shakespeare (the Schiller of the
Wallenstein trilogy and the Goethe of *Götz,* for example), and
though connections have been established between Brecht and
the panoramic form of the German "Jesuit and Reformation
drama,"[51] it is primarily Shakespeare one thinks of as one reads
this play and sees it acted. As critics such as Bentley,[52]
Grimm,[53] Klotz,[54] Parker,[55] Spalter,[56] Paul Rilla, and Brecht
himself have long since noted, this play is extraordinarily
reminiscent of his great Elizabethan forerunner. Brecht himself

noted of his subtitle ("a chronicle"): "The term *Chronicle* corresponds as a genre with the term *History* in the Elizabethan drama."[57] Quite correctly, Paul Rilla (a German critic whom Brecht knew and admired) said of Brecht's own 1954[58] production of the play: "Today the epic element means to him technically what it has meant to every great dramatist: a rhythmical principle. *Mother Courage* contains no more epic components than a Shakespearean history."[59] If one objectively considers the various elements of *Verfremdung* and "epic breadth" in the plays of Shakespeare, one sees that Rilla's point is well taken. If anything, Shakespeare is considerably more epic in his free use of time, space, and episodic construction. Even the leading authority on V-effects and epic construction in the microstructure of Brecht's plays agrees here. Though Reinhold Grimm does argue in one essay on *Mother Courage,* "It is perfectly obvious that such a world could not be contained in the old dramatic form,"[60] in another essay on the plays in general he observes: "In short: the 'verfremdende' drama structure is nothing more than the so-called 'open' form of the drama, which for hundreds of years has existed on equal terms with the 'closed' or classical drama—whether aesthetics likes to admit it or not."[61] If this be true, it is perfectly clear that Brecht's plays, even his most episodic plays,[62] can in fact be accommodated within a genre framework that already includes works as diverse as Schiller's *Wallenstein* trilogy and Aeschylus' *Prometheus Bound.*

In terms of structure, in terms of acting, in terms of its effect on audiences (the three main pillars of Brecht's "epic theater"), *Mother Courage and Her Children* fails to warrant the generation of a new descriptive term. In short, Brecht's *Mother Courage* constitutes another distinguished example of the fructifying influence of Shakespeare (directly or indirectly) on the German stage. Brecht's material is admirably accommodated by a form that Shakespeare used to accommodate all England and Italy, the "vasty fields of France," the whole of the Roman Empire, and fairy kingdoms undreamed of in Brecht's early philosophy. With skill unparalleled since Shakespeare, Brecht shapes his seventeenth-century materials to fit a seventeenth-century form, the chronicle play. Again the master playwright has given new life to an ancient form. Using this well-tried form and presenting it through the medium of his magnificent theater ensemble, it is really not surprising that the audiences who flocked to the several hundred performances given before Brecht's death were unable to maintain "epic calm" and distance. The turntable stage turned beneath their own feet.

CHAPTER SIX

A PORTRAIT OF THE ARTIST AS GRUBBY HUMANIST: *SCHWEYK*

"Though this dialogue (set in occupied Prague) is witty and lively, nevertheless, a viable play has not been constructed from the loose series of scenes [of the original]."

Carl Niessen[1]

Despite the fact that Brecht himself never staged his adaptation of the Czech novel, *The Good Soldier Schweik*, there are several reasons for including an examination of this play in this book. It is an obscure play, possibly because it has usually been simply written off as a crude steal of large and unassimilated sections of Hasek's great novel.[2] The play deserves better than this. Several facts about it suggest that it might be worth close critical examination. As Brecht assures us in a diary note made at the time he finished his version of the Schweyk (to use his spelling) material (June 24, 1943), the play is intended to be "a counterpiece to Mother Courage."[3] The suggestion would seem to be that the character of Schweyk may be seen as a viable alternative to Brecht's "hyena of the battlefield." We might expect, therefore, that *Schweyk in the Second World War* may illuminate Brecht's chronicle of the Thirty Years War. The time at which *Schweyk* was finished[4] should give us further pause, as it was written in the middle of the great period in which Brecht wrote *The Good Person of Sezuan* and *The Caucasian Chalk Circle.* Further, the adaptation is of considerable technical interest to students of "epic theater" because this is the only instance where Brecht reworks a text that had been produced (with his own active participation[5]) on Piscator's "epic" stage. A direct comparison, therefore, of the 1927 version of the material as it was produced in Piscator's theater and Brecht's 1943 adaptation can concretely illustrate how far Brecht has retreated by this time from what he had called "epic theater" in the twenties. Lastly, if the figure of Schweyk is, in many ways, as so many critics have maintained, a self-portrait of Brecht, and an archetypal figure who appears again and again in Brecht's work, then this "key figure" warrants close examination.[6]

The Czech novel which Brecht mines was written and published serially (beginning in 1920) and was simply broken off when Jaroslav Hasek died in 1923. Within a year of its publication in book form in 1926, this satirical portrait of the Austro-Hungarian empire, its generals, its aristocracy, the recently fought and lost war itself, was translated into eighteen languages and was on the bestseller list in all of them. Schweik, the anarchic but seemingly naive debunker of "The Great War," struck a responsive chord in those millions who had been touched, warped, or crushed by that massive debacle. Among those most impressed with Hasek's smart-simpleton and his genius for exposing the monstrous stupidity of his "superiors" was the great Berlin director—Brecht's mentor, Erwin Piscator. So taken was Piscator with Grete Reiner's German translation of the Czech work that he immediately attempted to obtain the German stage rights for Hasek's sprawling and unfinished masterpiece.[7] This novel was precisely the kind of political bombshell that Piscator loved to fling at his Berlin audiences.[8] In form also the work appealed to him. His stage, so overloaded with stage machinery that it quite literally began to collapse, was just the thing for mounting a work of such epic proportions as *The Good Soldier.* On the team of collaborators who prepared the work for the stage was Brecht.[9]

The distinction between Piscator's largely formless, epic revues of contemporary or recent historical events, and Brecht's own theater practice is clearly revealed in his reworking of the Schweik theme, *Schweyk in the Second World War.* A close examination of the Hasek novel, the Piscator 1927-28 revue, and Brecht's own texts reveals that Brecht has turned the Schweik material entirely to his own ends, and has used "epic" materials to form a closely knit drama.

When Piscator obtained the German stage rights to *Schweik,* he rejected a boulevard style theater presentation of the novel that had been prepared in Prague. Instead of accepting a boulevard drama about an officer's servant and that officer's love affairs (elements already present in the Hasek novel)[10] Piscator chose to emphasize the political implications of the adventures of "the good soldier." His ambitious intent was to bring the whole world of the Hapsburg monarchy onto his stage. In the words of one of his collaborators, he was not so much interested in a "dramatization" as in "bringing segments of the novel itself onto the stage."[11] In order to achieve this, Piscator had to resort to revolutionary means. He introduced, at enormous expense, a "laufendes Band," or moving sidewalk (fig. 42). As one of his co-workers, Felix Gasbarra, notes: "Thus, the problem was solved not only in terms of its mechanics but dramaturgically also. The rewriting team then no longer had to seek ways of building up [dramatic] scenes, in ways perhaps alien to the original material; they could now concentrate their attention on picking out the most dramatically effective scenes in the novel and preparing these for the stage."[12] John Gassner writes of the 1927-28 production by Piscator and his numerous and talented co-workers:

> Recognizing the satiric possibilities of the work, Piscator allowed it to assume its natural non-Aristotelian character, producing a thoroughly horizontal pattern of incidents strung

on the thread of Schweik's comic gaucheness. Since Hasek had not completed the novel, Piscator did not even strain for a conclusion—the play as it stood without a dramatic ending (and it had no Aristotelian "beginning" and "middle" either), was all the action that was needed to expose the absurdities of the Austrian-Hungarian empire and the confusing futility of the First World War.[13]

Summing up his impressions of the essentially formless production mounted by Piscator, Gassner notes: "The resulting play was inevitably 'epic' rather than dramatic in the Aristotelian sense of having a beginning, a middle, and an end."[14] Gassner echoes here Brecht's own use of the term "epic" in the 1920s. As we have earlier noted, "epic" meant in those days something close to one strand of meaning of the term in English: something huge, sprawling, monumental. It meant presenting "half the entire earth" on stage and thus allowing historical fact to speak for itself; it meant the use of documentary films;[15] it meant huge casts and large choruses—in a word, a presentation of "the massive subjects" (oil, the stock exchange, etc.) on the stage without shaping these "raw" materials to fit a specifically dramatic or "artistic" mold. Brecht himself wrote of it: "Piscator's theater constituted an object lesson. Here one could see how the revolution of 1918 [in Germany] collapsed, how battles for consumer markets and raw materials lead to wars, how wars are fought by nations not wanting these wars, and how successful revolutions are made."[16] Obviously Brecht could not have meant Piscator's theater when he observed of the practice of his contemporaries: "If one surveys the materials [treated in] the narrative and performing arts, one notes that 'the massive subjects' such as, war, money, oil, railroads, parliaments, working conditions, and land, are encountered but rarely and even then only as a decorative backdrop or as a stimulus to meditation."[17]

Though Piscator was one of those rare individuals who did in fact present the "massive subjects" Brecht yearned to see more frequently on the Berlin stage, each man had clear reservations about the other's work. Piscator did not find enough substantial political material in the work of the early Brecht, and Brecht seems not to have been entirely satisfied with the way in which Piscator presented just such materials.[18] The sociologist, Fritz Sternberg (a close friend of Brecht at the time Brecht was working with Piscator on *Schweik*), tells us that even then Brecht had other ideas as to what he wanted to do with the Schweik material. A few days after attending the *Schweik* premiere with Sternberg, Brecht outlined the following very ambitious, very "epic" treatment of the theme to his friend.[19] The plan called for two stories of a large building to be seen on stage simultaneously. On the top floor, Ludendorff was to stand before a gigantic map upon which he would work out the battle plan for German divisions engaged on both the Eastern and the Western fronts. "Nothing seems to function— and why did it not function?"[20] Brecht asked rhetorically. The explanation of why the plans of the "higher regions" never seemed to be properly executed lay in the "lower regions," a "huge, cellarlike room" below. The lower regions were to be filled with soldiers who all, in one way or another, looked like Schweyk. "These Schweyks," Brecht related to Sternberg, "are then set in motion. They do not openly resist, but they either do not arrive or do not arrive at the right time. There are incidents. Ever more and ever more diverse incidents that delay them; they need more time; they disappear. Nowhere is there active resistance; there is not even anything in their conversation that could be seen as being in direct opposition to the war; they obey all orders; they show respect to their superiors; when orders to march arrive, they begin to move. But they never arrive at the time and place preordained by Ludendorff above, and they never arrive with their numbers intact."[21] This particular version was never to be completed. It remains only as a sketch with something of the scale of Piscator's production and yet anticipating in some particulars the 1943 version. In the later version there would be, instead of the simultaneity of action proposed in the 1927 sketch, simply an intercutting of semi-alternate scenes in the "higher and the lower regions." The "massive subject" of all Europe at war would be scaled down to a size far more consistent with the traditional requirements of the stage. The substantial structural differences between Piscator's stage *Schweik,* Brecht's 1927 sketch, and the final 1943 version of the play, illustrate how radically Brecht retreated in the intervening years from "epic theater" as he had defined it and Piscator had practiced it during the twenties.

Before proceeding to Brecht's structural changes, a few words are essential on one of the most misunderstood characters of Brecht's creation, his—as distinct from Hasek's—Schweyk. Led astray by the name of Hasek's delightful rogue and the fact that Brecht borrows numerous sections of dialogue and much of his plot, most critics have, thus far, gone on to the unwarranted assumption that Brecht has simply "transferred Hasek's character to German-occupied Prague."[22] Were this error one that would only alter our reading of one play it might be tolerated. As it is, however, Schweyk is a figure who appears so often, under so many guises in Brecht's work that a precise definition of his character is essential if a misreading of "Brecht's Schweikian Philosophy"[23] (to use Martin Esslin's term) is to be avoided. Esslin defines the "Schweikian Philosophy" as one of "enlightened self-interest based on the conviction that survival and success are more important than the striking of heroic attitudes."[24] Several implications of this definition are clearly supported by Hasek's character but are not really descriptive of Brecht's creation.

A careful examination of the two long volumes of Hasek's unfinished novel reveals the simple fact that his Schweik is guided almost entirely by self-interest. The only exception to his self-interest is one short incident in Volume Two of the Czech novel.[25] In Hasek, the character Baloun gets himself into trouble by eating the rations of Schweik's former master, Lieutenant Lukasch. Aware of Baloun's uncontrollable appetite, Schweik claims that he has eaten the rations himself. He does not, of course, stand to get anything more than a box on the ear for this admission. In Brecht's play, Schweyk also tries to save

Baloun, but faces death rather than a box on the ear. In their new context, the "same acts" of Schweyk take on a radically different meaning and Schweyk becomes thereby a radically different character. One must beware, therefore, despite the large number of borrowed scenes—the discussion of the assassination, the dog-stealing scene, the wagon number trick where Schweyk confuses the Nazi railway guard (fig. 43), the scene of Schweyk's arrest, Schweyk's meeting with the kind old woman during the Anabasis, and Schweyk's meeting with the deserters —each one serves a new function in the new aesthetic construct. Linking all these changes is the basic change in the character of Schweyk himself.

A scene that admirably illustrates Brecht's genius for changing much by changing little (and thereby misleading his critics) is the dog-stealing scene (fig. 44). Though Brecht keeps long sections of Hasek's dialogue between Schweyk and the girl exercising the dog, he makes one small-large change. The Hasek incident takes place in the unreal world of comedy where injury to people can be done without its consciously registering upon us. Brecht makes Schweyk extremely aware of the implications of the theft. His Schweyk says of the girl and her relationship to her master, Votjta: "Votjta is mean to the servant girl; she is the third one he had had since Candlemas, and even she wants to leave, so I've heard, because the neighbors nag her for working for a quisling. She doesn't care, therefore, whether she comes home with the dog or not; the main thing is that she doesn't get into any trouble because of it."[26] It is clear that this Schweyk thinks about the fate of others and does what he can, even in small ways, to help others.

A larger scale illustration of change in Brecht's play and in Schweyk's character, is the scene where Schweyk attempts to help his friend Baloun. In the novel, it will be remembered, Schweik runs the risk of a box on the ear for his defense of Baloun; in the play, Schweyk defends his friend against the dreaded S.S. and thus risks torture and death. After his friends have been physically attacked by the brutal S.S. man, Bullinger, who demands to know how Baloun got his hands on a package of blackmarket meat, Schweyk steps forward and says: "Sir! Would like to report I can clear up the whole thing. The package doesn't belong to anyone here. I know that because I put it down myself"[27] (figs. 45 and 46). It is true that by fantasy, playing dumb, and exaggeration Schweyk hopes to save his own neck, but the significant difference, as I see it, is that Schweyk voluntarily places himself in an extremely dangerous situation. Intelligent, and fully aware of the risk he runs of exchanging the warm pub, "The Goblet," for the torture cellars of the S.S., and/or the holocaust of the Russian front, Schweyk risks his own life for his friend. After his arrest, one of the pub's patrons says flatly: "He won't get out of this alive."[28] Baloun himself bewails his own appetite and lack of courage and says of his courageous friend: "I've dragged my best friend so deep into this that if they can they'll shoot him during the night. If not, he can thank his lucky stars and they'll get him early in the morning instead."[29]

That this fundamental switch in Schweyk's character was a highly conscious move on Brecht's part is indicated by a diary note from the period when he was working on the play: "Returning from N.Y. last night, told Steff something about my Schweyk-plan. He said right away that the original Schweyk would not only not have bothered about Baloun's problems but would have advised him to join the German army instead."[30] Brecht then goes on: "Right away I decided to build Schweyk's unpolitical action into the story in a paradoxical kind of way."[31] I submit that in intention and in fact, Brecht's Schweyk is not the man Martin Esslin (led astray by Hasek's Schweik) would have us believe he is. The Schweyk who risks his life for his friends is not demonstrating a "philosophy of enlightened self-interest." The term "self-interest" applied to someone who is prepared to lay down his life for his friends loses all coherent meaning. Nor can Schweyk's voluntary heroism be squared with someone for whom "survival and success" (self-survival, that is) are the cardinal virtues.

As harmful as the critical myopia induced by seeing Brecht's Schweyk as a borrowing from Hasek, is that induced by reading into Brecht's tightly constructed play the episodic and fragmentary Hasek novel and Piscator's deliberately disjointed "revue." A typical misreading is that of the West German critic, Carl Niessen, who confidently maintains: "Though this dialogue (set in occupied Prague) is witty and lively, nevertheless, a viable play has not been constructed from the loose series of scenes [of the original]."[32]

Brecht's own notes reveal that he has very consciously shaped a tightly structured play. Brecht notes: "The center of the stage set is the inn, 'The Goblet,' in Prague. In the third act, part of the inn appears to him [Schweyk] in his thoughts and dreams. The Anabasis in this act moves in a circular fashion around this part of 'The Goblet.' "[33] Using the pub as a perfectly logical meeting place, Brecht brings together characters having only the loosest kind of connection with one another in either the Hasek novel or in Piscator's "epic" treatment. Further, Brecht combines several of Hasek's characters. Blahnik (who steals the dog in Hasek), the army engineer Woditschka (a close and bellicose friend of Hasek's Schweik), and Baloun (who in Hasek is only a fellow batman and not really a friend of Schweik's) are all combined in the single figure, Brecht's Baloun. Brecht then "ties" Baloun through his appetite to the owner of the pub, Frau Kopecka (what's in a name?), and to the serving girls (plural in Brecht) from whom the dog is stolen (with Baloun's help) through an arranged meeting at "The Goblet." The inn is then further used dramatically as a centripetal force, by staging the Razzia for the stolen dog there. Lastly, as Brecht himself notes, the inn ties together the Anabasis by its appearance whenever there is a danger of Schweyk falling asleep in the snowy wastes of Russia and dying from exposure. "The Goblet," it is clear, binds together the parts of the play and the individual characters.

Harold Lenz has observed of the function of "The Goblet": "The inn is the dream haven of the poor 'little man,' to whom Brecht dedicated the epigraph of the *Threepenny Opera:* 'First grub, then morality.' "[34] Surely Lenz is correct in seeing the inn as the modest dream of the little man. "The Goblet" (in Brecht but not in Hasek) is where the little man drinks his beer and asks for nothing more than peace, food, drink, and warmth.[35] Mrs. Kopecka and her patrons are not interested in the "higher" virtues, the things that in Brecht get you into trouble—things like honor, glory, and politics.[36] These are the "virtues" of the higher regions, the Wagnerian dream world of Hitler's bloody crew, that form the terrible and funny, deliberately grotesque backdrop to the world of the modest inn. What remains of the plan for the two-story set that Brecht had outlined to Sternberg in 1927 is a series of contrasting appearances of Hitler and his cohorts, presented in the Berliner Ensemble production as outsize puppets[37] (except Goebbels who is presented as an undersize puppet), that are wheeled onto the stage in showcases immediately after the half-curtain opens. As a prologue to the play, they stand around a globe while martial music blares in the background. These denizens of "the higher regions" then appear twice more in the play as interludes staged, according to Brecht's own directions, as "tales of horror." The plans of the mighty as presented in these interludes are then shown to come to nothing through the scenes in "the lower regions": "The Goblet," the Prague railway station, and the scenes of Schweyk's Anabasis, as he wends his circuitous way towards Stalingrad (fig. 47). The suggestion, sometimes explicit but often only subliminal, is that the plans of the mighty are consciously though deviously undermined by "little men" such as Schweyk. In the play's epilogue, Schweyk meets Hitler (now reduced literally to Schweyk's level), amidst the blinding snows that helped to defeat the German armies at Stalingrad. As Schweyk gives Hitler his marching orders, it is clear that the plans of the "mighty" have come to nothing and that the bitterest of defeats lies ahead.[38] To underline Brecht's intended message, the entire cast comes to the apron to sing as an epilogue the fatalistic "Song of the Moldau." We are, the song suggests, about to return to the kind of peace represented in the play by "The Goblet" and its non-political Czech patrons.

Within the play, Frau Kopecka says to an S.S. man who wants to talk of the "higher regions" (fig. 48) and thus of politics: "Here's your beer. We don't want any politics here. I'm a businesswoman. If someone comes in and orders a beer, I'll pour it for him, but that's all."[39] Making even plainer her view of "The Goblet" and inviting extension of its basic principles, Frau Kopecka sings "The Song of the Goblet." The song begins:

> Come dear guest and sit you down
> Join us at the table.

The song continues:

> You don't need references
> Honors will only do you harm,
> If you've a nose on your face,
> You're invited.
>> Be a little bit friendly
>> You don't have to be smart or ace someone out here.
>> Eat your cheese and drink your beer
>> And you'll be more than welcome here.
>> As will be your twenty cents.

The final verse of the song runs:

> There'll come a time when we'll look out
> To see if the weather's decent
> And we'll see the world of man
> Turned into a hospitable inn.
>> Each will then be looked upon as a human being
>> None will be ignored
>> Everyone will have a roof to shelter them from snow and wind
>> Because we are badly frozen now
>> Even with our twenty cents![40]

For twenty cents, concludes the song, everyone, everywhere, should be able to come in out of the cold to enjoy warmth, food, and friendliness. The whole world is to become "a hospitable house." The old virtues have been stripped of phony heroism in this deliberately non-heroic world. Echoing Mother Courage, she says explicitly, "Honors only harm you," but if you are friendly (though you may be ugly, dishonorable, and stupid) you are more than welcome (if you have twenty cents). She dreams in her song of a world where there is no need for heroes, honor, greatness, or politics; she dreams of a world where, as in the microcosmic ideal, "The Goblet" itself, friendliness and helpfulness overcome hate and stupidity.

The dream of the song of "The Goblet" is then underlined by another major "folk song" in the play, the beautiful "Song of the Moldau," already mentioned above. When it is first sung, it is in an attempt to dispel the black mood of a present hardly to be endured. The song advises endurance, demands survival, and points to the inevitability of a coming peace:

> The stones shift in the bed of the river Moldau.
> Three emperors lie buried in Prague.
> The great do not stay great, and the small do not stay small.
> The night has twelve hours and then comes the day.
> Times change. The mighty plans of the
> Mighty, end.
> And they, like bloody chickens, leave.
> Times change; it does not help to use force.[41]

The song ends with the repetition of the first verse. Sung first at the darkest point of the play when endurance seems as futile as victory seems impossible, the song is repeated at the play's close when Schweyk's survival seems relatively certain and Hitler's defeat assured. The trouble, of course, with this beautiful song is that, politically, it cuts both ways: great and small men can draw as much assurance from the same song. We are back in embarrassing proximity to Mortimer's sentiments expressed in *Eduard II* in his dissertation on "the slut fortune." Yet these sentiments as expressed in the "Song of the Moldau," capture Schweyk's own thoughts quite precisely. Speaking to a mongrel (Ajax!) that he has befriended on his way "to Stalingrad," Schweyk says specifically: "The war can no more last forever than can the peace."[42] Obviously, both Schweyk and Frau

Kopecka foresee a Prague, and by extension, a world whose peace will regularly be shattered, a world in which, with the monotonous regularity with which day follows night and night day, the "Song of the Moldau" can be repeated from generation to generation. All that will be necessary to bring the song up to date will be the addition of another tyrant (or bloody chicken) to the total mentioned in the song. Furthermore, the song suggests not only that peace and war are part of an eternal cycle but that there is nothing that one can do to change or to interrupt the cycle. The song says (and it is virtually the last line of the play): "It does not help to use force." Gone, apparently, is the assurance and the naiveté of the earlier counsel of the use of force "to good ends" that often dominated the plays of the didactic period and that will reappear much later in plays such as: *The Days of the Commune,* the incomplete adaptation of Shakespeare's *Coriolanus, Don Juan,* and *Drums and Trumpets.*[43] *Schweyk,* in contrast, belongs with the big plays of the exile period, plays that plead for change, for friendliness, but propose no concrete way to achieve it.

Schweyk, like Mother Courage, has a human complexity, a certain anarchical quality that is completely alien to any organized system of change for social betterment. Schweyk's only wish would seem, on the face of it, to be relatively modest: he wishes to be left alone to live his own life in the anarchic but friendly, lowly but warm, coarse but human world of "The Goblet." He does not want any other Utopia; his Utopia is almost wholly passive and not the least bit idealistic. It is in fact a world full of grubby humanists. The organized world of Pelegea Wlassowa, with her hard work and self sacrifice as she works with all her force to establish a Communist new millenium has given way. We then find ourselves, thematically and metaphysically, very close to the vision of the earlier apolitical Bertolt Brecht, the Brecht who created Mortimer and whose character, Kragler, in *Drums in the Night* said flatly, ignoring a call to join in and help the revolution for social betterment: ". . . I am a swine, and this swine is going home."⁴⁴ Yet Brecht's shift from *The Mother* to *Schweyk* is not a polar one but one of degree. Schweyk does not simply save his own skin (as did Kragler and Hasek's Schweik), he saves at least Baloun and Frau Kopecka as well. While crawling (and he certainly does crawl before the S.S.), while being despicable by "normal humanistic standards," he approaches heroism, pride, and humanitarianism. He falls, therefore, somewhere between Wlassowa (the unadulterated Communist heroine) and Kragler (the asocial swine). And therein lies Schweyk's interest; his humanity is in small things. He is like us, neither wholly good nor wholly bad. His problem, like those of Mortimer, Mother Courage, Shen Te-Shui Ta, Azdak, Galileo, and Keuner (hero of many of Brecht's short short stories), is the perennially modern one—how to be and to do "good" in the midst of evil. Schweyk, like the rest of us, has no real answer.

Though the play will close with Schweyk literally whistling the tune for the great, he will do this against the background of the sentiments expressed in the "Song of the Moldau." Other invaders, the song suggests, may even then be on their way to occupy the friendly inn and Prague itself. Will Schweyk "lick the hands" ⁴⁵ of the new invaders as he has licked the hands of Hitler's henchman, Brettschneider? Will he still say: "Don't ask too much of yourself. It is already a great deal still to be alive nowadays. One is so busy with surviving that one doesn't get to anything else."⁴⁶ Will he still counsel, as he has the mongrel Ajax: "If you want to live through the war, keep close to the others; do the usual, no volunteering for extra duty, but rather lie down until you can bite."⁴⁷ Schweyk does not tell Ajax when it will be possible to bite! Nor could he answer if he were asked what he would do if "the usual" and "sticking with the others" might involve guiding his fellow Czechs to gas chamber and to oven, the fate of many of a Czech "little man" under Hitler. It may be that Schweyk will avoid murdering as many people as the orders from above call for, but murder he will, with the rest, if his own survival depends on it. Schweyk's instructions to Ajax do, however, present Schweyk himself in the worst possible light and they are, of course, at odds with the selfless courage we have seen him display elsewhere. He may be tactically correct when he cautions against active resistance, but it is hard to argue with the woman in "The Goblet" who says of all cooperation, no matter how half-hearted, "we are guilty along with them."[48] And though Schweyk does hinder the "plans of the mighty" in numerous small ways,[49] his efforts are consistently compromised by his half-hearted support of a war that he knows is both stupid and none of the business of the inhabitants of the lower regions.[50] Consistently, as with the instructions to Ajax, Schweyk brushes aside the all-too-troublesome question of how one sticks close to the others without being forced to murder right along with them.

It is clear that Schweyk (in direct contrast to Brecht's claim that Schweyk is the opposite of Mother Courage) helps the cause of war much as Mother Courage did. Though such a comparison is not to Schweyk's advantage (if we want to make an old-fashioned hero of him), it does help us to understand our own response to Courage, the hyena of the battlefield. Are we really able to blame her any more or less than we can Schweyk for being involved in a stupid war? After all, Courage, Schweizerkäs, Eilif, and the soldiers are all doing the usual. She too says that she does not want to get too deeply involved in the war. She too longs for a quiet haven (remarkably akin to "The Goblet"), the inn at Utrecht to which she could retreat with the cook if she were only inhuman enough to suppress her motherly instincts and abandon her burdensome daughter. It is not too far-fetched to imagine Schweyk, in some mythical composite play of Brecht's, replacing either the cook or the chaplain, using Courage's wagon (as they do) as a haven in the midst of war.

Obviously, by pointing out Schweyk's many and very human ideological weaknesses, and the fundamental similarity of his behavior to that of the old reprobate, Mother Courage, I do not suggest total condemnation of his behavior. The terrifying thing about Schweyk is that whatever good he is able to do is always paid for with an ample measure of "evil." We have in Schweyk the paradigmatic statement, by the ideologically insecure exile, of the problem of the individual's helplessness in the face of all-pervasive corruption in the body politic. If we can (with some reservations)[5][1] extend Schweyk's metaphorical role to include both Brecht himself and the "little man" in general in the real political world, only two ideological interpretations of his behavior immediately present themselves. We might justify Schweyk's serving such dubious masters as the Nazi Brettschneider by saying that this is what one little man acting alone must do. He can expect no more of himself. Or we could make this very defense our attack and say that Schweyk was surely smart enough to see that the only way for him to change the harsh political facts of life would be not to act alone but to organize a party cell or collective around the patrons of "The Goblet." He might then, with the help of his comrades, begin the work of revolution that would topple, if necessary by force, the oversize puppets of the higher regions. Then the earth could indeed be turned into a friendly inn. But this is, fortunately or unfortunately, a blind alley as far as Schweyk and the text of the play are concerned. The last line states, may we repeat, "It does not help to use force." It is difficult to see this in ideological terms as anything but a specific rejection of the dynamic use of force to effect change that was at the heart of the Comintern movement. Schweyk, rather obviously, is a character completely alien to all such highly organized and forceful political structures. It is for this reason, of course, that East German critics (e.g., Müller, Knauth, Petr, and earlier Mayer) have looked askance at Schweyk and at those of Brecht's characters who share the "Schweikian philosophy." They question, quite correctly, the usefulness to the world Communist movement of a proletariat made up of Schweyks. Petr puts the position concisely when he says that "Schweyk would not actively participate in a future socialist revolution."[5][2]

Now if the above assessment is correct and if other critics are also correct when they see in Schweyk a portrait of his creator, then we are smack up against a central problem of Brecht criticism in general. How can a character who fits so poorly into the scheme of organized socialist revolution be a likeness of Brecht, whose allegiance to world Communism is beyond all debate? As long as access to personal memoirs and political documents in the Brecht Archive remains highly restricted, it is too early to form a complete view of Brecht the man; despite Esslin's work and the more recent studies of Frederic Ewen and Dieter Schmidt,[53] this must remain a highly speculative area. Nevertheless, there is enough evidence on hand to permit our drawing some parallels between Brecht's Schweikian characters and the character of the author himself. There is in fact a substantial link between Schweyk's essentially anarchic philosophy and Brecht's "Communism." That significant portions of this connection have been largely overlooked is due in part to ideological bias (East and West) and in part to falsely but widely held suppositions about the "Schweikian mentality" on the one hand and about the nature of Brecht's "Communism" on the other. If we modify the conventional view of Schweyk to grant his frequent lack of self-interest and his grubby humanitarianism, and if we modify our view of the exiled Brecht to include a vision of "Communism" having very little to do with Party politics, we may find it easier to identify Brecht with his fundamentally apolitical hero. As a term for what they share, possibly the neologism "Commune-ism" might prove helpful. Both Brecht and Schweyk are, I submit, Commune-ists, people eager above all else to live in harmony with their fellow men in a world which is "a hospitable inn." Such a world would certainly be classless, but its guiding principle would be friendliness, not its social and political organization.

A Commune-ist would, of course, look to nineteenth-century Marxist-Humanist theory for his inspiration. But he could also draw on the simple *caritas* of Ur-Christianity—for the dream of the nineteenth-century Utopian Marxists is not so very different from early Christianity's dream of peace and good-will.[54] This similarity, important in its own right, is of particular importance here, because it strongly underlines the specifically religious nature of nineteenth-century Marxism. Speaking of the early Marxists (the men who preceded the Apparatchiks) and here speaking only of theoretical Marxism, Bertram Wolfe states this religious essence very clearly: "It made a true gospel of its particular brand of salvation. It possessed singleness, exclusivism, dogma, orthodoxy, heresy, renegation, schism, excommunication, prophets, disciples, vocation, asceticism, sacrifice, the ability to suffer all things for the sake of the faith. Heresy or rival doctrine was worse than ignorance; it was apostasy. To the disciple even of so rational a doctrine as that of Marx, an *ipse dixit* was an irrefutable proof."[5] It is true that Wolfe, after likening early Marxism to a religious gospel which the believer accepts for the sake of future salvation, does call the doctrine "rational." But this "rationality" is open to question. Too many of the eminently "rational" predictions about what simply had to happen historically have failed for one to remain entirely unsuspicious of the basic logic of the argument. In addition to its appeal to faith, the passivity and dream-like naiveté, which are also part of the early doctrine, argue against its rationality. Sit back and relax, the gospel implies, for it is from the profoundest despair of the proletariat that its greatest hope springs. And, conversely, when the bourgeoisie seems strongest it is then at its weakest. The structure will inevitably fall of its own top-heavy weight. Once the old structure has collapsed we can then again relax, as Paradise will be upon us. The state will wither away; money and banks will be abolished; and people will practice brotherly love as a matter of course. To borrow the imagery of *Schweyk*, the friendly world that Frau Kopecka envisions in the "Song of the Goblet" will—also as a matter of course—become reality.

It is worth recalling that when Brecht had turned to Marxism in the late twenties and we find him studying the "Communist classics," the lovely humanistic dream of the early theoretical Marxists had by no means entirely faded. On the one hand the purges had not yet begun in the Soviet Union, and on the other the tottering Capitalist structures seemed to herald the fulfillment of Marx's predictions. Furthermore, as Capitalism crumbled while Marxism flourished, the Fascist movement grew so alarmingly that Brecht, like many another basically apolitical artist and intellectual of the period, saw in the world Communist movement the only effective counterforce to darkest reaction. Conversions to Marxism at that time were perhaps at least as emotional as they were rational. The fervor of Brecht's initial commitment supports the view that his heart was won at least as much as his head. Two of his closest friends from this period have spoken against seeing Brecht as a very logical thinker. Feuchtwanger, in the figure of Kaspar Prökl in the novel *Success,* challenges Brecht's ability to understand social problems by logical analysis. And Sternberg, a better authority on logic and political analysis than Feuchtwanger, says flatly (though without the least malice): "He did not, by nature, think systematically."[5][6]

Because of the time when Brecht adopted Marxism, because of his initial fanaticism, and because there is little evidence that he ever was a very logical thinker, I must agree with those critics who have seen his conversion as a profound religious-emotional experience. He found in Communism what he wanted to find there—the beautiful humanistic dream of an idyllic world which lay beyond the logical facade. If this is true, then we should not seek Brecht's creed or the creed of his most successful characters in the activist doctrines of Lenin, Stalin, and Ulbricht, men faced with the impossible task of reconciling the dream world of the theory with the harsh realities of everyday power politics. Rather, it should be clear that Brecht's creed is derived from a vision of the world to come when the Stalins and the Ulbrichts have outlived their usefulness and have passed away. An undated "political fragment" in the Brecht Archive shows (though proof is hardly needed) that he well knew the difference between the political realities of the far-from-ideal present and the eventual goal: "one cannot say that freedom prevails in the worker's state of russia. but one can say that the process of establishing freedom prevails."⁵ ⁷ One can challenge Brecht's prediction but not the fact that his loyalty is to the salvation promised rather than to the political structure of the present. What Brecht seems to have longed for—or so *Schweyk* and other plays of the same period would suggest—was a world of simple, quiet peace where there was no further need of heroes, of political parties (or even the Party), functionaries, or politics. What he wanted was not Ulbricht's wall and the Vopos guarding it but the hospitable, undisturbed world of "The Goblet."

With this we can return to where this chapter began. Schweyk is not Schweik; Schweyk is a figure who does serve to illuminate many another character in Brecht's work and the character of Brecht himself. Like Brecht's, Schweyk's actions are ambivalent, now heroic (in a quiet sort of way), now passive and compliant. Schweyk's vision of the world (made over in the image of the warmth and friendliness of "The Goblet") and the reality of the political world which always forces the little man to bend are two very different things. In a world of power, ambition, "higher and lower regions," brutality, and an endemic state of war there can be no clear strategy for realizing a goal which is beyond party, war, and class. In this world there can certainly be no active and ideologically consistent tactic for establishing a harmony which is apolitical and Utopian among men. Schweyk had no strategy, nor did Brecht when he wrote *Schweyk* and the other exile plays in one of his ideologically weak, least doctrinaire periods. But both dream the humanist dream of an undisturbed world of peace on earth. Both are Commune-ists who would like to live in the "hospitable house" of a world ruled by the anarchical god, Friendliness.

The complicated and very human figure that Brecht has drawn in his Schweyk deserves at last to live his own life in literature and on the stage. Likewise the play itself, radically different as it is in both content and form from its models, deserves more critical attention than it has received heretofore. The play, with its dramatic contrasts of the brutality of power and the down-to-earth humanism of "The Goblet"; of the warmth of the dream inn and the coldness of Czechoslovakia, Germany, and Russia at war; and with its simultaneously appealing and repulsive central character who provides a key to so much of Brecht's work and life, is of the greatest formal and human interest. Again Brecht has managed to turn borrowed materials entirely to his own ends. We may continue to remember Piscator's *Schweik* as a magnificent and bold extension of the capabilities of the physical and the actively political theater. We shall remember Brecht's *Schweyk in the Second World War* as a structurally conservative but profoundly disturbing image of a man like ourselves, whose dreams of peace are ground to nothing by the conflicting ideologies of this our time.

CHAPTER SEVEN

BRECHT AND THE ORIENTAL STAGE I:
THE GOOD PERSON OF SEZUAN

> "In structure, this is by no means 'epic' theatre: the plot is an
> extremely complicated affair rather than a concatenation."
> *Ronald Gray*[1]
> "The basic conflict of the play is carried, in an epic manner,
> through various stages of development and [various] levels."
> *Karl Heinz Schmidt*[2]

For those familiar with the recurrent motifs that run from first
to last through Brecht's poems, short stories, and plays, it is a
very short step from the Prague of Schweyk to the Sezuan of
Shen Te/Shui Ta. For all the changes in milieu, for all the
differences between Czechoslovakia "at war" and China "at
peace," we find ourselves face to face with a moral[3] problem
that knows no national boundaries and that is not restricted to
any specific time. How does one, anyone, anywhere, at any
time remain good in a world which predicates survival on
willingness to do evil?[4] Must the price paid for goodness and for
friendliness always be too high? Must the mere ounce of
goodness of a Schweyk or a Shen Te always be distilled from an
apparently inexhaustible quantity of evil? Before we turn to
Brecht's treatment of this theme in the parable play, *The Good
Person of Sezuan,* it may be helpful for us to wander freely in

time and space and look briefly at how Brecht came to choose certain devices from the Japanese and Chinese theater for two of his most important plays, the subject of this chapter and that of the next, *The Caucasian Chalk Circle*. Brecht was by no means alone in being overwhelmed by the various strands of the Oriental theater. By 1930, all Berlin was treated to two important productions that used techniques borrowed from the Chinese and the Japanese stage. Paul Claudel, who had lived for many years in China and Japan and had made a serious study of the Oriental stage, had his *Christophe Colombe* performed in Berlin in 1930.[5] The formal parallels between this "Catholic didactic opera" and the Japanese theater on the one hand and the "Marxist didactic operas" of Brecht on the other are, as John Willett has pointed out, very striking indeed.[6] Equally striking similarities obtain between the work of the great Soviet director, Vsevolod Meyerhold, and those of the Japanese theater, Claudel, and Brecht. Further, we know that in the very year that *Christophe Colombe* was performed in Berlin, Meyerhold brought his troupe to the German capital. Meyerhold's visit is of the greatest possible importance to Brecht's development, for Meyerhold combined two of Brecht's major interests: Marxism and the Oriental stage. It was Meyerhold who founded in the Soviet Union a whole school of theater that departed radically from the style of Stanislavsky and insisted on seeing theater as theater with no attempt at the kind of "fourth-wall" illusionism that we associate with Stanislavsky's name. Meyerhold directly influenced men such as Sergei Eisenstein[7] (now best known for his film work), Sergei Tretiakov[8] (a great specialist on both Chinese theater and politics and a close friend for many years of both Meyerhold and Brecht), Alexander Tairov (who brought his Moscow productions to Berlin as early as 1923 and whose major theoretical work, *Das entfesselte Theater* [*The Theater Un-chained*], became available in German the same year), Eugene Vakhtangov[9] (praised consistently in Brecht's theoretical writings), and Nikolai Okhlopkov (whose highly stylized "Oriental" production of Pogodin's play, *Aristocrats,* Brecht saw and liked on his visit to Moscow in 1935). Close ties were to develop between the "school of Meyerhold" and the Berlin avant-garde.[10] It was Meyerhold and his followers, one might add, who developed most of the stage practices which we in the West tend to associate either with the name of Brecht or of Brecht's own great teacher, Piscator. In the interest of historical accuracy it is worth reminding the general reader of something that John Willett[11] has long since pointed out, that several crucial terms in Brecht's critical vocabulary follow upon his several trips to the Soviet Union in the thirties. Yet, so thorough were Stalin's purges of all those who dared to tread other paths than the officially recognized one of "socialist realism" that we have all but forgotten that Moscow was recognized, during the first three decades of this century, as the world center of formal experimentation in theater.[12]

In order to help the reader's consciousness back beyond the searing experience of the purge trials, the murders of men such as Meyerhold and Tretiakov, the muzzling of Pasternak and Eisenstein, and the emergence of the era of "socialist realist" kitsch, we might look again at what it was that Brecht and others saw in that incandescent period of theatrical experimentation which preceded Stalin's and Zhdanov's brutal eradication of all "Formalist" experimentation in the mid- and late thirties.

As Meyerhold's work again becomes available (even, though in limited editions, in the Soviet Union), we are reminded that as early as 1902, Meyerhold had cited with vigorous approval the poet Valery Bryusov's slogan: "It is time for the theater to stop imitating reality."[13] Working from this premise (at a time when Brecht was but four years old), Meyerhold was already seeking to prevent his actors from following Stanislavsky and identifying themselves with their roles. He declared himself opposed to all psychologizing. He asked his actors to avoid emotional strain and to coin their words coldly.[14] The audience he sought for his productions was a critical one, an audience that would appreciate rationally the theatrical spectacle before them.[15] At the same time, grotesque exaggeration of types was encouraged on his stage. Theater equipment, he insisted, was to remain obvious and to be changed in full view of the rationally appreciative audience. To help this, all lights, he said, should be kept at full all the time. Study of the Oriental theater and Oriental art in general was encouraged in his troupe. Gesture, in his productions, began literally and figuratively to precede the spoken word.[16] Narrative exposition was encouraged and the radical rewriting of both Russian and Western European classics became standard on his stage. The fairground, the circus, the sports arena, music hall, and cabaret were all, he said, to be considered as models for the kind of theater he sought.

With the coming of the Russian Revolution, Meyerhold began to invest all his earlier aesthetic innovations with revolutionary purpose. His dress became resolutely proletarian. In appreciation of his work for the revolution, he (and not the "bourgeois" Stanislavsky) was made the director of all organized revolutionary theater activity in the Soviet Union. With a fine contempt for such atavistic and flagrantly bourgeois notions as author's copyright, the holiness of works of art or of artists, and the aesthetic integrity of any given work, Meyerhold now mounted mammoth political spectacles combining various texts (literary, political, and whatever took his fancy) with a massive technical apparatus which included the extensive use of film. A typical example of his work at this time is his 1924 production (at the time Brecht's *Eduard II* was running in Munich) of *The Give Us Europe Trust*. In the description of one critic: "The text of *The Give Us Europe Trust* was compiled by M. Podgyetsky from novels by Ehrenburg, Amp, Kellerman, and Sinclair. The play depicted the struggle of an American capitalistic trust with the radio trust of a Soviet republic. The American organization aimed at the complete 'destruction' of Europe to eliminate a dangerous competitor. There were seventeen episodes accompanied by political slogans."[17] It should be further noted that few characters appeared in more than one episode of the play and that there were long narrative commentaries on characters in the play. All this was accompanied by quotations from Lenin and Trotsky flashed on three screens with all the acting done in Meyerhold's grotesque or knockabout style. Rather obviously, everything about Meyerhold's work was a clear anticipation of the kind of thing that Piscator, Brecht, and others were to do in Berlin.

We now know that the various experiments carried on in Meyerhold's "school" in Russia were by no means lost to Bertolt Brecht. From Brecht's own *Writings on Theater* we know the esteem in which he held several Soviet artists of this school and we know from a few fragments of biography that he was, for a long time, very close to Sergei Tretiakov, the man who stood closest to Meyerhold after the suicide of the poet, Mayakovsky.[18] In 1930 (at the time he was most deeply involved in working out the relationship of his ideas on politics and those on Japanese drama) he saw Tretiakov's play, *Roar China,* when it was brought to Berlin by Meyerhold's student, Vasily Feodorov. At precisely this time he observed that Meyerhold had in fact worked out "a proper theory on the social function of the theater."[19] Later, when Brecht visited Moscow in 1935, he was in time to see the last magnificent flowering of Meyerhold's all-pervasive work in Moscow. Though the fight for life itself had already long since begun for those artists dedicated to the "Formalist" heresy, the Moscow stage was still dominated (always excepting the Moscow Art Theater itself) by Meyerhold and by his various students, now producers themselves. In that Indian Summer of experimental theater in Moscow, Brecht was to be profoundly influenced by two theatrical events that he saw there. Both deepened and extended his appreciation of the Oriental stage. One of these was the guest appearance of China's greatest contemporary actor, Mei Lan-Fang; the other was Okhlopkov's production of Pogodin's play, *Aristocrats.*

Probably in the company of the men who had invited Mei Lan-Fang to Moscow[20] (Tretiakov, Eisenstein, and possibly Meyerhold himself), Brecht saw the Chinese actor—in evening dress, and wearing no makeup, and with no special lighting—perform a series of women's parts (his specialty) from the classical Chinese repertory. Afterwards, Brecht said that as he had watched the actor perform, "The figure in the dinner jacket almost completely disappeared."[21] Though Brecht also noted that the actor seemed to stand beside the role and though the word "almost" is kept in his description of Mei Lan-Fang's astonishing transformations, it is interesting to see that for Brecht himself this textbook "epic" performance came close to closing the gap between actor and role that the early epic theory set such store by. If, under these conditions and for a real connoisseur of "epic distance," the gap almost disappears, we might ask parenthetically what hope there might be for achieving this distance under far less ideal conditions and with far less expert spectators; or, specifically, what are the chances for a cool response on a typical evening at Brecht's Theater am Schiffbauerdamm—with highly polished actors, with makeup, with scenery, with musical accompaniment, with men (usually) playing the men's parts and women the women's parts? Do the actors, for a typical audience, disappear? Or is the residual effect of Brecht's acting theory (dependent in part on the style of actors such as Mei Lan-Fang) discernible only to connoisseurs familiar with the finest details of what Brecht wants them to find there?[22]

But to return to Moscow in 1935 and the kind of production that helped Brecht to formulate his theory, let us look at one observer's description of Okhlopkov's production of *Aristocrats*. The American critic, Norris Houghton, who saw firsthand all major productions in Moscow in the 1934-35 theater season, writes:

> The action took place on two completely bare rectangular platforms set tangent to each other in the middle of the hall, with the upper left hand corner of one connecting with the lower right hand corner of the other. There was no scenery on

these two stages. The only decorations were painted screens done in the Japanese manner which lined the walls of the house. These suggested the changing seasons with oriental sparsity of detail—an owl on a snowy pine bough against a gray blue sky indicated that it was winter; apple blossoms against a lemon yellow background suggested that spring had come. The actual props required in the business were brought on in the full light by blue-masked and dominoed attendants who in function suggested the Chinese property man. They would run on in full stage light carrying a telephone, for example, and would hold it while a character made his call; when the business was completed they would run off taking the phone with them. Or when a table was required two of these men would enter with a piece of green baize which, squatting on the floor, they would hold taut between them to suggest the table top. The rest of the play, the dialogue, the costumes, were realistic, and the combination of these conventions with the realism I found disturbing. However, this production was hailed by most Moscow critics and many foreign ones as the Realistic Theater's finest performance.[23]

From Houghton's notes it is clear that Meyerhold's student, Okhlopkov, went very far indeed in the use of Chinese conventions—further, as we shall see, than Brecht would go in either of his two big "Oriental" plays, *The Good Person of Sezuan* and *The Caucasian Chalk Circle.* The deliberate contrast between "realistic dialogue" and extremely stylized Chinese convention that Okhlopkov insisted upon in producing *Aristocrats* is broken down in two major ways in Brecht's parable plays. First, he has very little "realistic dialogue" as such. Brecht's plays hover constantly on the brink of verse and often pass completely over from everyday prose to finely wrought lyric expression. Second, Brecht uses relatively few Chinese conventions, and when he does use one he usually Westernizes it enough that it comes close to conventions used in the traditional Western theater. By elevating his text and toning down convention, Brecht has his own productions work at a consistent aesthetic level. Usually no break is discernible between text and production style in Brecht's productions except where he wishes (largely in a traditional way), to underline irony or to make something or someone laughable. Technically, of course, the kind of discrepancy between text and playing style which Okhlopkov used fits very well with some of Brecht's early ideas on "epic theater," but again Brecht seems, in his theater practice from about 1939 on, to retreat from those theatrical devices that his early theory had set such store by.

If we review some of the "epic" or presentational devices of the Oriental stage,[24] we see quickly how few of them Brecht actually employed after the period of the didactic plays, and how many of them were in general use on the Soviet stage by 1935. To generalize about a richly diverse theatrical culture in China and Japan, one can point to a few traits shared by many strands of the classical tradition. Scenery is usually either not present at all or is represented by a stylized prop or picture. No attempt at conjuring up a "realistic" (in the Moscow Art Theater sense) playing locale is made. Masked and unmasked figures play in the same piece. Often all the roles are played by men; in one type of the Oriental theater, all roles are played by puppets of almost life size, manipulated by puppet-masters who are also in full view of the audience. Individual scenes of many plays can be dropped, as they relate only marginally to the main line of the dramatic action. Recitation or recapitulation before and after the plays and between individual "acts" is common. Exposition is often handled by means of direct audience address. The plays wander freely (both backwards and forwards) in time and space; spirit world and "real" world often become virtually indistinguishable. Stage barriers (mountains, oceans, rivers, etc.) are treated frankly as conventions with no attempt at realism. Musicians are often present on the stage in full view of the audience. Stage hands, often dressed in black (making them, by the conventions of the Oriental stage, invisible) change in full view of the audience whatever stylized props or scenery are present. Comic interludes and/or prose passages frequently relieve tense situations. Songs interrupt and comment on the stage action. The actor in such a theater recognizes frankly the theatricality of his performance and does not attempt to establish any "fourth-wall" or Stanislavskian identification of self with role. Obviously, what is true for human actors is even truer for the roles as played by puppets and manipulated by puppet-masters. Likewise, the spectators in such theaters had no notion (except in the most primitive sense) of seeing real events in a real world. The Oriental spectator comes to the often incredibly rowdy and bawdy popular (as distinct from courtly) theaters of Japan, China, and India, to see a performance and to judge it as a performance. Unhampered by fire marshalls, the spectator is free to smoke all through the performance. He is often even free to eat or have his hair shampooed in the theater! Despite all these "epic" elements, despite "epic" plays, performers, and smoking spectators, there is no evidence that these audiences remain unmoved. The Japanese or Chinese actor or dramatist, for instance, would be astounded at the naiveté of a view of theater that holds that stylized playing of highly episodic plays will fail *ipso facto* to move an audience to laughter and tears, or even to pity and to fear. It is virtually certain that Brecht, almost as soon as he evolves the abstract theory of "epic theater" and "alienation," comes to recognize that cool acting and cool plays by no means ensure a cool performance or a cool audience response. He certainly knew this at the time he completed *The Caucasian Chalk Circle* and *The Good Person of Sezuan.*[25] So much for the historical background of the playing style and dramaturgical form of Brecht's two most famous "Oriental plays." Now let us look at Brecht's Westernized treatment of a "Chinese" theme in the first of these plays, *The Good Person of Sezuan.*

From Brecht's notebooks we know that he first began work on the theme of a prostitute who disguises herself as a man[26] in the late twenties in Berlin. From the earliest sketches it is clear that the action of the story (it was not as yet cast in play form) was to take place in Germany and was to be a strictly economic study (from a Marxist point of view) of the relationship of prostitution to capitalist systems in general. The earliest title for the piece neatly sums up Brecht's objectives in writing it. The title, "Die Ware Liebe," with its play on "wahr" (true) and "Ware" (goods for sale) manages simultaneously to suggest two very different possibilities: "True Love" and "Love for Sale." Everything about the "Love for Sale" sketch points to the Brecht of the late 1920s, the Brecht who had recently been converted to Marxism, and the Brecht who had explored this same kind of demi-monde atmosphere in the two operas of this period, *The Threepenny Opera* and *The Rise and Fall of the City of Mahagonny.* Despite the similarity of the sketch to much of his other work of this time, it was to be almost ten years before he would be able to make any substantial progress with it. In these ten years his ideological commitment shifts and with this shift comes a change in his approach to the theater. Only in exile in 1939 is the locale of "Love for Sale" switched to China and does it become recognizably a draft of the play *The Good Person of Sezuan* with three gods[27] playing a significant role in the piece.

When Brecht first began to shape this work for the stage, he seems to have been both attracted and repelled by his own basic concept. As though he, the man who had made such a to-do about introducing science and reason to the theater, was now somewhat ashamed of himself, he notes in his diary in March, 1939: "The changes of clothes and makeup are enough to make this piece of work a charade."[28] After a great number of difficulties and changes in concept, Brecht begins in June 1940 to begin to be satisfied with the way he has shaped the "good" prostitute and her *alter ego,* the "evil" cousin. By January 1941 the play is finished and copies are sent from Finland to friends in the United States, Sweden, and Switzerland (figs. 49 and 50). There is by this time no one still alive in the Soviet Union to whom Brecht would dare send such a play. Having sent off the work to those he felt might be able to produce it, he had to wait eleven years before seeing it performed. Although the play was done in the East German city of Rostock by a satellite company of the Berliner Ensemble under the direction of Benno Besson, his most brilliant student, Brecht was unable to produce the play himself.[29] We do not know, therefore, what changes he might have introduced in the text, had he been able. The closest we can come to his stage concept of it is to look at Besson's production, moved to the headquarters of the Ensemble in 1957, a 1952 Frankfurt production that Brecht partially supervised, and the 1958 production in Milan by the director much admired by Brecht, Giorgio Strehler (fig. 51).

We can see from the photos of the Frankfurt, Berlin, and Milan productions that the Chinese setting of the fable has heavily influenced production style. Easily moved screens (except in the Milan production with its hints of Strehler's beloved commedia dell'arte) are used to create the barest and most stylized of settings (figs. 52-54). In this an attempt has been made not only to match the play's theme stylistically but also to give thereby some sense of the play's architecture, based, as it is, on Chinese models of dramaturgy (figs. 55-57). We should not, however, carry this particular view of the play too far. For all its "Chinese" tone, Sezuan is still in many, many ways the Berlin or Munich of Brecht's earliest sketches. Likewise, though the play's structure does indeed have something in common with the Chinese theater, it has at least as much in common also with medieval European dramaturgy, with the type of construction used frequently by Marlowe and Shakespeare, and, most of all, with Goethe's *Faust.*[30] In Brecht's play, from its beginning with the debate in Heaven to its end with the three gods singing a brilliant parody of classical German verse as they exit on their patently ridiculous pink cloud, and throughout the play in the divided soul of Shen Te/Shui Ta, we hear echoes of Goethe's drama of salvation, salvation even for those who are, in traditional terms, considerably less than perfect.

I suggest that *The Good Person of Sezuan* is a very German play set in a very German milieu. Even as the actors in the

Ensemble production are Germans disguised as Chinese, the play itself is a German work disguised as a Chinese costume piece. China[31] is here (as Persia was to Montesquieu and Italy to the Elizabethans, the Jacobeans, and to Schiller) a means of achieving some aesthetic, economic, and political distance from the events described or presented. The town of Sezuan, having no real existence on any map,[32] becomes the super-reality of a vaguely familiar somewhere and everywhere that we all have known.

Very consciously, *The Good Person of Sezuan* opens in an imitation of the style of highly conventionalized Chinese drama.[33] Wang, the waterseller, introduces himself directly to the audience, sketches the locale of Sezuan, and announces that three gods are expected in this "slightly Europeanized city" momentarily. With the appearance of the gods, Wang attempts to find them suitable lodgings. He starts with the rich and works down to the poor. He is rebuffed constantly[34] until he gets to the prostitute Shen Te, who, reluctantly and with considerable economic sacrifice, agrees to take the gods into her lodging. As a result of her kindness to them, the gods present Shen Te with one thousand silver dollars and enjoin the "good person of Sezuan" to use this money to do good. Through the tobacco shop that she purchases with the money, Shen Te proceeds to do her level best to attempt to be and to do good, but the greediness of those she tries to help and the sheer scale of want in the city of Sezuan make it obvious that neither goodness nor one thousand silver dollars is enough to help significantly. Threatened with the loss of her modest capital and with it the loss of any real chance of doing good, she invents (at the prompting of others) a business-minded "cousin," Shui Ta. Disguising herself as the ruthless Mr. Shui Ta, Shen Te, paradoxically, is able to do more good than before—and is able to stay afloat financially. The moral is obvious and profoundly disturbing: goodness, without at least a modicum of evil, is not possible in Sezuan. Appalled at this heretical conclusion but offering no solution to the dilemma of Shen Te/Shui Ta, the gods exit in indecent haste on a pink cloud. An actor then addresses the public directly in a brief epilogue that sets the spectator as difficult a task as the gods set for Shen Te: Find, if you can, a way out of the dilemma that Shen Te and you, the public, find yourselves in.

The profound metaphysical question of why evil is permitted, indeed encouraged, in the world has seldom been asked with such force. With his usual genius for finding the appropriate specifically dramatic gestus to point his question, Brecht creates the split character of Shen Te/Shui Ta. Totally incredible in terms of fourth-wall style theater, her change from the "good" and very naive Shen Te to the "bad" and exceedingly clever Shui Ta, unrecognized by anyone but the petty blackmailer Mrs. Shin, is credible only within the dungheap Utopia, the nowhere and everywhere of Sezuan. The ancient convention of the impenetrable disguise is exploited in Brecht's non-realistic parable to its fullest dramatic and tragic potential. The quintessence of both the best and the worst facets of Mother Courage[35] (businesswoman and mother), Shen Te/Shui Ta draws us close to her in pity and makes us recoil in fear. The closing scene of the play, where Shen Te cries out to the gods for some relief from the nightmare of this mad and vicious world, has much of the power of the scene in *Mother Courage* where the dumb drummer Kattrin pays for goodness with her life. It is no wonder that Reinhold Grimm asks of *The Good Person of Sezuan*: "Does not at least this play advance into the realm of tragedy?"[36] One wonders if Brecht, had he himself produced it, would have sought to prevent identification with Shen Te. The play as the Ensemble and other theater groups have produced it has been magnificently unsuccessful in eliciting a cool response from audiences east or west of the Berlin wall. It is no wonder that this play has become (in terms of number of productions and performances) the most popular play in the whole Brecht canon.

When we examine the play closely we find that the reason for the impact of the play is not faulty or "non-Brechtian" production techniques. The main problem, if this indeed be a problem, is the play itself. The play is so formed that it must be abominably produced indeed in order to elicit a cool response. The language of the play is too lively, yet in that typically Brechtian way that first struck Herbert Ihering in the early twenties, too raw, too well thought out to be easily forgotten. With its kind and foolish Shen Te, with Shui Ta who, like Schweyk and Galileo, does evil in order to do good, and with Sun, lovable somehow for all his brutality, the play demands our intense involvement. Further, beneath the surface of character and fable, there is woven a complex pattern of allegory and symbol based on the most ancient constituent parts of the storyteller's art: gods, devils, the symbolic use of weather,[37] the symbolic use of number, the frankly inexplicable power of a love that denies logic and rationality, and the intervention of fortune and of the "gods from the machine." Pitched very consciously[38] somewhere between the biblical tone of the story of Job and the dry facts of a German newspaper report, the story has an almost medieval quality; but it is a medieval tale as seen through a very sharp pair of twentieth-century eyes.

As is usual with Brecht's plays of the exile period, *The Good Person of Sezuan* is so carefully constructed that it is difficult to imagine it beginning or ending later or sooner than it in fact does. The opening scene serves as a model of compact exposition. Wang has waited, so we learn, three days for the three gods to appear. We the spectators, however, are only forced to wait as long as it takes for Wang to complete some essential exposition. We should not be asking ourselves while we wait why Wang has not utilized the three days to find suitable lodgings for the expected gods. Then, with a promptness reminiscent of the arrival of Agamemnon, or of the witnesses at the trial of Oedipus, or of the wagon of Mother Courage, the gods arrive. By the end of the first scene, Brecht has sounded every essential theme of the play at least once. The goal of the gods has been clearly explicated as has the reason for their embarking on a search for a "good person." The necessary "good person" is found in the opening scene. We are given a foretaste of the problems that goodness brings with it, as she must give up a customer in order to help the gods. Through Wang's first fruitless attempts to find lodgings, we have been given a panoramic view of the general heartlessness that prevails in the city of Sezuan. And, just before the gods exit in the first scene, Shen Te clearly states the problem which the rest of the play will illustrate.[39] She cries (and in this beginning is her end): "Of course I would like to be happy, to follow the commandments, to honor my father and my mother, and to be truthful. Not to lust after my neighbor's house would be a joy for me, and to be faithful to one man would be a pleasure. Also, I do not want to exploit anyone or to rob the helpless. But how am I to do all this? Even when I fail to keep a few of the commandments, I can hardly survive."[40] After the fairytale-like and wholly inadequate gift of the one thousand silver dollars (given at the insistence of the ever practical and cynical third god), the gods exit. They exit hastily, in precisely the way they will exit at the play's close, waving goodbye, and mouthing their impossible sentiments drawn from an outmoded humanist tradition. Just as we have seen with *Mother Courage* and we shall see with *Galileo,* all following scenes in *Sezuan* have been precisely anticipated in the opening scene. Like these other two plays, *Sezuan* proves to be classically circular in structure. And again as with these other two plays, this perfectly rounded aesthetic construct with its highly schematized world view will provide no philosophically or economically viable answers. Again we must content or discontent ourselves with a dramatic statement of an important and fundamentally human problem.

This talk of fundamental human and moral problems conjures up an image of a play perhaps forbiddingly Teutonic. And yet this it is not. The way in which Brecht has seasoned what might well have become a most unappetizing dish is a classic study of fulfillment of Horace's dictum, that the artist should combine the useful and the pleasurable. A key ingredient that Brecht uses to offset the taste of the wormwood he serves us (and something that Brecht criticism thus far has made surprisingly little of) is humor. Whenever the text begins to bog down, Brecht manages to lift it up again with the judicious use of his sense of the sheer absurdity of much of what we say and do. For the person attuned to Brecht's humor (and perhaps it is an aquired taste), Wang's opening monologue on the gods is typical. We find that Wang has learned of their coming, not from the traditional oracle, but from a buyer of cattle! When Wang finally spots the gods, he does not recognize them by their traditional "godlike" qualities but by the simple fact that they show "no sign of having any occupation at all."[47] This throwaway line captures the essence of Wang's smart-stupid, often almost "Schweikian" view of the world. At the close of the opening scene, the resolutely bourgeois first god cautions the prostitute, Shen Te, not to mention that they have paid very liberally for their lodging in her house. "This could," he observes, "be misunderstood."[42]

Other elements which impart a measure of lightness and a certain pleasing tonality are the use of dream (the gods appear to Wang as the patrons of "The Goblet" appeared to Schweyk), the use of symbol, the use of song, and the ancient device of the use of significant number. Often song and significant number are combined, as in the "Song of the Eighth Elephant." It will be remembered that in myth and fairytale the number seven[43] is traditionally associated (as is the number three and its multiple, nine) with good, whereas the numbers four and eight are frequently associated with evil. The numbers chosen by Brecht in the elephant song, in the play as a whole, and in his work in general, indicate his indebtedness to a tradition that has consistently used numbers symbolically to call forth specific psychological reverberations. We may particularly note the sheer frequency of the recurrence of the number three. Wang waits three days for three gods. Shen Te buys a shop three days after the gods leave. She borrows three hundred dollars. Sun calls three devils to witness. Sun also happens to become "capable of progress" during his third week of work at the tobacco factory. Then, he fully matures as an overseer in his third month. Every day Shen Te asks Mrs. Shin three times: "What will become of the baby?" Shui Ta complains that he has had to come three times. Or, to conclude a list which can be extended almost indefinitely, the play itself is divided into three sections between the prologue and the trial scene. This division corresponds, as Professor Berckman has noted,[44] to Shen Te's three major endeavors: to help her neighbor, to love Sun, and to save her small son from want. The inordinately frequent repetition of this and other significant numbers, helps to cast an almost medieval or biblical aura over much of Brecht's work. As we might expect in a medieval European, or a biblical or classical Oriental text, for instance, in the "Song of the Eighth Elephant," it is the eighth elephant (Sun) who drives the other seven into the darkness of the song's menacing refrain. This song, like Wang's song (used as a leitmotif throughout the play), or the extraordinary "Song of the Smoke,"[45] or the bitter yet achingly lovely "Song of St. Nevercome's Day" and the "Song of the Defenselessness of the Gods and the Good," is specifically related to the plane of dramatic action and is not set in the play like a plum in a cake.[46] Each summarizes a crucial development in the dramatic fable at the same time that it elevates the text beyond the specific and the mundane and places it at the level of the general and the rhythmically recurrent.[47] That Brecht knew exactly what he was up to with the use of songs in this particular play we know from a diary note made in January 1941: "Inasmuch as the play is very long, I shall add a poetic element, some verses and songs. It may become thereby lighter and not so boring even if it cannot be made shorter."[48] Giving new form and purpose to the ancient function of the chorus, Brecht succeeds in seducing us, through verse and music, into swallowing medicine that we might otherwise find too bitter.

As Brecht points out in his diary note, verse serves much the same function in his plays as song. When Brecht is not seducing us with the kind of songs that had won him so many admirers when he sang them himself in the early days in Munich and Berlin, then this man works on us through the medium of verse. Again and again in the play, we find mundane conversation passing imperceptibly into song or verse. It is no accident that the smart simpleton Wang, whose usual speech is as colorless as Brecht ever allows any character's to be, in describing the difficulties of Shen Te's position to the uncomprehending gods, passes from the pedestrian observation that times are indeed hard, to:

> Hardly was there a place shielded from the wind
> There came flying the whole wintry sky
> Of ruffled birds and
> Shoved for their place and the hungry fox bit through
> The thin wall, and the one-legged wolf
> Shoved over the small dish.[49]

Or Shen Te (basically a very simple sort of person) contemplating Wang's hand smashed by her oily admirer, the barber Shu Fu, turns to those who will not help and (in an ode that recalls Antigone's final address to the Theban Elders) says:

> Oh, miserable ones!
> Force is employed against your brother, and you squeeze your
>   eyes closed!
> He who is attacked calls loudly, and you are silent?
> The attacker prowls and picks out his victim
> And you say: he spares us because we show no dissatisfaction.
> What kind of city can this be, what sort of human beings are
>   you![50]

We, the inhabitants of any city on this earth are being addressed here; we are being chastised; it is we who recognized the aptness of her words applied to ourselves and we shrink a little in our seats as we hear her. Or, what are our feelings when Shen Te again, at the seesaw point that is the absolute psychological center of this drama of reason pitched against feeling, turns to the public and declares:

> I will go with him, whom I love.
> I will not calculate the cost.
> I will not meditate on whether it is good.
> I will not seek to know whether he loves me.
> I will go with him, whom I love.[51]

Finally, as Shen Te tries in the court scene to explain why she, the "good person of Sezuan," has had to turn herself into the "evil" Shui Ta, again Brecht's text passes from the prose of evil to the haunting melody of her longing for good. In a long verse passage she cries:

> Why
> Is evil rewarded and why do
> Such heavy penalties await the good?[52]

The question simply transcends the bounds of prose. Brecht the poet can only begin to hint at the depths of the agony of her question through the intense concentration and rhythmic sweep of verse. Are we, we wonder, supposed to remain rational and maintain our distance in the face of her cry? Or does the use of verse itself (with its atavistic echoes of the ebb and flow of the sea and the pulsing of our own life's blood) tend to awaken in us a primitive and profound excitement that compels us irrationally to move with its rhythms? With Shen Te's final cry we hear echoes of that something which called forth both terror and pity long ago in the sun-baked arenas of the Peloponnesus. We can no more remain aloof from her agony than we can from that of Kattrin or that of Oedipus.

Examined closely, *The Good Person of Sezuan* elicits the kind of response that we might well have expected had we carefully read Brecht's post-1940 criticism. By 1941 and the completion of his first major "Oriental" play, in both theory and practice the Brecht of the early "epic theory" has been left behind. It is clear that the play, whether measured against Brecht's own early theory or against the ancient dramatic tradition of the Orient, must strike one as conservative or non-epic. Ronald Gray, stressing the obvious fact that one scene grows directly out of the one before in Brecht's play, says flatly: "In structure, this is by no means 'epic' theater."[53] It is clear, as Gray intimates, that the individual scenes of this play could not, for the most part, be meaningfully rearranged or dropped. Shen Te does not turn into a robber baron suddenly; she does it slowly, with great reluctance and considerable pain.

Only gradually is she convinced that for goodness—any goodness—to survive, Shui Ta must stay for longer and longer periods. Brecht's careful deployment of his theatrical forces as he works toward an old-fashioned denouement is ordered and precise.

The unity of the dramatic curve of Brecht's play, so much clearer and more exact than much Oriental, medieval, and Elizabethan practice, hints at two other "unities" in Brecht's play, unities but rarely observed in non-Aristotelian theater. Compare for a moment the free wandering in time and space of the Oriental theater with Brecht's use of time and space in this play. In time the play covers a period a little short of nine months.[54] In space he confines himself to one section of one city. Though Brecht's work is non-Aristotelian when measured against neoclassical[55] interpretations of Aristotle, it is clearly much more "Aristotelian" in its use of the unities of time, space, and action than many a play of Shakespeare, of Marlowe, of the Orient—yes, even of Schiller and Goethe.

One could argue, however, that in one essential feature Brecht is almost more neoclassical than the neoclassicists. Seldom has the battle between the conflicting demands of head and of heart (so dearly beloved of Corneille and Racine) been presented with greater dramatic cogency than in the person of Shen Te/Shui Ta. Further, like the neoclassicists, Brecht has foregone "epic breadth and fullness" and has substituted dramatic tightness and intensity. We are shown only the intensely dramatic heart of Shen Te/Shui Ta's tightly circumscribed world. Retreating from the broad, sprawling, non-Aristotelian world of the Oriental stage, Brecht returns to that focused and intense area where the Hamlets and even the Cids and the Phaedras have had their hour or two[56] upon the stages of the Western world.

It will be remembered that Brecht's call for a new stage form in the 1920s was predicated on the principle that the old one did not permit the treatment of the kind of subject matter that the "epic" form would attempt to present. Speaking contemptuously of older forms, he had observed then: "If one surveys the materials treated in the narrative and performing arts, one sees but rarely the major subjects such as war, money, oil, railroads, parliaments, wage struggles and land. When these subjects do appear it is usually only as a decorative backdrop or to stimulate meditation."[5][7] What might the Brecht who wrote these words have thought of *The Good Person*? What has happened to the "present day world"? As Rischbieter notes of the setting of the play, it is "kept small and is easily surveyed." Instead of the "massive subjects" that the epic form was supposed to present, we have a simplified vision of the world, a world of gods and of fortuitous gifts, a world that has hardly changed (except for reference to Sun's plane) since the sixteenth or seventeenth century. As Rischbieter points out, "The breakdown of human relations through cash payments is presented in a small, easily encompassed area of personal relationships. It takes place in a pre-industrial or, at best, an early-industrial milieu."[5][8] This is not a world of gigantic cities, of galloping technology, of maneuvers on the stock exchange, of general strikes, or of military-industrial complexes. Instead, Brecht has chosen to cut through all this and explore problems that pre-date by millennia the world that his early epic theory demanded be presented on the twentieth-century stage. The social concern that caused him to generate the theory remains, as does the influence of his explorations of Oriental stage practice, but social concern and non-Naturalistic exposition are employed in *The Good Person of Sezuan*, not to present a world that has changed substantially since fifth-century Athens but to present a world that needs—desperately—substantial change. The play is not new in form, but it does not really need to be, for it deals with an ancient problem. The most profound tragedy of the play, perhaps, for Brecht is that the writing of tragedies was still, in 1941, both apt and necessary. Our tragedy, some thirty years later, is that Brecht's play is still at least as apt and still as necessary as in that dark year when it was written. The solution which the play's epilogue urges us to seek is still well beyond our grasp. The gods have vanished, their empty sentiments still hang on the air, and Shen Te and Shui Ta still await that world where goodness unimpaired will be suffered to survive.

CHAPTER EIGHT

BRECHT AND THE ORIENTAL STAGE II:
THE CAUCASIAN CHALK CIRCLE

> "The epic facet of theater is most fully developed in *The Chalk Circle.*"
>
> *Joachim Müller*[1]
>
> "Our task is as follows: we must replace supernumeraries with good actors. A good actor is worth a battalion of supernumeraries. That is to say, he is worth more."
>
> *Bertolt Brecht*[2]

Our examination of the first of Brecht's best known Oriental plays, *The Good Person of Sezuan,* has to remain somewhat speculative as we do not know exactly what Brecht might have done with the play if he had ever staged it himself. In the case of *The Caucasian Chalk Circle* we know in exhaustive detail how the play was rehearsed and staged.[3] We know what work went into the eight months of rehearsals which led up to the play's premiere on October 7, 1954. We know further what changes and cuts were made in the text and in the performance when Brecht took the play to France for the Festival of Paris in 1955, the year before his death. Having won the top prize in Paris the year before with his production of *Mother Courage and Her Children*, Brecht wanted to show the world in 1955 just how astoundingly rich the repertoire of the Berliner Ensemble was. *The Caucasian Chalk Circle,* polished and pared for almost a year before it opened at the Theater am Schiffbauerdamm, with its cast of some one hundred and fifty characters (reduced to fifty actual players by the use of masks and the doubling and trebling of roles), with the lightning swift scene changes required by such scenes as the "Flight into the Northern Mountains," was just the thing to show off the total effect of what was at that time the greatest theater ensemble in the world. It is with this production and the equally stunning production of *Mother Courage* that Brecht established his resounding international reputation. If we recall that after their triumphs in Paris, it was with *Mother Courage* and *The Caucasian Chalk Circle* that the Berliner Ensemble made its London debut in 1956 (opening in London two weeks after Brecht's death in East Berlin), and that it was with these same two plays that the Ensemble visited Moscow in 1957, then we can understand the magnitude of the impact the Ensemble made on highly sophisticated theater audiences in Eastern and Western countries. The two productions represented Brecht at the very zenith of his powers both as playwright and as director. But *The Caucasian Chalk Circle* was also his swansong, for he died the following year, in the midst of rehearsals of *Galileo.* Therefore, one might see the production of *The Caucasian Chalk Circle* as Brecht's last complete aesthetic testament.

In this play, in contrast to the dark tones of both *Mother Courage* and *The Good Person of Sezuan,* Brecht dreams a beautiful dream. The dream is of a time when war is over, when the partisans and exiles can return in peace to their own countries, when love and understanding can, however fleetingly, replace brutality, hate, and stupidity. In this dream Brecht allows himself, for a brief moment, in the never-neverland of a Caucasus that is largely a product of his own imagination, to think of a short but golden age where justice almost reigned. Significantly, as Eric Bentley has pointed out, Brecht set the play in a time in advance of the actual time of its composition. The play was commissioned for Broadway production[4] (a production that never took place) in 1943 and was completed in its final form by 1945. Yet, the prologue of the play is set in postwar Russia.

The lovely dream that forms the main body of the play is prefaced by another dream, the dream of a collective farm (Kolkhos) in the Caucasus where people settle their disputes in a rational and amicable fashion and where (wonder of wonders) the playing of a play helps the process of reason and helps to lead to peace (fig. 58). The dream that precedes the dream has been attacked by Communists and non-Communists alike. Western critics approach the prologue aesthetically and note the schematic nature of the characters presented and the tenuous relationship of the prologue to "the play itself."[5] Eastern critics object to the prologue on political grounds and claim that the Kolkhos members are not convincing as members of a real Kolkhos in a real Georgia.

If the prologue is played with the care with which it was presented in Brecht's production, we are gradually moved from the real world (ourselves in the theater) to the "real" world of the supposed here and now of the Kolkhos. The "real" farmers then lead us into the frankly "unreal" world of the ancient tale of Azdak and Grusche and the frankly theatrical presentation of that tale, with its stylized masks, sets, and deliberately exaggerated playing style. Viewed and acted thus, the prologue can form a kind of decompression chamber as we step from the here and now into the never-never. The advantages in the Western theater of playing the prologue are considerable. Considerations of time, however, might well force a director to lop it off and thus reduce the playing time of this very lengthy play.

The prologue of Brecht's play tells us that we are about to watch a performance, by amateur actors, of an adaptation of a fourteenth-century Chinese play, *The Chalk Circle*.[6] Actually Brecht's play has but little in common either with the Chinese play itself, or with his friend Klabund's German version of the original Chinese work, or with the more stylized conventions of the Chinese stage. Brecht has switched the locale of the play from China to the crossroads of the East and West, pre-Soviet Georgia. With the change of locale, he throws out the largely decorous language of both his models, flatly rejects the sentimental tale of the former prostitute who ends up as an empress, and switches the ending of the play so that the bitchy, rich biological mother of the child loses him in the circle test to the impoverished girl who loved and cared for him after his "real" mother had selfishly abandoned him.[7] Besides throwing out most of the content of his models, Brecht introduces the long, lovely, and involved tale of the cowardly and inebriated, clever and sober judge, Azdak. With all these changes, it is clear that Brecht's play has, in terms of content, virtually only the chalk circle test itself in common with its Chinese and German models. Even in terms of narrative style, however, Brecht departs from his models. Again, as with *The Good Person of Sezuan,* he uses only those non-naturalistic or "presentational" devices of traditional Chinese dramaturgy which help him to present his necessary expository materials in a form which is both condensed and explicit. Highly reminiscent of *Sezuan,* for instance, is the fact that the first drafts of the treatment of the *Chalk Circle* material were not set anywhere in the Orient. Written in exile in Sweden, the very earliest version was called "Odenser Kreidekreis." When he next returned to the theme, Brecht placed the story in Augsburg, the town of his birth. This short story version, completed in 1940, is called simply "Der Augsburger Kreidekreis." In this version, a maid by the name of Anna rescues the child and takes it to a neighboring village where her brother lives on a farm owned by his wife. In the chalk circle test an extraordinary judge, Ignaz Dollinger, loved by the local farmers for both his learning and his bawdy sense of humor, awards the child not to the rich Frau Zingli (the natural mother of the child) but to Anna. Of some interest is the fact that in this version the judge tells Anna before the trial that she will be awarded the child. Thus, no tension is allowed to build up, an idea wholly consistent with Brecht's early epic theory. In contrast, as we shall see, tension is allowed to build in the later play version as we are not at all sure of what Azdak might be capable of doing under stress. More important than this, however, is the simple fact that the "Oriental" tale of the circle of chalk can, as Brecht himself demonstrated twice, be easily transferred to an occidental milieu. As with *Sezuan,* only enough of the flavor of the original is kept to give the play an interesting touch of the exotic and a certain measure of aesthetic distance. Again Brecht will use only some of the scenic and acting conventions of the Chinese stage. Again he will use these conventions only in a much modified or Westernized form.[8] The style of his text and his production of that text would eschew the detailed "Realism" of an Ibsen or a Stanislavsky but would stay well away from a style so alien to a European audience that it might be baffled by something too unfamiliar.[9]

If we recall the placards which introduced Brecht's *Eduard II* and *Mother Courage,* the traditional chorus in *Antigone,* the use of a chorus and of direct address in *The Mother,* the "narrator" Wang in the *Good Person,* and the four-line verses that introduce the separate scenes of the next play to be examined, *Galileo,* we will recognize the singer who links and introduces the tale of the *Chalk Circle* as a summing up and extension of all these devices. Abandoning the implicit exposition of an Ibsen in a play like *The Wild Duck,* Brecht returns to a far more ancient, far more widespread form of dramatic exposition, the explicit method used by the Greeks, by most Oriental playwrights, by the medieval theater, and by Shakespeare[10] and most of his followers. Volker Klotz has pointed out the similarity of the singer's function in Brecht's play to Aeschylus' use of the chorus.[11] Like the chorus of the great Greek tragedian, Brecht's singer does not act; he plays no part; he simply sings. There is however one interesting Brechtian innovation connected with this singer. Although he is basically "outside" the action, he is also right in the middle of it (fig. 59). With his chorus of helpers (singers and musicians) he speaks the thoughts of Grusche when she is forced by circumstances or her own overpowering emotion to remain silent. He assumes at these moments both the ancient function that was served by the overheard monologue or choral ode and the modern function that is called in film "voice over narration." Throughout the play, the singer will introduce and comment upon each scene and, finally, will sum up what he (Brecht) believes to be the lesson that the staged presentation should have taught to its Kolkhos and theater audiences.

If we go on from the text itself to Brecht's magnificent staging of the play in 1954, there is one further point about the singer that deserves some mention. Brecht cast the greatest male actor and singer available, Ernst Busch (fig. 60), as both the singer ("outside" the play) and Azdak (very much "inside" the play).[12] In performance, therefore, we can postulate an intensification of the specifically dramatic (in Brecht's terms, the non-narrative or non-epic element of the play) at the expense of the purely narrative or epic. Ernst Busch (in the fifth scene)[13] joins the magnificent Grusche (Angelika Hurwicz) on the dramatic plane of the play. Henceforth, the part of the singer, though still of some importance as a role, is reduced in stature in Brecht's production as the strongest member of the "narrative" team changes his role and function and lends his enormously powerful personality to the dramatic side of the play. More subtly, of course, his switch in roles tends both to theatricalize the production by stressing role-playing as role-playing and to link the various parts of the play together. Thus, the appearance of a "new" character, Azdak, first appearing halfway through the play, is deliberately foreshadowed from the first line by the voice and the unmistakable gestures of Ernst Busch.[14] The roles of singer and of Azdak can, of course, be separated and given to different actors, but then we have a different aesthetic construct from the one Brecht chose to present in 1954. I am simply noting here Brecht's play as he presented it. This is a case where the text alone gives only subtle hints of what in performance became a very important aesthetic move on the part of the creative artist.

Viewed as Brecht staged it, his play moves from the plane of "reality" into the world of the drama in several major stages. First, in the Kolkhos we have a supposed one-for-one relationship of character to player.[15] The Kolkhos workers, with the aid of a professional singer, play the roles in the ancient tale (figs. 61-62). This first part of the play is balanced between action (Grusche) and narration (the professional singer and his amateur helpers). We move deeper (in performance) into action as Busch switches roles in scene five. From this moment on the performance is dominated by its active (dramatic) rather than passive or narrative (epic) elements. We have been gradually transferred from one plane of action, "The Kolkhos," to another, "The Circle of Chalk."

The happenstance of having Busch available to play the singer and the role of Azdak casts some interesting light on the text of the play. Brecht the playwright-director was fully aware that his text supports the casting move he makes in scene five. The relative importance of the singer in the two halves of the play is demonstrated by a small experiment. Remove all the lines of the singer from scenes one through four[16] and then try to make some sense of the text. Not only would the remainder be barely comprehensible, it would also lack a large measure of poetic power. We would miss, for instance, those heightened scenes where the singer provides the voice over narration of Grusche's thoughts. We need the singer in these scenes to "give voice" to the "dumb" Grusche. In scenes five and six, as the wily and articulate Azdak comes to the fore, we no longer need any voice over narration; he is perfectly capable of voicing his own thoughts. Except for the short song in the trial scene, where Grusche is again struck dumb with emotion, the singer has but little to do in scenes five and six. The role could be cut in these scenes with almost no damage being done to the basic plot line. It is not, therefore, simply an accident of Brecht's own production that he shifted (with Busch) the balance of the play from the narrative-dramatic to the overwhelmingly dramatic plane in the closing scenes.

The insight that performance gives to text in the case of the singer is by no means an isolated one. As I look carefully at the selection of photographs and notes on Brecht's production that Angelika Hurwicz has assembled,[17] I am stunned again and again by the emotive power of even these still (how expressive a word!) black and white pictures of a production that was obviously highly colorful and highly moving. Note, for instance, the skilled transition (by means of wrapping the child in a blanket) from the baby that arrives at the small hut in the mountains and the small boy we see in the spring (fig. 63). Miss Hurwicz notes of this scene: "In order to suggest the coldness of the pantry, the child is wrapped in a blanket. But this also serves to make, for the spectator, the transition from infant to larger child less crass or glaring."[18] A little later, in the scene where Grusche is torn between "her" explanation to her returned fiance, Simon Chachawa, and the threat to "her" child, a soldier of the governor, Brecht does not let her stand there very long, torn between her two loves. He has her dash off after the child and the governor's henchman in precipitous haste. Instead of "naturalistic" delay, a delay that would make her painful psychological choice credible, Brecht had something else in mind. Miss Hurwicz notes: "Brecht avoids developing the scene of Grusche's interesting dilemma. What was of more interest to him was *dramaturgically linking this scene with the later trial scene* [my italics], where Grusche, with all the forcefulness she can muster, will assert her rights to the child."[19]

The small but important details that Brecht used to tie the action together and which are so admirably explicated by Miss Hurwicz's analysis of the photos of the production, are then supported by Brecht's use of the most important technical device available to him at the Theater am Schiffbauerdamm: the huge turntable stage that he had used with such telling effect in his *Mother Courage* production. Karl von Appen, who designed the *Chalk Circle* production for Brecht, notes how the turntable was used for Grusche's flight into the Northern Mountains:

The turntable ran in the opposite direction to Grusche's line of flight; thus, though she kept running, she remained visible [at all times] through the proscenium arch. Towards her came the individual way stations of her flight, and the turntable was stopped as the individual scenes were played, and then set in motion again. While Grusche continued her journey, the set moved away. The back third of the stage was set off by a backdrop. Behind the backdrop, where the audience could not see this, the individual set segments were loaded on the turntable and run around the backdrop to the front of the stage. In the same way, segments disappeared behind the backdrop and behind this shield were taken off the turntable. In this way, the long and eventful flight could be presented without interruption. As it was necessary to be able to take off set segments and set new ones on the turntable in a matter of seconds, the result was that all the parts that had to be so moved were made of paper-mâché.[20]

As is absolutely plain from this description, the basic function of the turntable was to tie the scene together as closely as possible. The effect sought was flawless continuity and with this, chronological compression. In effect, therefore, we may postulate that the transitions from scene to scene in Brecht's "epic" play were far smoother than the kind of delayed changes (necessitated by major set changes) that we see so often in more "realistic" productions. Brecht's play was not sliced up by the "guillotine" (to use Brecht's own term for the device) of the heavy curtain used even today in many "Naturalist" productions.[21]

The smooth continuum of action established first by Brecht's choice of visual details (wrapping the child in a blanket for the hut scene), second by his not permitting "Naturalist" delay (Grusche's swift flight after the child and away from Simon), and third by the use of the turntable stage itself, is then reenforced by the music that Paul Dessau composed (on Brecht's instructions)[22] for this scene. Brecht himself notes of this music: "For the second act ('Flight into the Northern Mountains'), the theater needs a driving kind of music that will hold this very epic act together."[23] Not only did this driving music hold the act together, it also tended to reenforce the tension generated by the flight itself. "The Flight into the Northern Mountains" is very much a "chase sequence" in a style close to that of the old American films Brecht so dearly loved.[24] Grusche's escape, as the text never for a moment permits us to forget, is a nip and tuck affair. What is true of the text is, however, even truer of Brecht's staging. Instead, for instance, of completely stylizing the crossing of the two thousand feet deep chasm (a scene that would probably be done in the Chinese theater, full as it is of V-effects, solely with gestures and with no props at all),[25] Brecht gave the scene additional emotional drive by introducing an actual rickety bridge.[26] With the soldiers in hot pursuit, Grusche, almost too tired to move at all, approaches the makeshift rope bridge (figs. 64-66). Other characters, scared to death by the rotten ropes and completely loose end of one side of the bridge, stand around, refusing to attempt to cross and urging Grusche not to try anything so suicidal. Laden as she is with her bundle and her child, the bridge will, they assure her, collapse under their combined weight. But for Grusche to stand there and not cross is perhaps even more suicidal. The soldiers, one of whose heads she has smashed in the previous scene, can be heard approaching and they will, as one bystander assures Grusche and us the audience, "make hamburger out of her"[27] if she is caught. Under these circumstances she is willing to attempt to cross the bridge. Tension mounts as she resolutely decides not to leave the child behind and thus increases the danger considerably. Amid the gasps and prayers of the bystanders she makes the hazardous crossing safely and, just as she reaches the other side and the loose end of the bridge is once again allowed simply to dangle over the chasm, the soliders appear on the side she has just left. The scene and its staging are obviously so designed that we cross that bridge with Grusche; we see the two thousand foot drop below; we feel the breath of the pursuing soldiers on our necks. In a word, we are forced to identify fully with the heroic Grusche. We then follow her on her seven-day journey as the stage turns (as with Mother Courage)[28] against her progress. We are with her as she reaches her brother's hut, and we are there as, all her heroic efforts and sacrifices notwithstanding, the child is taken from her by the soldiers at the end of the act.

As the child is led away and Grusche makes her swift decision to follow and leave her beloved Simon standing agape, the scene closes (as is usual in Brecht at heightened moments, in verse), with the singer asking:

> Who will decide the case, to whom will the child be given?
> Who will be the judge, a good one, a bad one?
> The city was burning. On the seat of judgment sat Azdak.[29]

When a song is introduced in Brecht, we think (often erroneously, notes Miss Hurwicz) that this should signal a V-effect; indeed this is the usual way in which songs such as the above have been treated by critics working with *The Caucasian Chalk Circle*. Miss Hurwicz, who knows a great deal about *The Caucasian Chalk Circle* and other postwar productions, notes:

> Often the songs are interpreted as V-effects. They interrupt the dialogue; it follows therefore, so the conclusion is drawn, that they also interrupt the action (*Spiel*). However, Brecht wanted, for instance, in the scene where Grusche again meets her fiance, the actors to mime, with the most polished expression, the text of the singers. Distrust, reproach, disappointment, should be mirrored in their faces. The song as the poetic expression of silence. At the same point [in the play], the singers, as they give expression to the reproachful thoughts of Simon Chachawa, should not sing, as at other times, as though they were telling a tale and were not part of the action, but rather angrily, accusingly.[30]

"This moment," concludes Miss Hurwicz, "cannot by classified under any stylistic principle, it is simply a poetic, beautiful, and self-contained aesthetic moment." We have, therefore, if Miss Hurwicz is correct in her view, at the conclusion of the supposedly most narrative or "epic" section of Brecht's play, a clear anticipation of the action of the concluding two scenes.

Again, a staging device is used to help the audience make a transition from scene to scene rather than to draw the audience's attention to act or scene divisions.

The myriad aesthetic "knots" introduced deliberately by the playwright-director to offset scenic division and to eliminate breaks between dialogue and song, indicate how far the later Brecht had departed from the earlier theory. The pleasure of the spectator (the guiding principle of the 1948 *Short Organum*) and the pure aesthetic satisfaction that the later Brecht sought and found in the theater, seemed to have played a greater role here than the early theory with its discrete parts, its anti-aesthetic bias, and its calm and largely unmoved spectators. Brecht's own reading of his text is specifically dramatic and profoundly moving. The separate parts of the play become in production indissolubly welded together. Even leaving aside for a moment Brecht's casting innovation, it is obvious, in dramaturgical terms, that the break in the Grusche story, coming at the time it does, hurries us as precipitously as Grusche into the last lap of the play where the destinies of Grusche and Azdak converge in the test of the circle of chalk.

When Brecht shifts the scene to Azdak and the corrupt judge's rise to power, the spectator does not simply forget Grusche or the fact that the poor girl is in danger of losing her child to a wretched governor's wretched wife. Scene four closes very cleverly with Grusche running after her child as the singer, using one of the oldest devices known to storytellers in any media, asks: "What will happen now?" Everything depends on getting a just judge to decide Grusche's claim to the child; who will that judge be? We are then introduced to the man who is vital to Grusche's cause. Thereafter, with brilliant use of retardation as we are amused and frightened by and for Azdak, as we see Azdak's rise to power and how tenuous his power is, we continue to be nagged by the question: What is going on "back at the ranch"? Will the mad, sensuous, cowardly, brave, and eminently Schweikian Azdak be able to save the child for Grusche or will he be removed and slaughtered at whim before the case comes to trial? If he tries the case, will he be swayed by power or threats from the wealthy wife of the governor or will he stick his neck in a noose in order to save the child for the "true" mother? His earlier decisions in the case of the "rape" trial and the case of the miraculous ham lead us to hope that he will help the poor and heavy laden; but he is, at the same time, too cowardly, too whimsical for us to be wholly sure (fig. 67). We are raced by Brecht in the closing two scenes of the play, as surely as Racine ever raced an audience in his climactic and precipitous fifth acts, toward the denouement. But if we move too fast in our analysis, we shall miss some rather lovely, some profoundly moving substrata of Brecht's production and of the text of the play itself. Symbolic and linguistic devices in both text and playing point to as rich and paradoxical a use of semi-biblical language and imagery as any to be found in *Eduard II, Mother Courage,* or *The Good Person of Sezuan.*

Albrecht Schöne has pointed out the connection, in Brecht's production, of Azdak and Christ. As Azdak is arbitrarily installed by the rebellious soldiers as a judge, Schöne observes of the scene: "Now it happens in the play that in elevating Azdak to the position of judge, the soldiers dress him in the purple robe of the just executed former holder of the office. They place an upturned basket on his head and address him, saying: 'What manner of judge is this?' "[31] Schöne sees, quite correctly I think, a connection between this scene and these words and the scene in the Gospels where Christ is dressed in a purple robe and a crown of thorns and is then mocked by the soldiers and the crowd.[32] Numerous other scenes in the play support this interpretation of Azdak. He works among the poor, he brings comfort to the heavy laden. As the singer observes of Azdak: "and so he broke the laws, like bread, so that he might comfort them."[33] Immediately before the vital test of the chalk circle, when it seems overwhelmingly likely that he will be deposed as a judge and hanged (crucified) for his good works, he cries to his followers: "I beg you on my knees to take pity on me. Don't leave, I can hardly dribble any more.

I fear death."[34] The parallels with Christ in Gethsemane and the final words of the crucified Christ are too close for this to be merely coincidental. It is difficult to quarrel with Schöne's conclusion that these "associations create a messianic aura around him," and that further: "They contribute to this scene a magnification of impact, and they lend to the dramatic figure a power that suspends all disbelief, a power which breaks down the distance or reticence of the observing and smoking spectator."[35] The English critic, Ronald Gray, notes one further scene in the play that has profound religious implications. When Azdak sings to a poor woman who claims to have obtained a ham "by a miracle," Brecht has Busch place the woman in his judge's seat and sings seated at her feet. Gray notes, "he [Azdak-Busch] addresses her as though she were the Virgin Mary and begs mercy for such damned creatures as himself—a strange translation from religious into human terms which still has an atmosphere of genuine devotedness."[36]

If Brecht's text and production of *The Caucasian Chalk Circle* permit an interpretation of the rogue Azdak as a parodistic yet strangely devout Christ figure, then surely an even stronger case can be made for viewing Grusche as a more devout than parodistic echo of the other major figure of Christian symbology, the virgin mother, Mary. The viewer-reader steeped in the Western literary and religious tradition (as Brecht himself so obviously was) cannot help but be moved by this humble and somewhat "dumb" girl who receives a child from "on high," saves it from certain death by flight "into a far country," and must explain to the man she loves how she, a virgin, happens to be "with child." Was there, I wonder, any viewer of the Berliner Ensemble production who was not profoundly moved when this simple and loving girl, magnificently played by the somewhat homely portrayer of Kattrin in *Mother Courage,* Angelika Hurwicz, paused dangerously in her flight from the soldiers of the governor and offered, too poor to offer anything else, her barren breast to the princely but hungry child (fig. 68)? There is no hint of this significant act in the bare literary text of the play, yet surely Rülicke and Palitzch understate the case when they observe of a Polish production of the play in Poland: "It is understandable that in predominantly Catholic Cracow, Grusche's love of the child brought to mind the Mary legend."[37] It is obvious that the play itself supports the Polish interpretation. Grusche, with her mixture of biblical and peasant speech, her archetypical motherliness, her chasteness in her relationship to her beloved, Simon, and her "husband" Jussup, is a devout and apt virgin mother.

When Brecht combines, in his climactic final scene, the chaste and simple Grusche and his bawdy, cowardly, corrupted but kindhearted "Christ," and pits Grusche against the grasping "real" mother and her slimy cohorts, he creates a scene of tremendous dramatic intensity (figs. 69-75). Heinz Politzer, in an essay that asks (but does not answer) the question, "How Epic is Brecht's Epic Theater?" notes of the final scene of the play: "As if to stress the climactic character of this scene, Brecht constructed the two parts of the play so that the life histories of both Grusha and Azdak are crowned by it. The time sequences of both actions converge here and break the parallel structure of the epic drama."[38] It is obvious that if one of the hallmarks of the non-Aristotelian or epic drama be that such drama does not build toward a climax, does not work toward magnificent "curtains," then Brecht's play bears no trace of this hallmark. If prevention of "identification" be necessary, we look in vain for anything in the play to prevent our total subscription to Grusche's feelings and the "almost" justice of Azdak. Surely Grossvogel is correct when he claims that after the frametale of the Kolkhos is complete, "the conventional dramatic suasions take over. . ."[39] (fig. 76).

The standing ovation which was accorded the play in Paris says something more compelling than the early theory of the street scene and of the cool and primarily rational spectator. To this international theater audience, Brecht spoke as a man of the theater. As most members of this audience well knew, Brecht's production was a far cry in subject matter and in mode of presentation from an austere, halting, cool, fragmentary, and simple presentation of a "major contemporary subject." In view of this, is it wise to attempt to fit this 1955 production to a theater model constructed to fit the particular political circumstances of the 1930s? This is especially true if we recall that the earlier model had called for non-professional and unrehearsed actors, with no makeup or props, with no script, with no time to cast their description of the "street scene" in polished form (certainly not in verse!), and with no musical accompaniment, lighting, or costumes. Brecht was himself, of course, perfectly aware of the professional polish and expertise that was needed in order to produce the big exile plays properly. He noted of his own production of *The Caucasian Chalk Circle* for instance: "Roles such as those of Azdak and Grusche cannot, in our time, be created by the work of a director. No less than five years at the Berliner Ensemble were necessary in order to give the extraordinary Angelika Hurwicz the necessary prerequisites. And Busch's whole life, from his childhood in a proletarian milieu in Hamburg through the battles of the Weimar Republic and in the Spanish Civil War to the bitter experiences after 45, were necessary in order to create this Azdak."[40] This point of view was, of course, shared by others besides Brecht. Miss Hurwicz herself speaks consistently of the downright luxuriousness of Brecht's work with the Ensemble on plays such as *The Caucasian Chalk Circle.* It is not every theater which can permit itself, as Miss Hurwicz points out, rehearsal periods of up to an entire year and props any one of which would qualify as "a genuine museum piece."[41] For theater on this scale and of this complexity, Brecht's street scene sketch is less relevant critically than his later *Small Organum* and that excellent compendium of the Ensemble's practical work in theater, *Theaterarbeit.* In these works, as Rudolf Frank has pointed out, we find with astonishing frequency words such as: "noble, poetic, naive (in the sense the word is used by Schiller), graceful, soft or delicate, sweeping, sublime, charm, distinction, elegance, selectivity, beauty, precision, mythological grandeur, and a sense of reasonableness."[42] It is this critical vocabulary which helps us to describe Brecht's last and most famous productions. Apparently forgetting now the rational pauses his earlier theory had set such store by, Brecht said frankly in 1955: "In order to put a final polish on the production for our visit to Paris, cuts were made in the text and the tempo of the performance was increased." He then added: "The increase in tempo served not only to shorten but even more to enliven the production. The majority of scenes and figures were *improved* by means of this tempo."[43] As the Paris critics and Brecht watched this precise and highly polished production, they were fully aware that the rather plain caterpillar of the "Street Scene" had become the lovely butterfly of high dramatic art.

CHAPTER NINE

REFLECTIONS OF HIROSHIMA:
THE LIFE OF GALILEO

> "In conformity to the rules of his epic theater, of which *Galileo* is the most finished example, the life of the great scientist is split into autonomous scenes."
>
> *Walter Weideli*[1]

> "*Galileo* is perhaps Brecht's most poetically accomplished work. It is a high point of the epic-dialectic theater, and at this high point it becomes a closed drama again but without losing its alienating distance."
>
> *Joachim Müller* [2]

> "Technically, *Galileo* is a large step backwards; like *Frau Carrar's Rifles* it is much too opportunistic."
>
> *Bertolt Brecht*[3]

After returning from his enormous personal triumph at the Festival of Paris in 1955, Brecht began rehearsals of his *Life of Galileo*. Over a span of almost twenty years he had addressed himself no less than four different times to the task of hacking from the massive block of the life of the historical Galileo the epic drama he saw in his mind's eye.

Brecht had written his first version of the play in Denmark in 1938-39 at the very time that Nils Bohr was making his epochal discoveries in atomic theory. Brecht was apparently unaware at the time (as was virtually everyone else) of the spectral vistas that would be opened as a result of these discoveries. It is clear from Brecht's first dramatic treatment of Galileo that he saw the seventeenth-century scientist as a lineal ancestor of men like Bohr and that he felt a great deal of sympathy for Galileo as a man. In the first version we have a man who seems to be following Schweyk's admonition to the mongrel, Ajax, "crawl until you are able to bite." We have a Galileo whose recantation in the face of torture is eminently Schweikian, for this abject humiliation is followed by his writing the seminal *Discorsi*. From the diary notes of the period and the text of the play itself we see, however, that Brecht simply could not declare himself satisfied with the shape that the material, almost against his will, seems to have taken.[4] Then, in exile in Los Angeles, as the theme of the relationship of research to the most profound moral and social questions was blindingly illuminated by the reflections of Hiroshima and Nagasaki, Brecht attempted once again to cast his materials in a suitably "epic" form. Suddenly, large segments of the scientific population were echoing J. Robert Oppenheimer's cry as he had watched the first test explosion of an atomic weapon: "I am become death, the destroyer of worlds." Never had the words of the ancient Indian epic had such totally literal aptness. With just such a bleak vision of "scientific progress" Brecht seeks to portray Galileo, the man who, in Brecht's view, had made the work of the twentieth-century "destroyers of worlds" possible. The scene of recantation becomes thereby not an example of eminently practical behavior but a clear case of a scientist allowing the powers that be to use him for their own non-humanistic ends.

With a view to a major production of the play in the United States with Charles Laughton in the title role, Brecht began, with Laughton's cooperation,[5] to prepare an English version of the text that would reflect his new and almost wholly negative view of a man he now regarded as an "intellectual prostitute." Understandably, this new version has a darker tone than the pre-Hiroshima version of the text. Instead, however, of making the new version more "epic," Brecht seems partially to have bowed to the realities of American commercial theater and to have tightened and condensed the play.[6] When this new version was produced first in July 1947 in Los Angeles and then in December of the same year in New York, Brecht was himself morally outraged that the audiences who saw the play seemed *not* to be morally outraged by Galileo's behavior (figs. 77-78).

With the American experience in mind, Brecht sought to ensure that his own changes in the text of the play and his many hints on how to produce it would make a Cologne production in 1955 that he partially supervised, a signal warning to all the nearby Bonn militarists. Brecht's intentions remained one thing and critical response quite another. Again Galileo was seen as a very sympathetic figure; again audiences clearly identified with the author of the *Discorsi*. After this experience in Cologne, Brecht returned to Berlin to stage the play with the Berliner Ensemble, with Caspar Neher to design sets (figs. 79-81), Ernst Busch to play the lead, and Erich Engel as his co-director. He was determined that this time identification would definitely be broken down.

Before we pass to a close examination of the ways in which Brecht sought in rehearsal to shape the villain that he now wanted Galileo to be, it will help us considerably to look closely at the text he was attempting to turn to these ends. The passage of Galileo from forgivable and lovable rogue to, in Brecht's estimation, the intellectual prostitute he is supposed to be in the last known version, is accompanied also by a steady focusing of historical materials so that they might achieve their maximum dramatic impact.[7] Brecht's play passes steadily from the breadth and fullness of history to the density or *Dichtung* or *condensare* we have, since Aristotle, associated with dramatic art. Let us measure, at least initially, Brecht's Galileo (person and play) against the scale of what we know, with reasonable accuracy, about the historical figure and his milieu.[8] Four basic areas are germane (as Brecht's early epic theory made plain) to an historical or "epic" formulation of such a subject. First we would have to consider the whole of Galileo's physics—the entire universe as Galileo saw it. This view would include not only his numerous scientific errors and his resounding triumphs but also his long and far from exemplary life beyond his "scientific" endeavors. Second, we would have to consider other tillers of the same field, men like Ptolemy, John of Holland, Nicole Oresme, Copernicus, Tycho Brahe, Kepler, and Newton. Our third concern would be the mental anguish of the Catholic Galileo as he attempts to reconcile the heavens that the telescope brings close to him and the heavens that medieval Catholic cosmology had presented. This Galileo would be sympathetic to the problems of devout Catholics attempting to reconcile scientific fact with fundamental doctrinal questions of Holy Mother Church—doctrinal problems worked out in terms of the cosmology of Ptolemy and of St. Thomas Aquinas. Finally this Galileo, himself both Catholic and scientist, would surely be sympathetic to the problems of a Barberini, also Catholic and scientist, who, once elevated to the papacy, must speak for all Catholic Christendom and for all time. It is this opposite formulation of the historical problem which serves the American playwright, Barry Stavis, as the basis for his Galileo play, *Lamp at Midnight.* Stavis goes to great lengths to preserve the historical integrity of his raw materials. By so doing, in the view of some critics, he allows his drama as drama to suffer. Brecht, however, "vulgarizes"[9] history in order to get at the particular great drama that he wishes to read into that history.

In Brecht, instead of the whole of Galileo's physics we have only his essential discoveries. Instead of the whole of Galileo's life (including his notorious womanizing[10]), we have a prudish treatment of Galileo, a treatment that begins fortuitously with the vital and pregnant situation of the newly discovered telescope.[11] Instead of Galileo's broad intellectual milieu, the work of his contemporaries is played down and the discoveries of Galileo deliberately exaggerated in importance. If he is to be a great villain he must then make epochal discoveries first in order to deny them villainously later. The internally divided Catholic-and-scientist Galileo is scrapped. A divided Galileo, while he might be useful for a Shakespeare in a Hamlet-like drama concerned with interior states, is of little use to a playwright who wants first and foremost in this play to stress the physical world and Galileo's potential for modifying it in a humanistic way.

There is a red thread running through all these changes introduced by Brecht. Both Brecht the dramatist and Brecht the Marxist demand all these changes. Each successive reworking constitutes an increase of dramatic density but is, at the same time, a new attempt to come to grips in Marxist terms with the materials. Brecht's Galileo is deliberately changed into an embryonic Marxist because Brecht as a Marxist subscribes to the dogma that religion (unreason in his view) and science (reason itself) are antithetical elements. If this be so, Galileo *ipso facto* cannot be both scientist and Catholic; the one necessarily forces out the other.[12] This "Marxist" Galileo, determined no doubt in part by Brecht's own doctrinal position, produces two specifically dramatic, nondoctrinal windfalls for the playwright. First, the dogma demands that the whole notion of mental division (Catholic-scientist) be scrapped. Brecht can then exteriorize and/or demonstrate the actions of Galileo as he goes about his research and teaching before the eyes of the spectator in the theater. Second, Galileo seen overwhelmingly as scientist, as exteriorized action, can be used as a dramatic foil in a collision between science (Galileo) and religion or "the establishment" (the Pope and the Grand Inquisitor). Instead of a delicate and complex moral problem, we have the kind of fundamental moral clash that aestheticians, Brecht's beloved Hegel among them, have seen since time immemorial as the very stuff the drama is made of.[13] Rigging the historical situation to fit both his own Marxist cosmology and his instincts as a playwright, Brecht avoids the historical problem, the specifically undramatic (in a stage sense) problem of Galileo and the Church groping their way to a practical compromise between the faith and reason that all parties in the dilemma share.[14]

From various notes on the different versions and productions of his play, it is clear that Brecht was fully aware that in structural terms the play was not a new form, and that in terms of performance the play elicited sympathy and evoked a highly emotional audience response that included identification with Galileo. Of the 1938 Danish version Brecht had written:

> The only difficulty was created by the last scene. I needed a theatrical trick at the end, similar to the one used in *St. Joan,* in order to be sure to force the spectator to keep the necessary distance. Even the playgoer who tends to identify unthinkingly, at least must now, while on the way towards identification, sense a V-effect. If the performance is kept rigorously epic, a certain identification, of a permitted kind, will take place.[15]

Again we are back (as in the "Drum Scene" in *Mother Courage*) with an emphasis on epic performance rather than epic structure and with "identification of a permitted kind." Yet, as three productions of *Galileo* demonstrated to Brecht, his own dictatorial position on what identification was to be "permitted" was totally ignored by critics and audiences alike.[16] There is, as we shall see, the gravest doubt that things would have been any different had Brecht managed to complete his own production of the play with the Berliner Ensemble.

Besides the whole problem of "identification" and the need for "theatrical tricks," Brecht was well aware that in several other particulars the play did not fit very well with his early epic theory. In February 1939 he writes categorically of the whole play: "Technically, *Galileo* is a large step backwards, like *Frau Carrar's Rifles* it is much too opportunistic. This work would have to be completely rewritten if one wished to have this 'breeze from new coasts,' this red sunrise of science."[17] This new play, Brecht went on, would have to be something as follows: "Everything more direct, without the interiors, the 'atmosphere,' the emotional involvement. And everything directed towards a planetary demonstration. The divisions could remain, even the basic character of Galileo, but the work, the pleasant work, can only be done with proper contact with a physical stage."[18] Yet, as Schumacher notes in his thorough examination of the various versions of the Galileo text, even when Brecht had "proper contact with the physical stage," first in America with Laughton and then in East Berlin with the Ensemble (perhaps in the latter case because of his failing health), Brecht failed to make any essential structural changes in the play. Instead, Brecht kept in all the later versions all the interior scenes and all the "atmosphere" of the Danish original. Evidently, almost the entire burden of preventing identification was to come not from the text but from the production, especially from Ernst Busch's almost singlehanded attempt to stamp out any good qualities in the role of the great scientist. In view of Brecht's failure to introduce substantial structural changes, we detect more resignation than surprise in an observation he made in January 1945: "In *Galileo*, with its interiors and 'atmosphere,' the structure of the scenes, which is taken from the epic theater, seems strangely theatrical."[19] Some six months later Brecht was prepared to state flatly: "Formally I do not defend this play very strongly."[20]

A close examination of the play confirms the soundness of Brecht's own view. With the fifteenth scene (Andrea's crossing of the frontier) and the plague scene, both of which Brecht omitted in the performance text, the play covers 195 pages of the *Stücke* text. Without these scenes the play runs to about 180 pages. Of these, 103 are played in Galileo's study. Another 50 pages are also interior scenes. Even if we cut the two scenes which are left out in the Ensemble performance version, the text as given in the *Stücke* and the *Collected Works* is still very deceptive. In Brecht's directing copy a large number of lines are simply cut, and the play is thereby "considerably condensed."[21] It may be that we should simply see this continual process of condensation, of paring the text down, as being a reflection of external circumstance—in America, the economics of the theater; in Berlin, Brecht's failing health. But it may have been something much more basic than mere circumstance that called forth these changes. It is possible that it was Brecht's instinct for what worked best on the stage that inexorably pushed the Galileo material into an ever smaller, ever more specifically dramatic compass.

In my close reading of the opening scenes of several of Brecht's plays, I have tried to show the large number of traditional devices of dramatic condensation, linkage, and exposition which Brecht consistently employs. A similar examination of the opening scene of *Galileo* shows why Brecht himself felt the play to be a large step backwards. He uses there a whole bag of some of the very oldest tricks of the dramatist's trade.

The Life of Galileo opens with a placard which tells in verse what is to happen in the scene that follows. We first meet the great scientist, stripped to the waist in his "somewhat bare study in Padua." It is morning, and he is washing himself as he lectures his landlady's son Andrea on the new (mainly Copernican) cosmology. The year is given as 1609. Galileo is now forty-six years old. Later, Andrea's mother will enter, make Galileo's bed and announce a young man who wants to take private lessons with the celebrated teacher (fig. 82). After introducing the young man she exits, but returns later to announce the arrival of the Dean of the University of Padua. Galileo then, on the basis of information fortuitously given him by his first visitor of the morning, designs a telescope and sends Andrea off to get lenses ground. The boy returns with the lenses immediately after the Dean leaves. The scene closes with the announcement that Galileo plans to sell (in the next scene) "his" new invention to the state of Venice.

Brecht has begun his play, as Schumacher notes, "with a decisive phase in the life of the historical Galileo." The long, dull, undramatic history of the relatively unimportant early years is chopped off. The playwright, with totally different purposes from those of the historian, goes instantly to the heart of a dramatic conflict. He then organizes even these highly selected elements in a specifically dramatic manner.

The play opens on a particular day—indeed at a particular time of day. Why at that time of day? Why that particular day?

Why, on that very day does Galileo happen to explain for the first time to Andrea the Ptolemaic and Copernican systems? Why has Andrea, with his consuming interest in astronomy, never seen before the model of the Ptolemaic system that Galileo keeps there? Has Galileo never talked to this boy before? The context makes it quite plain that he has spoken with him innumerable times. If this be so, why does Galileo have to make his enormously long (four pages of text), frankly expository speech to the boy on the various cosmologies? The boy does not need this information, but the audience does. Why on this day of days does this particular private student arrive? Coincidentally, this otherwise completely empty-headed young man who is really not the least bit interested in studying, happens to come in (immediately after the description of the cosmologies and immediately before the appearance of the Dean) and happens to bring with him a rather complete description of a telescope that happened to go on sale the day before he left Holland. Why is it that this particular young man will later become a suitor for Galileo's daughter, Virginia?[22] Why does he come when, by his own admission, his only real interest is in horses? Reluctant to study at all, why did he not delay a few days after returning from Holland, telling others what he had seen there, and then come days later and suitably late in the day to begin the studies which his parents were forcing him to undertake? Why does the Dean arrive immediately after Ludovico's departure? Why does the Dean come to Galileo rather than Galileo going to the Dean? Why does Galileo then realize, right after discussing with the Dean the deadly dangers of astronomical research and how poorly paid it is, that the telescope, already fully assembled by the end of the scene, will help him to raise some much-needed cash and get him involved ever more deeply in a topic considered heretical and highly dangerous in that place at that time? Brecht can no more let the action flag while Galileo waits for another visitor than Sophocles can let Oedipus and the audience wait for the witnesses to appear at his criminal investigation. Brecht, following traditional modes of exposition, has, by the end of his first scene, given the audience all the facts they need to know to follow the play.

There is at least one more factor in this opening scene that deserves further analysis. In a number of notes (written in English) on the American version of the play, Brecht sets up the following chart to illustrate the symmetrical structure of the play:

> similia in 1) and 12).
> there is a morning in 1), and an evening in 12)
> there is a gift of an astronomical model in 1), of a goose in 12)
> There ist [sic] a lecture for Andrea, the boy in 1), and a lecture for Andrea, the man in 12)
> there is a woman going around watching [sic] in 1), and a woman going around watching in 12).[23]

Ernst Schumacher observes of this orderly little table which he found in the Brecht Archive: "Symmetry is an essential feature of the classical drama." He then goes on: "The uses of symmetry in *Galileo* underline, as structural elements of his dramaturgy, the 'conservative' character of the work."[24] Taking his cue from Brecht's own notebooks, Schumacher notes:

> In the first scene, in the morning, the beginning of not only a new day, but also of a new era, the bed is being made in Galileo's room. In the next to last scene [the last scene in the Ensemble version!] in the evening, not only of a day, but in the evening of a life of high ideals, the bed is being prepared for the night. In the first scene Galileo is "singing" the "aria" of the new era. In the next to last scene he expresses his conviction that this new era has begun, even if it looks like the old.[25]

It is clear that Brecht knows that his *Life of Galileo* is, like *Mother Courage,* classically circular in structure—the end brings us back to the beginning.

It should not really surprise us that this finely wrought play, constructed as it is from only the most telling episodes in the life of the great but cowardly Galileo, should move us profoundly as we see this many-faceted figure pass from health, vigor, and hope to blindness, old age, and bitter cynicism about himself and about the role of physics in the new world that he sees on the horizon. Precisely because Brecht gives us a figure, like ourselves "neither wholly good nor wholly bad," we respond this way to him. In the final Berliner Ensemble version of the play enough of the "good" Galileo of the first Danish version still shines through the dark layers painted over him in successive versions for the portrait to have considerable depth and ambience. The character becomes most sympathetic precisely because he has such depth. This then is the raw material which Brecht the playwright gave Brecht the director.

Beginning in mid-December 1955, Brecht conducted some fifty-nine rehearsals of *Galileo* before his health forced him to turn the production over to his co-director, his old friend Erich Engel. Because of his failing health, Brecht usually rehearsed the play for only two hours a day. Everything about the rehearsals was stripped down to essentials. There were, as was usual with Brecht's work at the Ensemble, almost no discussions with the actors of epic theory and practice.[26] The slide projections which had been used in the Los Angeles and New York productions were abandoned with the explanation given that with all lights at full they were too faint to be seen.[27] The text itself was approached strictly in terms of what was essential to the basic "Fable" or story. The opening scene was rehearsed eleven times. The final scene of the stage version (the handing over of the *Discorsi*) occupied nine rehearsal sessions. These two scenes, plus the pivotal recantation scene, absorbed most of Brecht's interest.[28]

Again and again as Brecht worked with the Ensemble in the last months of his life, he stressed the necessity of seeing his *Life of Galileo*, not as a historical work from the far away and long ago, but as one of a most pressing contemporary urgency.[29] He would, for instance, always stop rehearsals when the actors reached the line: "My task is not to prove that I have been right thus far, but to question whether I have been."[30]

For a Marxist, he said, this is the most important line in the play. This is worth remembering as it is a line opposed to all dogma, whether it be Copernican, Papist, Stalinist, or even perhaps, Brechtian.[31] At the rehearsals themselves dogma was never enough. Though Brecht did not suffer fools gladly and could be incredibly blunt when the spirit moved him,[32] he showed an almost "Chinese sense of politeness"[33] with those whose talents he admired. One of the talents he admired most was that of Ernst Busch, and Busch was simply too great an artist, too sure of his own sense of a major role to allow himself to be overawed in the slightest by a director who also happened to be the author of the play being rehearsed. In fact, we know from several contemporary accounts that Busch flatly disagreed with Brecht's view of Galileo's character.[34] Had Brecht wished to turn his view of Galileo into dogma, Busch was perfectly capable of telling him that their job in the rehearsals was not to prove that Brecht had been right so far but to find out whether he had been. Out of Busch's predominantly positive view of Galileo and Brecht's predominantly negative view would emerge dialectically a character of great depth and complexity. That Brecht himself knew what he was about in engaging in this intellectual tug-of-war with Busch would seem to be confirmed by the fact that after devoting a number of rehearsals to bringing out the negative side of Galileo's character, Brecht himself later switched and devoted considerable time to treating Galileo as a positive figure.[35] Even had he not done this, however, it is improbable that Busch would have been willing to play the part of a two-dimensional villain.

The composer Hanns Eisler reports that "Busch prepared himself thoroughly for the role of Galileo. He read books about classical and modern astronomy and physics."[36] Eisler also notes that Busch began to take on Galileo's "lecturing style and it became the most natural thing in the world for him to argue about astronomy, and the jargon of physics and astronomy became part of his ordinary speech."[37] The composer's account of Busch's preparation then concludes with the following anecdote which could almost have been taken from the notebooks of Stanislavsky himself: "A friend, who was in Rome at the time, told me this story: 'I saw a bust and thought, that's Ernst Busch. How did that bust get here? Already? As I came closer I saw that it was a bust of Galileo.' "[38] In view of this, one wonders whether Busch's acting did not owe at least as much to Stanislavsky's *An Actor Prepares* or his *Building a Character* as to Brecht's ideas on keeping a visible gap between actor and role.

Given Busch's view of the role of Galileo, let us look at the recantation. What scope is there in the text for Busch to present the great scientist in a positive way? Many critics have argued that Brecht has deliberately stripped the recantation scene of high drama by not showing us directly Galileo's confrontation with the officers of the Inquisition. But this approach ignores the imagination of the spectator, an imagination fueled by the constant speculation of Galileo's closest associates, as they wonder what horrors the Inquisition might be perpetrating upon him. Their fear may trigger a greater emotional response in an audience than a direct view of Galileo facing the instruments of torture. If we plot the emotional curve of the scene this way, we see that it rises inexorably as Andrea, Federzoni, the Little Monk, and Galileo's daughter all await the five o'clock bell that is to announce the recantation. One critic who does interpret the scene in this way speaks of it as having a "brilliant contrapuntal structure" in which the "frenzied prayers" of Galileo's extremely religious daughter are played off against the "agony of suspense"[39] of Galileo's scientific co-workers. When the bell does indeed ring (not before Brecht lets the suspense be screwed one notch tighter as the bell does not ring promptly at five), Galileo's daughter rejoices as she knows her father's life is saved while Andrea almost collapses in disbelief that a "great man" can do so despicable a thing in order to "save his big fat gut."[40] At precisely this moment Galileo (Busch) enters. Brecht's stage direction tells us that the scientist has been "completely changed, almost to the point of unrecognizability by the trial."[41] Which way will we now incline? The idealist Andrea who would have preferred Galileo's death before the great teacher's dishonor cries: "Unhappy the land that has no heroes!" To which Galileo responds with the Schweikian counter-proposition: "No, unhappy is the land that needs heroes."[42] We might incline towards Andrea's view here if we were able to believe Brecht's proposition (made in an essay on the play rather than in the play itself) that Galileo had such a following at this time that he could have successfully resisted the church. However, at the beginning of the recantation scene, Brecht has Andrea say explicitly: "They will kill him. The writing of the *Discorsi* will not be completed."[43] The play tells us one thing and Brecht's essays on the play another. The evidence of the play itself points to justification of Galileo's behavior. All Brecht's horror notwithstanding, it is Galileo's Schweikian response that wins us, not Andrea's idealism. Busch understood this very well.

When Busch's Galileo was pitched against Ekkhard Schall's Andrea in the final scene of the stage version, the confrontation was electric. The great teacher demonstrated for the last time his charismatic power over his former disciple. According to Brecht's own notes, we find that after Galileo hands over the *Discorsi* and delivers judgment upon himself (a scene reminiscent in some striking ways to the final scene of *Oedipus*), Andrea is so "shaken, he can hardly speak."[44] He must then almost be led out of the room, and his own last words are: "But I cannot think that your murderous analysis will be the last word."[45] It is quite clear that the scene is designed to work in a shattering way on Andrea. Brecht himself told Schall to play the scene with pathos as though it were a scene from Schiller,[46] and said further that the handing over of the *Discorsi* "must have a colossal effect, like the H-Bomb."[47] Brecht's choice of this particular image, at this particular point, in this particular play could hardly have been more apt.

Both from Brecht's own notes on the two final scenes of the stage version of the play, and from what we know of

Busch's view of Galileo's character, we can see why Brecht's "fire brigade" was simply unable to reduce more than a very few degrees the H-Bomb temperature of the final two scenes of the play. We know also from contemporary accounts that the Ensemble's "failure" meant that an emotional response to the villain-hero was really all that was left for most spectators. Most people, we may assume, came to the theater simply to see the play and had not armed themselves in advance with a battery of Brecht's early theoretical pronouncements on what they were to be "permitted" to feel and to think. One critic who did do his homework before the play wrote of the production:

> But besides all this, what do I actually see on the stage during this intellectual battle? I see a man who has weakened his eyes at the telescope and who is now almost blind as a result of working, illegally, by moonlight, in order to make a copy of a work extremely useful to mankind. This is not merely spoken; this is demonstrated. I see further, a man ruined by the burden of thought and work that has driven him like an uncontrollable itch into ever more dangerous situations, while, all the time, he is being spied upon by his shrewish and stupid daughter. And I am supposed to hate this man? To condemn him? I don't care how many directives are issued demanding that I do so, I simply cannot![48]

Precisely the same response was elicited in Paris when the Ensemble took the production there and audiences demonstratively responded to and for Galileo. The left-wing Paris critics were incensed at this and went so far as to accuse the poor Ensemble and Erich Engel (Brecht himself now being dead) of having "dramatized" what was supposed to be an "epic" play and of having given it a "tragic focus"[49] (figs. 83-84). It is my carefully considered opinion that had these critics examined closely the history and structure of the text itself and what Brecht had done with it in rehearsal, they would not have directed their wrath at the helpless fire brigade, but against the man who had set the fire.

Had those critics who objected to the way in which Erich Engel completed the *Galileo* production after Brecht's death not been quite so deafened by Brecht's deliberately overstated slogans of his last pre-exile years in Berlin—those years when he had been more concerned with effectively opposing Hitler than in presenting finely honed aesthetic formulae—they might have heard the much quieter voice of the post-1938 Brecht, the Brecht who wrote *Galileo*, the other famous exile plays, and the *Short Organum for the Theater*. As Ernst Schumacher points out: "At the time that Brecht wrote the Galileo play, he had already taken a significantly more dialectic position on the problem of identification and of emotional release through events on stage than he had taken in his notes on those plays written before 1933."[50] In support of this contention Schumacher draws our attention to various notes from Brecht's diary of the exile period. We learn, for instance, that in Finland in 1940, Brecht had had to explain to an actor who told him that he understood by the term *Verfremden*, a "performance without emotions," that this was not what he meant at all. The same day he noted in his diary: "On the one hand, even when rational elements are used we find *the act of identification,* and on the other hand, a V-effect can be achieved strictly through the moderate use of emotion."[51] Some eight years then pass between the writing of this diary note and the completion of the semi-Aristotelian *Short Organum.* These years mark the gradual but steady whittling away of most of the crude excrescences of the earlier theoretical pronouncements.

If we closely follow Brecht's work through the exile years, looking at the diary entries, the theoretical essays, the recorded conversations, and above all at the plays themselves, we can trace the curve of his movement from the anti-Aristotelian notes on the *Mahagonny* opera, to his gradual rapprochement with classical aesthetic theory. It is this Brecht, a Brecht who is drifting, often seemingly against his will, from aesthetic nihilist to not only a warm defender of the "Aesthetic" but the self-conscious author of an aesthetic—it is this man who composes, revises, and begins to stage *The Life of Galileo*. It should not, therefore, have surprised either the Berlin or the

Paris critics that the play in the Ensemble's magnificent production could not be fitted to the procrustean bed of Brecht's more extreme anti-aesthetic pronouncements of the late 1920s and the early 1930s. Galileo as Brecht created him is a massive, memorable and modern figure, but a figure cut with one eye fixed upon a most ancient and tragic pattern. We should not feel guilty if we are as moved by this figure as we are by Brecht's great models, the figures of the Greeks and the Elizabethans.

The reverberations of Brecht's play are cosmic. Once again, as had been possible in the drama of the Greek and the Elizabethan periods, a single exemplary figure has been made to reflect the furthest reaches of the known universe. The movement of the planets in space is again linked in the Great Chain of Being with the movement and the destinies of human atoms on the earth. We are led by the logic of the play to believe that Galileo's life is at least as important in the shaping of our destiny as the death of Caesar, of Hamlet, of Faustus, or of Edward II of England. Again, a single guiding world view has been used to help shape historical materials to a clear dramatic and moral purpose. *Galileo* is no more a play for the play's sake than are its great seventeenth-century Christian models. Though there are, of course, things about the play which stamp it as a specifically twentieth-century construct, one wonders if one is not dealing in *Galileo* and several other plays of the exile period, with a full-blown renascence of the best aspects of seventeenth-century dramaturgy. In the eighteenth century, Johann Elias Schlegel tried to define, as simply as possible, what it was about the English drama which distinguished it from the neoclassical mode. He wrote:

> If I am to judge from what I have read of the English stage, I would say that their plays are more imitations of certain persons than imitations of certain actions. They search first for a number of persons whose lives have been interconnected. When they have let them talk about the most important events in their lives for long enough to entertain a number of spectators for some hours, or until one reaches a decisive point in their lives or the characters finally die, then one ends the play.[52]

This marvelously naive description of English sixteenth- and seventeenth-century dramaturgy, with its clear recognition of the English departure from the neoclassical view of Aristotle, fits in several essential particulars most major plays of Brecht's exile period. To claim "newness" in either structural or in performance terms for these plays is, to say the least, shortsighted. To pin the "epic theater" label on these plays is, as the later Brecht himself knew, but to give a new and confusing name to a very ancient game. *Galileo,* if we may read it as the very last (if unfinished) aesthetic testament of Brecht as playwright and as director, tells this plainly enough. The Brecht of the chronicle *Life of Galileo* has, similar to this and most of his best plays, come full circle. We are close once again in Brecht's production of *Galileo* to the play and the production with which we began, Brecht's adaptation of *Eduard II* in Munich in 1924. The essential Brecht has remained essentially the same.

In concluding this examination of a handful of Brecht's plays, as I look over the full range of his achievement on the twentieth-century stage, I am reminded of the eighteenth-century humanist Lessing's call for a drama of the future, a drama that would attempt "to blend the gigantic characters and conflicts of Shakespeare with the restrained, lucid, and really classical form of Sophocles."[5][3] In his finest plays, Brecht answers Lessing's call. His characters are gigantic and his conflicts are mighty, yet he consistently eschews bombast and retains lucidity while reintroducing in his beautifully formed plays the theater's ancient and lovely partners—poetry, song, dance, and a strong sense of the theater's humanizing potential. All its imprecision notwithstanding, this is perhaps the final justification of Brecht's early iconoclasm and its product, his epic theater creed. In his greatest plays, his early iconoclasm and his later stress on clarity and reason are combined not only with an astounding mastery of all major forms of poetic expression but also with his gluttonous passion for the theater and his unerring sense of dramaturgical form. The combination is an excessively rare one; we encounter it only a very few times in the long history of the dramatic medium. It is not for everyone to turn the dross of tradition and the conflicting ideologies of a complex age into rich jewels of the living stage. Only rarely does the work of any man burn so brightly that both our past tradition and our problematic future are illuminated. Bertolt Brecht—playwright, poet, singer, drama theorist, director, and very much engaged humanist—was such a man.

A SHORT CHRONOLOGY

1898 Brecht is born into a middle-class family in the small southern German town of Augsburg.

1917 Ostensibly a student of medicine at the University of Munich, Brecht actually begins to study theater history with the famous Wedekind biographer, Professor Kutscher. It is in Kutscher's classes that Brecht meets Wedekind personally.

1918 Brief military service as a medic. Writes his celebrated lampoon of the military, "The Legend of the Dead Soldier." Already active as a drama critic. Meets Lion Feuchtwanger. Writes *Baal* and begins *Drums in the Night.*

1919 Takes a bit part in the famous Munich political cabaret of Karl Valentin. Completes *Drums in the Night.*

1921 Brecht visits Berlin for the first time. Writes several wonderful one-act plays under the influence of Valentin.

1922 Directs, until the cast quits en masse in dismay at Brecht's high-handed approach, Arnolt Bronnen's *The Patricide* in Berlin. *Drums in the Night* produced in Munich and thereafter in Berlin. Begins to write *In the Jungle of Cities.* Awarded the Kleist prize by Herbert Ihering.

1923 *In the Jungle of Cities* produced in Munich and *Baal* in Leipzig. Hired as Dramaturg at the Munich Kammerspiel. Supposed to direct *Macbeth* but begins work instead (with Lion Feuchtwanger) on an adaptation of Marlowe's *Edward II.*

1924   The Hitler putsch in Munich virtually coincides with the premiere of *Eduard II* in the same city. Moves "permanently" to Berlin to work as a Dramaturg for Max Reinhardt. Begins work on *A Man's a Man.* Meets Elisabeth Hauptmann.

1925   Friendship with the boxer Samson-Körner and the artist George Grosz. Much of Brecht's income now derived from short story writing.

1926   Berlin production of *Baal* under Brecht's direction. *A Man's a Man* produced in Darmstadt. First volume of Brecht's poems appears. Begins reading the Communist classics. Brecht begins to use the phrase "epic theater."

1927   Work with Piscator on *Schweyk* (a loose adaptation of the Hasek novel). Intensive work with several avant-garde composers. First version of *Mahagonny* performed in Baden-Baden. As usual, Brecht's work stirred up enormous debate.

1928   Marries Helene Weigel, who becomes the great interpreter of his major female roles. Brecht's greatest popular success, *The Threepenny Opera,* with music by Kurt Weill, breaks records at the Theater am Schiffbauerdamm, the scene-to-be of Brecht's postwar triumphs with the Berliner Ensemble.

1929   Great period of the didactic plays. An attempt to repeat the previous year's success of *The Threepenny Opera* with *Happy End* fails dismally.

1930   Final version of *Mahagonny* produced at Leipzig. *The Threepenny Opera* film lawsuit. First two volumes of the *Versuche* (Essays) appear. Premiere of *The Measures Taken.*

1931   Brecht works on the revolutionary film, *Kuhle Wampe.* Brecht's famous production of *A Man's a Man* with Peter Lorre as Galy Gay is mounted in Berlin.

1932   First production of *The Mother.* Open street fighting between Communists and Nazis.

1933   Brecht's plays interrupted by supporters of Hitler in several different German cities. Burning of the Reichstag on February 28. Brecht, with a price on his head, flees to Switzerland via Prague and Vienna. Later in the year he moves to Denmark.

1934   Brecht travels widely in Europe speaking out boldly against the Nazi government of Germany. Much of Brecht's major theoretical writing on "epic theater" is first drafted in this same period.

1935   Returns to Denmark to settle in Svendborg. Visits New York to supervise a production of *The Mother.* Extensive propaganda activity against the Third Reich. Nazis officially deprive him of his German citizenship. Visits Moscow and sees Mei Lan-Fang perform there.

1936   His anti-racist play *The Roundheads and the Peakheads* produced in Copenhagen. As was true of most of his plays in this period, the Copenhagen production was a very limited popular success.

1937   *The Threepenny Opera* and the anti-fascist play *The Rifles of Mrs. Carrar* produced in Paris.

1938   Several scenes from *The Fear and Misery of the Third Reich* produced in Paris. Brecht begins work on his *Life of Galileo* and continues work begun earlier on *The Good Person of Sezuan.*

1939   Threatened by the Nazis, Brecht moves from Denmark to Sweden. Writes *The Trial of Lucullus* (an opera), *Mother Courage,* and his important essay on unrhymed verse.

1940   Begins work on *Puntila and his Servant Matti.*

1941   *Mother Courage* produced in Zürich with Therese Giehse in the lead role. Flees from Sweden and briefly visits Moscow before crossing to Vladivostok to take a freighter to San Pedro, California. Joins the German exile community in Los Angeles and attempts to make a living selling film scripts.

1943   *The Good Person of Sezuan* and *Galileo* produced in Zürich. Writes the film script, *Hangmen Also Die.* Works on versions of both *Schweyk* and *The Caucasian Chalk Circle.*

1944   Completes *The Caucasian Chalk Circle.*

1945   *Fear and Misery of the Third Reich* produced in New York. Works with Ferdinand Reyher on an American version of *Galileo.*

1946   Works with Charles Laughton on an English text of *Galileo.* Travels frequently between California and New York; Brecht attempts to establish a toehold in the center of American theater, New York.

1947   *Galileo* produced with Charles Laughton in both Los Angeles and New York. Competes on Broadway with Barry Stavis's *Lamp at Midnight.* Brecht called to testify before HUAC. Immediately after testifying, Brecht flies back to Europe with all his texts on microfilm.

1948   Brecht produces his own version of *Antigone* (with Helene Weigel in the lead and with sets by Neher) in the small Swiss town of Chur. Writes *Days of the Commune* and his major theoretical work of this period, the *Short Organum.* Visits, on a Czech passport and via Prague, East Berlin.

1949   Produces *Mother Courage* in East Berlin with Helene Weigel playing the lead. Establishes the Berliner Ensemble as a repertory theater troupe but is not given his own theater as yet by the East Berlin government.

1950   Both Brecht and his wife take out Austrian passports. *Mother Courage* produced in Munich. Brecht complains that critics and audiences rave at all the wrong things.

1951   Intensive work with the Ensemble and with other theater groups. Brecht's production of *Mother Courage* taken to Paris.

1952   Tour of the Berliner Ensemble to Poland. Brecht produces *The Rifles of Mrs. Carrar* with the Berliner Ensemble.

1953   The East German uprising.

1954   The Ensemble is given the renovated Theater am Schiffbauerdamm as a permanent home. Brecht produces *The Caucasian Chalk Circle.* Brecht's production of *Mother Courage* wins the First Prize at the Festival of Paris. Brecht is awarded the Stalin Peace Prize. Considerable propaganda work for the German Democratic Republic.

1955   Travels to Moscow to accept the Stalin Peace Prize. Brecht's production of *The Caucasian Chalk Circle* wins a further major prize for the Ensemble at the Festival of Paris.

1956   Rehearsals for a Berlin production of *Galileo* with Ernst Busch in the title role. Brecht dies on August 14. Helene Weigel continues to direct the fortunes of the Ensemble. Erich Engel completes "Brecht's" production of *Galileo.*

A SHORT GLOSSARY

Aristotelian Theater. Usually, Brecht's concern is not so much with describing what is Aristotelian as with what it is not. From various clues, however, the following picture of "Aristotelian theater" emerges: The "Aristotelian theater" encourages illusion and seeks to have its audience identify (preferably emotionally) with the characters on stage. In this theater, each scene builds from the preceding one and everything is geared toward a final curtain. Brecht would seem to understand the terms "dramatic" and "Aristotelian theater" as virtual synonyms. At times one gets the impression that Brecht means by "Aristotelian theater" the theater of the Naturalists and of Stanislavsky. This is particularly unfortunate as it is reasonably certain that Aristotle would not have thought the theater of the Naturalists "Aristotelian."

Bearbeitung (plural: Bearbeitungen). The term is used in German criticism to describe plays closely modelled on an already existent classic of world literature. To cite a well-known example from the classical Greek period, Euripides' treatment of the Orestes theme is a *"Bearbeitung"* or "reworking" of Aeschylus' *Choëphoroe*. Shakespeare, obviously, is the greatest writer of *"Bearbeitungen"* for the English stage.

City Supported Theater. The English and American reader should be given to understand that most German theater is either state or city subsidized. Though the state or city can and does sometimes try to intervene in a theater's planning, such interference is surprisingly rare. The best example of a city or state supported theater is, rather obviously, the Berliner Ensemble Theater am Schiffbauerdamm in East Berlin. State interference,

I might add, is rather more frequent in East than in West Germany. East German theaters are expected to give a "progressive" twist to all their productions.

Constructivism. When used of the stage this term is most frequently associated with the name of the Russian director, Meyerhold, a man famous for giving classical plays a fresh and modern interpretation. Meyerhold often used bare scaffoldings and even gym and circus equipment on his stage. With his contemporary, Tairov, he fought against the "excessive reality" of the Moscow Art Theater and sought instead to create consciously theatrical theater. It is worth noting (see Norris Houghton, *Moscow Rehearsals,* p.18) that Meyerhold used gongs, unmasked spotlights, a half-curtain some twelve feet high, segments of "real" rooms standing free in space, all combined with detailed realism of stage requisites. This was a theater, as Houghton observes, that did not allow one to forget either during or between scenes that one was in a theater. At the same time, the "Constructivists" were associated with both a glorification of their technological age and of the Bolshevik revolution. It is important to note that Meyerhold visited Berlin with his troupe in 1930 and that a close friend of Meyerhold, Sergei Tretiakov, was also a close friend of Brecht. My separate study on the close ties of Brecht to "Constructivists" and other strands of the Russian theater appears in *Brecht Heute/Brecht Today,* Vol. II (1972).

Dadaism. "Dadaism" as an identifiable movement is associated with the period 1916-1924. Though eventually an aesthetic and some order emerged from what was felt at first to be a movement devoted to disorder and an anti-aesthetic, the importance of the early movement to the young Brecht should be stressed.

Dialectic Theater. Brecht's first use of the term is in the late 1920s. At that time Brecht deliberately refused to define the term. Probably Brecht was very sensible in doing this as he was then able to keep the term as a "joker in his deck." Whenever he gets into logical difficulties with his criticism, he tends thereafter to plunk down this particular card and to assign forthwith a new meaning to it. My own feeling is that when Brecht started to use it with increasing frequency at the end of his life, he was attempting a subtle rapprochement with the classical theater and with the aesthetics of his beloved Hegel. "Dialectic theater" means so much that it means virtually nothing concrete.

Dramaturg. In the German theater, the *"Dramaturg"* functions as both play-reader and play-doctor. He can also be called upon to direct productions. A large number of German playwrights have held such positions. Brecht's own theatrical career began with his serving as *"Dramaturg"* in Munich. Unfortunately, English and American theaters can but rarely afford the "luxury" of a *"Dramaturg."* A major exception is the Tyrone Guthrie Theater in Minneapolis.

Epic Theater. In the 1920s the term was used to describe a theater of ample scope, treating contemporary materials in all their epic complexity. The "epic theater" was usually political, tendentious, and employed a large number of documentary and "narrative" devices. A good practical example of such a theater was that of Piscator who used the terms "epic" and "political" as virtual synonyms. As used in Brecht's later aesthetic theory, the term lacks, as Bentley and Willett (among others) have observed, coherent meaning. Brecht himself seems, late in life, to have agreed with this latter view.

Expressionism. In literature, "Expressionism" as a movement gathered force in Germany during the years, c. 1910-1925. Quite consciously the "Expressionists" sought to *express* the inner man that had been largely neglected by the Naturalists with their emphasis on man's exterior state and/or his environment. To oversimplify radically, it might be argued that the outside world is determined, shaped, even distorted by the mind and the feelings of man in "Expressionist" dramaturgy and staging. In contrast, in Naturalist plays and with "realistic" staging, it is the environment that determines, shapes, and distorts the mind and feelings of man.

Identification or Einfühlung. According to Brecht's early theory of the dramatic or "Aristotelian theater" (q.v.), the spectator in such a theater is robbed of his own freedom of will as he is hypnotized by the dramatic event and is made to "creep into the skins" of the actors on the stage. Brecht's own concern, therefore, became means of inhibiting such "identification." He sought to write and stage plays that would be "cool" in their effects, plays that would permit the spectator to retain his intellectual freedom.

Mitarbeiter or Co-worker. Many of Brecht's plays were written in conjunction with one or more "co-workers." The role of the "co-worker" was sometimes nominal; at other times, Brecht's role was perhaps nominal. The question of Brecht's contribution to many plays issuing from his theatrical workshop can only be tackled on a broad front when the East Berlin archive materials are made available without restriction.

Modellbuch or Model Book. Brecht, like many a worker in the theater before him, was profoundly disturbed by the ephemeral nature of most theatrical productions. The "model books" attempt to capture for posterity some sense of Brecht's productions as aesthetic wholes. Not only did Brecht urge others to make and to use "model books," he frequently both made and used them himself. The influence of the wartime Zürich production of *Mother Courage* (which Brecht did not direct) on his own postwar East Berlin production of the play is particularly striking in this regard.

Naturalism. A movement of the late nineteenth century, stemming from Realism and often indistinguishable in both form and content from works of the earlier (mid-nineteenth century on) Realistic movement. On the stage, both Realism and "Naturalism" owe much to the pioneer efforts of the Duke of Saxe-Meiningen and later, to Stanislavsky and Nemirovich-Danchenko. In extreme cases, the "Naturalist" stage would reproduce every detail of a "real" environment. On such a stage the actor was asked to "become" the character he was playing and the audience was asked to believe that they were seeing "real" people in "real" settings. In Stanislavsky's technical writings he often stresses the fact that one sees on his stage "real" rooms with the fourth wall removed. This extreme position of Stanislavsky came under heavy fire very early from Chekhov himself and was railed against all through the 1920s. In the 1930s, however, this style was officially endorsed by the Soviet government and one could depart from it thereafter only at considerable peril. Many great artists of the period (including Meyerhold) paid for "formalist" departures from the official creed quite literally with their lives.

Playwright or Stückeschreiber. It may seem foolish to define a word as simple as "playwright," but Brecht's interpretation of his own role in the theater is illuminated by analysis of this deceptively simple word. Brecht liked to stress in the 1920s his view of creative writing as simply another form of work rather than as an inspired and arcane gift from above reserved for the very few (again Soviet theory may have been decisive here). He consciously rejected the term poet or *Dichter*, and used instead a term that stressed his craft rather than his art. The English term "playwright" with its relation to wheelwright and like terms, exactly matches Brecht's early view of himself as "artisan" rather than "artist."

Schriften or Writings. The *Writings on Theater* are available in German in three major forms. There is an early, one-volume edition first published in 1957. Then there is a seven-volume edition which first appeared in 1963. The most recent edition (1968) of the writings is contained in the *Gesammelte Werke.* This adds but little to what is contained in the 1963 edition.

Story or Fable. For Brecht, as for Aristotle, the "story is the heart of the drama." It is noteworthy that Brecht's agreement with Aristotle on this one crucial point of dramatic composition and presentation seems to have led him, however deviously, to agreement with Aristotle on a large number of other important details.

The Street Scene. In attempting to define certain essential characteristics of his theatrical style, Brecht frequently used "the street scene" as his model. Brecht asks us to imagine that there was an accident involving a car and a pedestrian. Spectators rushing to the scene interrogate an eyewitness who proceeds to describe what he has seen. This eyewitness, Brecht stresses, does not "become" the injured pedestrian or the driver of the car, he simply "acts out" in a rudimentary sort of way the salient details of the event. Of cardinal importance to the "street scene" model is Brecht's insistence on the documentary nature of the scene, the narrative quality of the description that ensues, and the non-professional "acting" of the eyewitness. Theoretically, or so the "street scene" model would seem to imply, anyone (even with no actor training) can play in this epic theater (q.v.) model. In fact, of course, Brecht's Berliner Ensemble was and is a theater of stars. These stars are highly trained and rehearse any given (presumably "epic") text for up to a year before presenting it to the general public. Though vestigial remains of the "street scene" model may remain in a typical Berliner Ensemble performance, it takes a highly trained, exceedingly well informed, and far from typical audience member to spot these remains.

Stücke or Plays or Pieces. These have been published in so many versions and editions that the publishing history of them cannot be treated here. I have usually used the text of the *Werkausgabe,* Suhrkamp, 1968. The reader should be warned that the texts of the "pieces" are often as unreliable as those of the *Writings.* Obviously, this problem is compounded in translation. For the sake of consistency, I have, therefore, translated all German quotes given in the text myself. English versions of most of the plays examined are available in Grove or Methuen editions and will soon be available in a Pantheon edition.

Teaching or Learning or Didactic Plays. Most of these plays stem from the late 1920s and the early 1930s. They are often severely stylized and contain long sections of descriptive or narrative materials. These plays (of which *The Mother* is stylistically a good example) come closest to actually achieving what Brecht was theoretically after when he first began to use the term "epic theater."

Verfremdung. This term is usually rendered into English as "alienation." John Willett consistently translates the word thus in his otherwise very useful volume, *Brecht on Theater.* In my view, the original term is much more complicated than the single English term "alienation." Surely Professor Grimm is correct in seeing *"Verfremdung"* as the cornerstone of the whole "epic theater" (q.v.) edifice. As an epigraphical introduction to his *Brecht, The Structure of his Work,* Grimm cites as follows the German Romantic poet Novalis: "To make, in an appealing way, an object strange, yet at the same time to make it familiar and attractive, that is Romantic poetry." This two-part formulation exactly parallels the "Preface to the Lyrical Ballads" where we find that the purpose of the ballads is to make the familiar strange and the strange familiar. I would like to suggest here that Brecht's understanding of *"Verfremdung"* has an enormous amount in common with the romantic formulations given above. I stress this here because, for most critics (Grimm is a prominent exception), the "alienating" or "distancing" connotations of the word have virtually squeezed out its oxymoronic connotations of attraction and identification. The term itself, and the master dialectician surely relished this, has two complementary though diametrically opposed meanings. If we can once grant this, there is then ample scope for dialectical studies of Brecht's plays that stress either alienation or attraction or both.

For the technically minded, it should be noted that the word *"Verfremdung"* is found, as Reinhold Grimm has pointed out, in only one German dialect, the Swabian, Brecht's own.

A SELECTED BIBLIOGRAPHY

The following bibliography can make no claim to completeness. Those seeking fuller information on either Brecht's own writings or on those who have written about Brecht would be well advised to directly consult the following comprehensive bibliographies:

Grimm, Reinhold. *Bertolt Brecht.* Stuttgart: Metzler, 1961. This volume is periodically updated and reissued and is perhaps the single most reliable source of bibliographical information on and about Brecht.
Nellhaus, Gerhard. "Bertolt Brecht Bibliography." *Sinn und Form. 1. Sonderheft Bertolt Brecht.* Berlin: Rütten and Loening, 1949. An important list of articles about Brecht in English.
Nubel, Walter. "Bertolt Brecht-Bibliographie." *Sinn und Form. 2. Sonderheft Bertolt Brecht.* Berlin: Rütten and Loening, 1957. This bibliographical list has been much admired for its completeness in the area of Brecht editions and in German writing on Brecht.
Petersen, Klaus-Dietrich. *Bertolt-Brecht-Bibliographie.* Bad Homburg: Verlag Gehlen, 1968.

Further, annual bibliographies in Brecht studies may be found in *The Year's Work in Modern Language Studies, PMLA,* and, from Volume Three on, in the yearbook of the International Brecht Society: *Brecht Heute/Brecht Today.* Further information on the *Brecht Heute/Brecht Today* bibliography may be obtained by writing to the Brecht Society's bibliographer, Professor Gisela Bahr, Department of German, Douglass College, New Brunswick, New Jersey 08903.

For the reader with little German it may be convenient to note a basic list of those publishers, translators and editors whose work is easily obtainable. Eric Bentley has served as general editor for the Grove Press and has personally translated a large number of Brecht's plays and many of his poems. In England, under the general editorship of John Willett, a large number of plays and significant sections of Brecht's theoretical writings have been published by the Methuen Company. More recently, Methuen in England and Pantheon Books (a division of Random House, New York) have begun publication of many Brecht plays. Edited by Ralph Manheim and John Willett, Volume One of the British and American editions of the plays is now available. Inasmuch as different translators have worked on the American and British editions respectively, this means that a choice of three different versions (Grove, Methuen, and Pantheon) will be available in English for most of Brecht's more important plays.

Anders, Günther. *Bert Brecht: Gespräche und Erinnerungen.* Zürich: Arche, 1962.

Arlington, L.C. *The Chinese Drama.* New York: Benjamin Blom, 1966.

Aufricht, Ernst Josef. *Erzähle damit du dein Recht erweist.* Berlin: Propyläen Verlag, 1966.

Bach, Rudolf. "Marlowe, Eduard II und Bert Brecht." *Die Rampe,* No. 7, 16 Nov. 1926, 137-148.

Baxandall, Lee. "Brecht on Broadway: A Commercial System at Work." *Prompt,* No. 5 (1964), 38-40.

Beckermann, Bernard. *Shakespeare at the Globe: 1599-1609.* New York: Macmillan, 1962.

Beckley, R.J. "Adaptation as a Feature of Brecht's Dramatic Technique." GL&L, 15 (1962), 274-284.

Benjamin, Walter. *Schriften.* 2 vols. Frankfurt: Suhrkamp, 1955.

———. *Versuche über Brecht.* Suhrkamp, 1966.

Bentley, Eric. "Brecht, Poetry, Drama and the People." *The Nation,* 157, 31 July 1943, 130-131.

———. "What is Epic Theatre." *Accent,* 6, No. 2 (Winter 1946), 110-124.

———. "Epic Theater is Lyric Theater." *The German Theater Today.* Ed. Leroy R. Shaw. Austin: Texas UP, 1963.

———. "Are Stanislavski and Brecht Commensurable." TDR, 9, No. 1 (Fall 1964), 69-76.

———. "Brecht und der 'Zonk.' " *Listen* (March-April 1964).

Berckman, Edward M. "The Function of Hope in Brecht's Pre-Revolutionary Theater." *Brecht Heute/Brecht Today*. Ed. R. Grimm, E. Bentley, J. Fuegi, et al. Frankfurt: Athenäum, 1971.

Boeddinghaus, Walter. "Bestie Mensch in Brechts *Mutter Courage.*" *Acta Germanica*, 2 (1968), 81-88.

Brashko, S. "Die letzte Inszenierung Bertolt Brechts." *Kunst und Literatur*, 6 (1958), 835-850.

Brecht, Bertolt. *Gesammelte Werke*. 20 vols. Frankfurt: Suhrkamp, 1967.

———. *Schriften zum Theater*. Zusammengestellt von Siegfried Unseld. 7 vols. Frankfurt: Suhrkamp, 1957.

———. *Schriften zum Theater*. Ed. Werner Hecht. 7 vols. Berlin and Weimar: Aufbau, 1964.

———. *Couragemodell 1949*. Berlin: Henschelverlag, 1958.

———. *Aufbau einer Rolle–Busch und Laughton*. Berlin: Henschelverlag, 1956.

———. "Tagebuchnotizen." *Spectaculum III: Sieben moderne Theaterstücke*. Frankfurt: 1960.

———. *"Mutter Courage und ihre Kinder" (Eine Chronik aus dem Dreissigjährigen Krieg): Bühnenfassung des Berliner Ensembles*. Ed. Joachim Tenschert. Berlin: Henschelverlag, 1968.

———. *"Der kaukasische Kreidekreis": Bühnenfassung des Berliner Ensembles*. Ed. Joachim Tenschert. Berlin: Henschelverlag, 1968.

———. *"Der gute Mensch von Sezuan" (Parabelstück): Bühnenfassung des Berliner Ensembles*. Ed. Joachim Tenschert. Berlin: Henschelverlag, 1969.

———. *Die "Antigone" des Sophokles: Fassung der Churer Aufführung*. Ed. Werner Hecht. Berlin: Henschelverlag, 1969.

———. *"Die Mutter": Leben der Revolutionärin Pelagea Wlassowa aus Twer (Nach dem Roman Maxim Gorkis): Bühnenfassung des Berliner Ensembles*. Ed. Joachim Tenschert. Berlin: Henschelverlag, 1970.

———. *"Leben des Galilei" (Schauspiel): Bühnenfassung des Berliner Ensembles*. Ed. Joachim Tenschert. Berlin: Henschelverlag, 1970.

———. *"Leben Eduards des Zweiten von England": Vorlage, Texte und Materialien*. Ed. Reinhold Grimm. Frankfurt: Suhrkamp, 1968.

———. *Seven Plays*. Ed. Eric Bentley. New York: Grove, 1961.

———. *Mother Courage and Her Children*. Trans. Eric Bentley. New York: Grove, 1955.

———. *Edward II: A Chronicle Play*. Trans. Eric Bentley. New York: Grove, 1966.

———. *The Caucasian Chalk Circle.* Trans. Eric Bentley. New York: Grove, 1965.

———. *The Good Woman of Setzuan.* Trans. Eric Bentley. New York: Grove, 1965.

———. *The Mother.* Trans. Lee Baxandall. New York: Grove, 1965.

———. *Collected Plays, Volume I: 1918-1923.* Ed. John Willett and Ralph Manheim. London: Methuen, 1970.

———. *Collected Plays, Volume I.* Ed. Ralph Manheim and John Willett. New York: Pantheon, 1971.

——— with Caspar Neher. *Antigonemodell 1948.* Berlin: Gebrüder Weiss, 1949.

Brod, Max. "Jaroslav Hasek und sein Schwejk." *Schulter am Schulter: Blätter der Piscatorbühne.* Berlin: 1927.

Bronnen, Arnolt. *Tage mit Bertolt Brecht.* Vienna, Munich, Basel: K. Desch, 1960.

Brustein, Robert. *The Theatre of Revolt.* Boston: Little Brown, 1962.

Büdel, Oscar. "Contemporary Theater and Aesthetic Distance." *Brecht: A Collection of Critical Essays.* Ed. Peter Demetz. Englewood Cliffs, N.J.: Prentice-Hall, 1962.

Bunge, Hans-Joachim, Werner Hecht, Käthe Rülicke-Weiler. *Bertolt Brecht: Leben und Werk.* Berlin: Volk und Wissen, 1963.

———. *Fragen Sie mehr über Brecht: Hanns Eisler im Gespräch.* Munich: Rogner and Bernhard, 1970.

———. "Antigone-Modell 1948 von Bertolt Brecht and Caspar Neher: zur Praxis und Theorie des epischen (dialektischen) Theaters Bertolt Brechts." Diss. Greifswald, 1957.

———. " 'Hegelisches' in Brechts *Antigone.*" *Antigone* program of the Schaubühne am Halleschen Ufer. Berlin, 1965.

Chiarini, P. "Lessing und Brecht. Einiges über die Beziehung von Epik und Dramatik." *Sinn und Form,* 9 (1957), 188-203.

Clurman, Harold. *The Fervent Years: The Story of the Group Theatre and the Thirties.* New York: Hill and Wang, 1957.

———. "The Achievement of Bertolt Brecht." *Partisan Review,* 26 (1959), 424-428.

Cohen, I. Bernard. *The Birth of a New Physics.* Garden City, N.Y.: Anchor, 1960.

Crumbach, Franz Hubert. *Die Struktur des epischen Theaters: Dramaturgie der Kontraste.* Braunschweig: Waisenhaus, 1960.

Dekker, Thomas. *Guls Horne-Booke.* London: 1609.

Demetz, Peter (Ed.). *Brecht: A Collection of Critical Essays.* Englewood Cliffs, N.J.: Prentice-Hall, 1962.

Desuché, Jacques. *Bertolt Brecht.* Paris: Presses universitaires de France, 1963.

Dickson, Keith A. "Brecht: An Aristotelian malgré lui." *Modern Drama,* 11 (1967), 111-121.

Dietrich, Margret. *Das moderne Drama: Strömungen, Gestalten, Motive.* Stuttgart: A. Kröner, 1961.

Dort, Bernard. *Lecture de Brecht.* Paris: Éditions du Seuil, 1960.

―――. "Le réalisme épique de Brecht." *Les Temps Modernes,* 15 (1959-60), 67-83.

Downer, Alan S. *The Art of the Play.* New York: Holt, 1955.

Einem, Gottfried von and Siegfried Melchinger (Ed.). *Caspar Neher.* Velber near Hannover: Friedrich Verlag, 1966.

Eisenstein, Sergei. *The Film Sense.* Ed. Trans. Jay Leyda. New York: Harcourt, Brace, 1947.

―――. *Film Form.* Ed. Trans. Jay Leyda. New York: Harcourt, Brace, 1949.

Eisler, Hanns. "Schweyk und der deutsche Militarismus." *Sinn und Form: Eisler Sonderheft.* Berlin: Rütten and Loening, 1964.

Ekmann, Bjørn. *Gesellschaft und Gewissen: Die sozialen und moralischen Anschauungen Bertolt Brechts und ihre Bedeutung für seine Dichtung.* Copenhagen: Munksgaard, 1969.

Erpenbeck, Fritz. "Episches Theater oder Dramatik?" Theater der Zeit, 9, No. 12 (1954), 16-21.

―――. "Verurteilung oder Mitleid?" *Theater der Zeit,* 12, No. 3 (1957), 8-13.

Esslin, Martin. *Brecht, A Choice of Evils.* London: Eyre and Spottiswoode, 1959.

―――. *Brecht: The Man and his Work* (Rev. ed. of *Brecht, A Choice of Evils*). New York: Doubleday, 1961.

―――. *Brecht: Das Paradox des politischen Dichters* (rev. and updated version of *Brecht, A Choice of Evils*). Munich: DTV, 1970.

Ewen, Frederic. *Bertolt Brecht: His Life, His Art, and His Times.* New York: The Citadel Press, 1967.

Fassmann, Kurt. "Brecht: Eine Bildbiographie." Munich: Kindler Verlag, 1958.

Fergusson, Francis. *The Idea of a Theater.* Garden City, N.Y.: Anchor, 1949.

―――. "Three Allegorists: Brecht, Wilder and Eliot." *The Sewanee Review,* 64, No. 4 (Oct.-Dec. 1956), 544-573.

Fleisser, Marieluise. "Aus der Augustenstrasse." *Süddeutsche Zeitung* (Munich), No. 129, 8 June 1951.

Flemming, Willi. *Epik und Dramatik.* Munich. Lehnen-Verlag, 1955.

Fradkin, I. "On the Artistic Originality of Bertolt Brecht's Drama." *Brecht: A Collection of Critical Essays.* Ed. Peter Demetz. Englewood Cliffs, N.J.: Prentice-Hall, 1962.

Frank, Rudolf. "Brecht von Anfang." *Das Ärgernis Brecht.* Ed. Willy Jäggi and Hans Oesch. Basel and Stuttgart: Basilius, 1961.

Frey, Daniel. "Études Brechtiennes *Schweyk.*" *Études de Lettres,* 9 (1966), 125-148.

―――. "*La Mère* de Gorki à Bertolt Brecht à travers trente ans d'histoire." *Études de Lettres,* 6 (1963), 125-151.

Friederich, Werner P. *German Literature.* New York: Barnes and Noble, 1948.

Frisch, Max. *Tagebuch 1946-1949.* Frankfurt: Suhrkamp, 1958.

Fuchs, George. *Die Schaubühne der Zukunft.* Berlin: 1903.

―――. *Die Revolution des Theaters.* Munich: 1906.

Fuegi, John. "*The Caucasian Chalk Circle* in Performance." *Brecht Heute/Brecht Today,* 1. Ed. Eric Bentley, Reinhold Grimm, John Fuegi, et al. Frankfurt: Athenäum, 1971.

Fuller, Edmund. "Epic Realism: An Analysis of Bert Brecht." *The One Act Play Magazine* (April 1938), 1124-1130.

Galilei, Galileo. *Discoveries and Opinions of Galileo.* Trans. Stillman Drake. New York: Doubleday, 1957.

Gaskell, Ronald. "The Form of *The Caucasian Chalk Circle.*" *Modern Drama,* 10 (1967), 195-201.

Gassner, John. *The Theatre in Our Times.* New York: Crown, 1954.

―――. "Varieties of Epic Theatre in Modern Drama." *Comparative Literature Studies,* Special Advance Issue. 1963.

Geissler, H.W. "Das Leben Eduards II., Uraufführung in den Münchner Kammerspielen." *München-Augsburger Abendzeitung.* No. 80, 21 March 1924.

Geissler, Rolf. "Versuch über Brechts *Kaukasischen Kreidekreis.*" *Wirkendes Wort,* 9 (1959), 93-99.

Ghisselbrecht, André. "Bertolt Brecht und die Güte." *Aufbau,* 13 (1957), 571-589.

Gorchakov, Nikolai A. *The Theater in Soviet Russia.* Trans. Edgar Lehrman. New York: Columbia UP, 1957.

Gorelik, Mordecai. *New Theatres for Old.* New York: Dutton, 1962.

Gorki, Maxim. *Gesammelte Werke,* vol. 5: *Die Mutter.* Trans. Adolf Hess. Berlin: 1926-30. Vol. 5: 1927.

Gray, Ronald. *Bertolt Brecht.* New York: Grove, 1961.

Grimm, Reinhold. *Bertolt Brecht: Die Struktur seines Werkes.* Nuremberg: Hans Carl, 1959.

———. *Brecht und die Weltliteratur.* Nuremberg: Hans Carl, 1961.

———. *Strukturen: Essays zur deutschen Literatur.* Göttingen: Sachse and Pohl, 1963.

———. "Naturalismus und episches Drama." *Episches Drama.* Ed. Reinhold Grimm. Cologne and Berlin: Kiepenheuer and Witsch, 1966.

———. "Von Novum Organum zum Kleinen Organon: Gedanken zur Verfremdung." *Das Ärgernis Brecht.* Ed. Willy Jäggi and Hans Oesch. Basel and Stuttgart: Basilius, 1961.

———. "Ideologische Tragödie und Tragödie der Ideologie." *Interpretationen deutsche Dramen von Gryphius bis Brecht.* Frankfurt: Fischer, 1965.

Grossvogel, David I. *Four Playwrights and a Postscript: Brecht, Ionesco, Beckett, Genet.* Ithaca, N.Y.: Cornell UP, 1962.

Haas, Willy. *Bert Brecht.* Berlin: Colloquium Verlag, 1958.

Hamburger, Käte. *Von Sophokles zu Sartre: Griechische Dramenfiguren antik und modern.* Stuttgart: Kohlhammer, 1963.

Hardy, Thomas. *The Dynasts: An Epic-Drama.* London: Macmillan, 1909.

Hartung, Günter. "Brecht und Schiller." *Sinn und Form; Sonderheft I: Probleme der Dramatik.* Berlin: Rütten and Loening, 1966.

Hašek, Jaroslav. *Die Abenteuer des braven Soldaten Schwejk.* 2 vols. Trans. Grete Reiner. Reinbek: 1926.

Hasenclever, Walter. *Antigone.* Berlin: Paul Cassirer, 1917.

Hauptmann, Elisabeth. "Notizen über Brechts Arbeit 1926." *Sinn und Form. 2. Sonderheft Bertolt Brecht.* Berlin: Rütten and Loening, 1957.

Hecht, Werner. *Brechts Weg zum epischen Theater: Beitrag zur Entwicklung des epischen Theaters 1918 bis 1933.* Berlin: Henschelverlag, 1962.

———. *Materialien zu Brechts "Der gute Mensch von Sezuan."* Frankfurt: Suhrkamp, 1968.

———. *Materialien zu Brechts "Leben des Galilei."* Frankfurt: Suhrkamp, 1969.

———. *Materialien zu Brechts "Der kaukasische Kreidekreis."* Frankfurt: Suhrkamp, 1966.

———. *Materialien zu Brechts "Mutter Courage und ihre Kinder."* Frankfurt: Suhrkamp, 1964.

———. *Materialien zu Brechts "Leben des Galilei."* Frankfurt: Suhrkamp, 1963.

———. *Materialien zu Brechts "Leben des Galilei."* Berlin: Henschelverlag, 1970. This edition differs in many essential particulars from the 1963 Suhrkamp version of materials on *Galilei.*

———. *Aufsätze über Brecht.* Berlin: Henschelverlag, 1970.

Hegel, G.W.F. *Hegel on Tragedy.* Ed. Trans. Anne and Henry Paolucci. Garden City, N.Y.: Anchor, 1962.

Henel, Heinrich. "Szenisches und panoramisches Theater." *Episches Theater.* Ed. Reinhold Grimm. Cologne and Berlin: Kiepenheuer and Witsch, 1966, 383-396.

Hennenberg, Fritz. *Dessau-Brecht: Musikalische Arbeiten.* Berlin: Henschelverlag, 1963.

Hill, Claude, and Ralph Ley. *The Drama of German Expressionism. A German-English Bibliography.* Chapel Hill, N.C.: N.C. UP, 1960.

Hinck, Walter. *Die Dramaturgie des späten Brecht.* Göttingen: Vandenhoeck and Ruprecht, 1959.

Hoffmann, Charles W. and John Fuegi. "Brecht, Schweyk and Communeism." *Festschrift für Detlev W. Schumann.* Ed. Albert R. Schmitt. Munich: Delp, 1970, 337-349.

Högel, Max. *Bertolt Brecht: Ein Porträt.* Augsburg: Verlag der Schwäbischen Forschungsgemeinschaft, 1962.

Hölderlin, Friedrich. *Werke.* Ed. Fritz Usinger. Hamburg: n.d.

Holthusen, H.E. "Brecht's Dramatic Theory." *Brecht: A Collection of Critical Essays.* Ed. Peter Demetz. Englewood Cliffs, N.J.: Prentice-Hall, 1962.

———. "Dramaturgie der Verfremdung. Eine Studie zur Dramentechnik Bertolt Brechts." *Merkur,* 15 (1961), 520-542.

Hoover, Marjorie. "V.E. Meyerhold: A Russian Predecessor of Avant-Garde Theater." *Comparative Literature,* 17 (1965), 234-250.

Houghton, Norris. *Moscow Rehearsals: An Account of Methods of Production in the Soviet Theatre.* N.Y.: Harcourt-Brace, 1936.

Hultberg, Helge. *Die ästhetischen Anschauungen Bertolt Brechts.* Copenhagen: Munksgaard, 1962.

———. "Bertolt Brecht und Shakespeare." *Orbis Litterarum,* 14, No. 2-4 (1959), 89-104.

Huntford, Roland. "Brecht in the North." *Industria International.* Stockholm: 1963, 44-45, 154, 158-160.

Hurwicz, Angelika. *Brecht inszeniert: "Der kaukasische Kreidekreis."* Text by Miss Hurwicz and photos by Gerda Goedhart. Velber bei Hannover: Friedrich, 1964.

Ihering, Herbert. *Bertolt Brecht und das Theater.* Berlin: Rembrandt, 1959.

———. *Von Reinhardt bis Brecht: Vier Jahrzehnte Theater und Film.* Berlin: Aufbau-Verlag, 1958.

———. *Berliner Dramaturgie.* Berlin: Aufbau-Verlag, 1947.

———. "Gorki, Pudowkin, Brecht." *Berliner Börsen-Courier.* No. 28. 18 Jan. 1932.

Jones, Frank. "Tragedy with a Purpose: Bertolt Brecht's *Antigone.*" TDR, 2, No. 1 (Nov. 1957), 39-45.

Kahler, Ernst. "Zweimal Pawel." *Theaterarbeit: Sechs Aufführungen des Berliner Ensembles.* Ed. Berliner Ensemble (Leitung Helene Weigel). Dresden: Dresdner Verlag, 1952.

Kaufmann, H. *Bertolt Brecht: Geschichtsdrama und Parabelstück.* Berlin: Rütten and Loening.

Kayser, Wolfgang. *Das sprachliche Kunstwerk.* Bern: Francke Verlag, 1948.

Kern, Edith. "Brecht's Epic Theatre and the French Stage." *Symposium,* 16 (1962), 28-35.

Kerzhentsev, V.M. *Tvorchesky Teatr.* Petrograd: 1918. An early and seminal formulation of Proletkult theater theory and practice.

Kesting, Marianne. *Bertolt Brecht in Selbstzeugnissen und Bilddokumenten.* Reinbek: Rowohlt, 1959. Werner Hecht has told me that he plans to publish a list of well over a hundred errors of fact found in the Kesting volume.

———. *Das epische Theater. Zur Struktur des modernen Theaters.* Stuttgart: Kohlhammer, 1959.

Klotz, Volker. *Geschlossene und offene Form im Drama.* Munich: C. Hanser, 1960.

———. *Bertolt Brecht: Versuch über das Werk.* Darmstadt: Gentner, 1957.

Kluev, Viktor Grigorevich. *Bertolt Brecht—Novator Teatra.* Moscow: 1961.

Knauth, Joachim. "Viele Wege führen zu Brecht. *Schweyk im zweiten Weltkrieg* von Bertolt Brecht in Erfurt." *Theater der Zeit,* 13, No. 4 (1958), 36-39.

Königshof, Kaspar. "Über den Einfluss des Epischen in der Dramatik." *Episches Theater.* Ed. Reinhold Grimm. Cologne and Berlin: Kiepenheuer and Witsch, 1966, 279-289.

Kopelev, L. *Brecht.* Moscow: Lives of Remarkable People, 1966.

Kopetzki, Eduard. "Das dramatische Werk Bertolt Brechts nach seiner Theorie vom epischen Theater." Diss. Vienna, 1949.

Kortner, Fritz. *Aller Tage Abend.* Munich: Kindler, 1959.

Laboulle, L.J. "A Note on Bertolt Brecht's Adaptation of Marlowe's *Edward II.*" MLR, 154 (1959), 214 ff.

Lebel, Jean-Jacques. "On the Necessity of Violation." TDR, T 41 (Fall 1968), 89-105.

Lenz, Harold. "Idee und Bild des Friedens im Bertolt Brecht." *Der Friede, Idee und Verwirklichung: Festschrift für Adolf Leschnitzer.* Heidelberg: 1961, 281-289.

Ley, Ralph John. "The Marxist Ethos of Bertolt Brecht and its Relation to Existentialism." Diss. Rutgers, 1963.

Li Hsing-tao. *Kreidekreis.* Trans. Klabund (Pseud. for Alfred Henschke). Berlin: I.M. Spaeth, 1925.

Ludwig, Emil. *Gesammelten Schriften.* Leipzig: 1891.

Luft, Friedrich. "Brecht's *Galileo* von beklemmender Aktualität." *Die Welt.* 17 Jan. 1957.

Lukács, G. "Grundlagen der Scheidung von Epik und Dramatik." *Aufbau,* 11, No. 11-12 (1955).

———. *Beiträge zur Geschichte der Ästhetik.* Berlin: Aufbau Verlag, 1954.

———. *Essays über Realismus.* Berlin: Aufbau Verlag, 1948.

Lyons, Charles R. *Bertolt Brecht: The Despair and the Polemic.* Carbondale, Ill.: S. Ill. UP, 1968.

Macgowan, Kenneth and Robert Edmund Jones. *Continental Stagecraft.* N.Y.: 1922. Reissued N.Y.: Blom, 1964.

Marlowe, Christopher. *Christopher Marlowe: Five Plays.* Ed. Havelock Ellis. N.Y.: Hill and Wang, 1956.

———. *Eduard II. Tragödie.* Trans. A.W. Heymel. Leipzig: n.d. [1914].

Mayer, Hans. *Meisterwerke deutscher Literaturkritik.* Stuttgart: Goverts, 1962.

———. *Ammerkungen zu Brecht.* Frankfurt: Suhrkamp, 1965.

———. *Bertolt Brecht und die Tradition.* Pfüllingen: Neske, 1961.

Melchinger, Siegfried. *Drama zwischen Shaw und Brecht.* Bremen: Schünemann, 1957.

Melngailis, V. Dreimanis. *"Leben Eduards des Zweiten von England: Bertolt Brecht's Adaptation of Marlowe's Edward II."* Diss. Harvard, 1967.

Mennemeier, Franz Norbert. "Mother Courage and Her Children." *Brecht: A Collection of Critical Essays.* Ed. Peter Demetz. Englewood Cliffs, N.J.: Prentice-Hall, 1962.

Meyerhold, V.E. *Meyerhold on Theatre.* Ed. Trans. Edward Braun. N.Y.: Hill and Wang, 1969.

Michener, Wendy. "The Plays of Bertolt Brecht." *Queen's Quarterly,* 67 (1960), 360-366.

Mittenzwei, Werner. *Bertolt Brecht: Von der "Massnahme" zu "Leben des Galilei."* Berlin and Weimar: Aufbau Verlag, 1965.

Monecke, Wolfgang. "Hugo von Hofmannsthal und Bertolt Brecht: Zur Genesis des Verfremdungseffekts." *Orbis Litterarum,* 20, No. 1 (1965), 32-51.

Morsch, H. *Goethe und die griechischen Bühnendichter.* Berlin: 1888.

Motekat, Helmut. "Bertolt Brecht: Von der Freundlichkeit der Welt." *Orbis Litterarum,* 19, No. 2 (1964), 145-151.

Müller, André. "Weil man die Menschen davor warnen muss. *Schweyk im zweiten Weltkrieg* von Bertolt Brecht in Frankfurt/Main." *Theater der Zeit,* 14, No. 8 (1959), 48-50.

―――. "Echte oder vorgetäuschte Naivität. Der Schweyk bei Hasek, Burian und Brecht." *Theater der Zeit,* 14, No. 8 (1959), 15-18.

―――. "Dramatisches und episches Theater: Zur ästhetischen Theorie und zum Bühnenwerk Bertolt Brechts." *Wissenschaftliche Zeitschrift der Friedrich-Schiller Universität Jena,* 8, No. 2-3 (1958-59), 365-382.

Münsterer, H.O. *Bert Brecht: Erinnerungen aus den Jahren 1917-22.* Zürich: Arche, 1963.

Niessen, Carl. *Brecht auf der Bühne.* Colone: 1959.

Ohly, Hans. "Ein Anti-Theologie. Zur Frage des Verhältnisses des Werkes von Bert Brecht zur Theologie." *Junge Kirche,* 21 (1960), 585-590.

Parker, R.B. "Dramaturgy in Shakespeare and Brecht." *University of Toronto Quarterly,* 32, No. 3 (1963), 229-246.

Parrott, Thomas Marc and Robert Hamilton Ball. *Short View of Elizabethan Drama.* N.Y.: Charles Scribner's Sons, 1943.

Pauli, H. "Brechts Bearbeitungen von klassischen Dramen." Staatsexamen Arbeit. Berlin, 1956.

Petersen, Juluis. "Zur Lehre der Dichtungsgattungen." *Festschrift für A. Sauer.* Stuttgart: 1925.

Petr, Pavel. *Haseks "Schwejk" in Deutschland.* Berlin: 1963.

Petsch, R. "Die innere Form des Dramas." *Euphorion* (1930), 19-39.

Piscator, Erwin. *Das politische Theater.* Berlin: 1929. Work reissued with modifications by Felix Gasbarra by Rowohlt Verlag (Reinbek bei

Hamburg), 1963. A facsimile edition of the original text, however, was issued by Henschel (East Berlin), 1968.

Plato. *Great Dialogues of Plato.* Trans. W.H.D. Rouse. N.Y.: New American Library, 1956.

Politzer, Heinz. "How Epic is Brecht's Epic Theater?" MLQ, 24 (June 1962), 99-114.

Pudovkin, V.I. *Film Technique and Film Acting.* London: Mayflower, 1958.

Puknat, Siegfried B. "Brecht and Schiller: Nonelective Affinities." MLQ, 26 (1965), 558-570.

Ramthun, Herta. *Bertolt-Brecht-Archiv: Bestandsverzeichnis des literarischen Nachlasses, Band I, Stücke.* Berlin and Weimar: Aufbau Verlag, 1969.

Rasch, Wolfdietrich. "Bertolt Brechts marxistischer Lehrer. Aufgrund eines ungedruckten Briefwechsels zwischen Brecht und Karl Korsch." *Merkur,* 17, No. 7 (1963), 988-1003.

Reich, Bernhard. "Erinnerungen an den jungen Brecht." *Sinn und Form. 2. Sonderheft Bertolt Brecht.* Berlin: Rütten and Loening, 1957.

———. *Im Wettlauf mit der Zeit: Erinnerungen aus fünf Jahrzehnten deutscher Theatergeschichte.* Berlin: Henschelverlag, 1970.

Rilla, P. *Essays.* Berlin: 1955.

Rischbieter, Henning. *Bertolt Brecht.* 2 vols. Velber bei Hannover: Friedrich Verlag, 1966.

Roy, Claude. "Des erreurs commises sur Brecht," *Nouvelle Revue Française,* 13 (Jan. 1965), 114-118.

Rühle, Jürgen. *Literatur und Revolution: Die Schriftsteller und der Kommunismus.* Cologne and Berlin: Kiepenheuer and Witsch, 1960.

Rülicke-Weiler, Käthe. *Die Dramaturgie Brechts.* Berlin: Henschelverlag, 1966.

Rus, Vladimir. "Brecht's *Schweyk im zweiten Weltkrieg* and Hasek's *Good Soldier Schweik.*" Diss. New York University, 1963.

Ryan, Lawrence. *Friedrich Hölderlin.* Stuttgart: Metzler, 1962.

Sagar, Keith M. "Brecht in Neverneverland: *The Caucasian Chalk Circle.*" MD, 9 (1966), 11-17.

Sartre, J. P. "Brecht et les Classiques." *World Theatre,* 7 (Spring 1958).

Sayler, Oliver M. *The Russian Theater.* N.Y.: Brentano's, 1922.

Schaefer, H. "Der Hegelianismus der Brechtschen Verfremdungstheorie in Abhängigkeit von ihren marxistischen Grundlagen." Diss. Stuttgart, 1957.

Schmidt, Dieter. *"Baal" und der junge Brecht. Eine textkritische Untersuchung zur Entwicklung des Frühwerks.* Stuttgart: Metzler, 1966.

One of the most interesting books yet written on the early Brecht. Explodes several of the early myths which Brecht himself had set in circulation.

Schöne, Albrecht. "Bertolt Brecht, Theatertheorie und dramatische Dichtung." *Euphorion*, 52, No. 3 (1958), 272-292.

Schumacher, Ernst. *Drama und Geschichte, Bertolt Brechts "Leben des Galilei" und andere Stücke.* Berlin: Henschelverlag, 1965.

———. *Die dramatischen Versuche Bertolt Brechts: 1918-1933.* Berlin: Rütten and Loening, 1955. Remains one of the two or three most useful books on Brecht's pre-exile plays.

———. "Piscator's Political Theater." *Brecht, A Collection of Critical Essays.* Ed. Peter Demetz. Englewood Cliffs, N.J.: Prentice-Hall, 1962.

Seidel, Gerhard. *Die Funktions- und Gegenstandsbedingtheit der Edition: untersucht an poetischen Werken Bertolt Brechts.* Berlin: Akademie-Verlag, 1970. A courageous if somewhat utopian attempt to describe an ideal edition of Brecht's total writings.

Serreau, Geneviève. *Bertolt Brecht: Dramaturgie.* Paris: Ed. L'Arche, 1955.

Shaw, Leroy R. Ed. *The German Theater Today.* Austin: Texas UP, 1963.

Shelley, Percy Bysshe. *Shelley's Literary and Philosophical Criticism.* Ed. J. Shawcross. London: 1909.

Sokel, Walter. "Brecht's Split Characters and his Sense of the Tragic." *Brecht, A Collection of Critical Essays.* Ed. Peter Demetz. Englewood Cliffs, N.J.: Prentice-Hall, 1962.

Sophocles. *Antigone.* Greek text ed. W. Rabehl. Leipzig and Berlin: 1927.

———. *Three Tragedies: "Antigone," "Oedipus the King," "Electra."* Trans. H.D.F. Kitto. London: Oxford UP, 1962.

Sorensen, Otto M. "Brecht's *Galileo:* Its Development from Ideational into Ideological Theater." MD, 11, No. 4 (Feb. 1969), 410-422.

Spalter, Max. *Brecht's Tradition.* Baltimore: Johns Hopkins UP, 1967.

Spielhagen, Friedrich. *Neue Beiträge zur Theorie und Technik der Epik und Dramatik.* Leipzig: 1898. This book was in Brecht's personal library.

Staiger, Emil. *Grundbegriffe der Poetik.* Bern: Francke Verlag, 1946.

Stark, G. and G. Weisenborn. *Die Mutter.* Published as a private *Bühnenmanuskript.* n.p., n.d. Copy of text in BBA 441.

Steer, W.A.J. "Brecht's Epic Theatre: Theory and Practice." MLR, 63 (1967), 636-649.

Steffensen, Steffen. "Der Theoretiker Brecht." *Orbis Litterarum,* 19, No. 2 (1964), 152-160.

Steiner, George. *The Death of Tragedy.* N.Y.: Knopf, 1963.

Stern, Guy. "The Plight of the Exile: A Hidden Theme in Brecht's *Galileo Galilei.*" *Brecht Heute/Brecht Today,* 1. Frankfurt: Athenäum, 1971.

Sternberg, Fritz. *Der Dichter und die Ratio: Erinnerungen an Bertolt Brecht.* Göttingen: Sachse and Pohl, 1963.

Suvin, Darko. "The Mirror and the Dynamo: On Brecht's Aesthetic Point of View." TDR, 12, No. 1 (Fall 1967), 56-67. A complex and very useful piece of analysis of the post-epic Brecht.

Svendsen, Juris. "The Queen is Dead: Brecht's Eduard II." TDR, 10, No. 3 (1965), 160-176.

Szondi, Peter. *Theorie des modernen Dramas.* Frankfurt: Suhrkamp, 1956.

Tailleur, Jean. "Brecht und das elisabethanische Drama." Diss. Paris, 1959.

Tairoff, A. *Das entfesselte Theater.* Potsdam: 1923.

Tank, Kurt L. "Hier mahnt ein verhinderter Christ: Religiöse Wurzeln des politischen Radikalismus." *Sonntagsblatt* (Hamburg), No. 35. 26 Aug. 1956.

Tretjakow, S. M. *Ich will ein Kind haben: Ein Produktionstück in 10 Scenen, 5 Akten.* Autorisierte Übersetzung von Ernst Hube bearbeitet von Bert Brecht. Freiburg: Max Richard Verlag, n.d. This "stage text" is available in BBA 662. Brecht's version (as yet unpublished) is sometimes given as *Die Pioniere.*

―――. "Bert Brecht." *Brecht, A Collection of Critical Essays.* Ed. Peter Demetz. Englewood Cliffs, N.J.: Prentice-Hall, 1962. The factual authenticity of much of the information that Tretiakov presents in this essay is now open to question.

Tynan, Kenneth. *Curtains.* N.Y.: Atheneum, 1961.

Völker, Klaus. "Brecht und Lukács: Analyse einer Meinungsverschiedenheit." *Kursbuch 7.* Frankfurt: Suhrkamp, 1966, 80-101.

Weber, Carl. "Brecht as Director." TDR, 12, No. 1 (Fall 1967), 101-107.

Weideli, Walter. *The Art of Bertolt Brecht.* Trans. Daniel Russell. London: Merlin, 1963.

Weisstein, Ulrich. "From the Dramatic Novel to the Epic Theater: A Study of the Contemporary Background of Brecht's Theory and Practice." GR, 38, No. 3 (1963), 257-71. This article is particularly useful for the light which it sheds on Piscator's theater practice.

―――."The First Version of Brecht/Feuchtwanger's *Leben Eduards des Zweiten von England* and its Relation to the Standard Text." JEGP, 69, No. 2 (April 1970), 193-210.

Wekwerth, Manfred. "Auffinden einer ästhetischen Kategorie." *Sinn und Form. 2. Sonderheft Bertolt Brecht.* Berlin: Rütten and Loening, 1957.

Wellek, René. *Concepts of Criticism.* New Haven: Yale UP, 1963.

———, and Austin Warren. *Theory of Literature.* N.Y.: Harcourt-Brace, 1956.

Willett, John. *The Theatre of Bertolt Brecht: A Study from Eight Aspects.* London: Methuen, 1959.

———. "Martin Esslin on Bertolt Brecht: A Questionable Portrait." *Massachusetts Review,* 1 (1960), 589-596.

Wirth, Andrzej. "Über die stereometrische Struktur der Brechtschen Stücke." *Sinn und Form. 2. Sonderheft Bertolt Brecht.* Berlin: Rütten and Loening, 1957.

———. "Die Funktion des Songs in *Mutter Courage und ihre Kinder.*" *Sinn und Form. 2. Sonderheft Bertolt Brecht.* Berlin: Rütten and Loening, 1957.

Witzmann, Peter. *Antike Tradition im Werk Bertolt Brechts.* Berlin: Akademie-Verlag, 1964.

Wolfe, Bertram D. *Three Who Made a Revolution.* Boston: Beacon, 1955.

Wulbern, Julian H. *Brecht and Ionesco: Commitment in Context.* Chicago, Urbana, London: Ill. UP, 1971.

Zucker, A.E. *The Chinese Theater.* Boston and London: 1925.

Zuckmayer, Carl. *Als wär's ein Stück von mir.* Frankfurt: Fischer, 1966.

Zwerenz, Gerhard. *Aristotelische und Brechtsche Dramatik: Versuch einer ästhetischen Wertung.* Rudolstadt: Greifen-Verlag, 1956.

NOTES

Introduction

1. G. B. Shaw and Frank Wedekind are consistently singled out for praise in Brecht's early critical writings. Both men, as Brecht himself acknowledged, profoundly influenced his view of the style and the function of the theatrical event in the twentieth century.
2. The influence of Shakespeare on Brecht is so all-pervasive as to warrant Symington's book-length study. The English reader should note that in Germany Shakespeare is considered, through the medium of superb translations, virtually a German classic.
3. Toward the end of his life, Brecht began a very serious attempt to revive a large part of the classical German repertory. He consistently urged his co-workers neither to be overawed by the classics nor to treat them with disrespect.
4. These notes are often printed separately and are available in English in John Willett's translation in the volume of major critical writings, *Brecht on Theatre.* Of particular interest in the *Mahagonny* notes is the fact that Brecht's major concern would seem to be with audience response rather than with differences in dramatic form per se.
5. The *Short Organum,* with addenda, is also available in Willett's translation in *Brecht on Theatre.*
6. This is often referred to as Brecht's "nihilistic period." Though partly true of the early Brecht, somehow "nihilism" does not seem an appropriate descriptive term when applied to Baal's untrammeled

lust for life. It would be more accurate perhaps to say that many of the early characters are selfish or asocial or apolitical (Kragler in *Drums in the Night* would serve as an apt example of this) but not nihilistic. The early Brecht would seem to anticipate the much later Brecht in his interest in an almost Chinese view of the life cycle. He is frequently enchanted, for instance, with the paradoxical strength of weakness and the weakness of apparent strength. I would very seriously suggest that this early love of the paradox of passivity prepared him for a reading of both the Chinese philosophers and of Marx. In Marx, out of the deepest despair of the poletariat comes their greatest hope; inversely, it is when the bourgeoisie becomes strongest that it is most vulnerable. In a sense, as the Brecht of *The Measures Taken* is well aware, the doctrine cautions against action and demands a large measure of passivity. Things must be allowed to get worse if they are to have a chance of getting permanently better. The parallels, for instance, with *The Book of Changes* are both too obvious and too complex to need or permit further explication here.

7. Estimates differ as to degree, but there is general agreement among Shakespearean authorities that almost all of Shakespeare's plays are "adaptations" of borrowed materials. The same can be said of Brecht's plays. The best work thus far on Brecht's sources is Reinhold Grimm's brief but thorough *Brecht und die Weltliteratur* (Nuremberg, 1961).

8. Though more biography than close textual analysis is available to the English and even the German reader, it should be pointed out that attempts to write reliable biography have been hampered by the fact that an enormous amount of archive material on Brecht has not yet been cleared for publication. We are only now beginning to get behind the myths Brecht wove around himself and to the historical figure. Significant steps in this direction are Dieter Schmidt's *"Baal" und der junge Brecht: eine textkritische Untersuchung* (Stuttgart, 1966), and Klaus Völker's *Brecht-Chronik* (Munich, 1971).

9. There is a definite sense of the possible romantic origins of Brecht's theory of *Verfremdung* (though no specific reference is made to Wordsworth) in Reinhold Grimm's *Struktur* book. Grimm cites (p.4) Novalis's famous statement: "Die Kunst, auf eine angenehme Art zu befremden, einen Gegenstand fremd zu machen und doch bekannt und anziehend, das ist die romantische Poesie." ("To make, in an appealing way, an object strange, yet at the same time to make it familiar and attractive, that is romantic poetry.") Grimm also cites

(p.8) Shelley's observation: "Poetry lifts the veil from the hidden beauty of the world, and makes familiar objects be as if they were not familiar." *Shelley's Literary and Philosophical Criticism,* ed. J. Shawcross (London, 1909), p.131.

10. John Willett, *The Theatre of Bertolt Brecht: A Study from Eight Aspects* (London, 1959), p. 187. Hereafter to be referred to as: Willett, *Eight Aspects.*

11. The *Dialogues* are available in German in both the seven-volume *Schriften zum Theater* and in the more recent *Gesammelte Werke* (GW) in twenty volumes. The reader with no German may consult John Willett's translation, *The Messingkauf Dialogues,* now available as a Methuen paperback.

12. Also available in both the *Schriften* and in volumes 15-17 of the *Gesammelte Werke.* An English translation of the work is available in John Willett's anthology, *Brecht on Theatre.*

13. The recommendation is made in the notes, "Additions to the *Short Organum.*"

Chapter I

1. "Kunst ist Scheisse." Erwin Piscator, *Das politische Theater,* first published in Berlin in 1929. My citation is from the more readily accessible Rowohlt edition of 1963, p. 37.
2. Jean-Jacques Lebel, "On the Necessity of Violation," *TDR,* XIII, No. 1 (Fall, 1968), 105.
3. "Auch die nachsichtigsten Opportunisten werden nicht die Stirn haben zu behaupten, dass das Augsburger Stadttheater ein Kultur-faktor ist—nicht einmal für Augsburg. Zweifellos ist es das Geld nicht wert, das die Stadt dran hinhängt. Geführt von einem Geschäftsmann, einem ehemaligen Provinzschauspieler, dem jedes geistige Format abgeht, hat es mit seinem üblen Laviersystem, seinen Ausflüchten, Hinweisen auf die Stupidität des hiesigen Publikums alle die Jahre her nicht vermocht, auch nur die selbstverständlichsten Pflichten einer städtischen Bühne zu erfüllen." GW, XV, 23.
4. "Die *Jedermann*-Regie lehnt sich bis auf die bengalische Verkitschung des Schlusses eng an die des Münchener National-theaters an." GW, XV, 26.
5. Brecht became nationally famous in 1922 when Herbert Ihering awarded him the prestigious Kleist Prize. With the success of *The Threepenny Opera* in 1928, he speedily became internationally known. This first burst of international fame was, however, fairly shortlived. When he arrived in America in 1941 he was asked by new acquaintances to spell his name.
6. I am thinking particularly of men such as Georg Fuchs, Meyerhold, Evreinov, Tairov, Mayakovsky, Blok, and G.B. Shaw.
7. The work of Weisstein, Willett, Grimm, and Gassner has long since conclusively demonstrated Brecht's lack of any "originality" in a positivistic sense. However, the dust-jacket of a 1968 book on Brecht still refers to him as "the originator of the epic theater."
8. See Willett, *Eight Aspects,* pp.112-113. Willett also notes productions of Reinhardt's that anticipate some of Brecht's later practice. Willett writes: "In Reinhardt's 1907 production of *Twelfth Night* the stage rotated with the curtain up, while the actors stood in front and mimed the gist of the episode to come. In his *Danton's Death* players were scattered among the audience, and several episodes took place at once." p.106.
9. See note 2 above.

10. "Ich habe an allen seinen Experimenten teilgenommen." GW, XV, 289. The use of the word "experiments" with reference to Piscator's work parallels closely Brecht's own use of the term *Versuche*.

11. "Vor allem war die Wendung des Theaters zur Politik Piscators Verdienst, und ohne diese Wendung ist das Theater des Stücke-schreibers kaum denkbar." GW, XVI, 598-99. A further observation of Brecht's in this same passage sheds considerable light on the early and apolitical Brecht. He notes of the abortive revolutionary attempts in Germany in 1918: "Er hatte am Krieg teilgenommen, der Stückeschreiber jedoch nicht. Die Umwälzung im Jahre 18, an der beide teilnahmen, hatte den Stückeschreiber enttäuscht und den Piscator zum Politiker gemacht. Erst später kam der Stückeschreiber durch Studium zur Politik." ("He [Brecht] took part in the war, the playwright, however, did not. The upheaval of the year 1918, ir which both took part, disillusioned the playwright but made Piscator politically oriented. Only later, through study, did the playwright become politically oriented.") This is an unusually frank biographical and political statement of Brecht concerning his early years. Elsewhere he claims to have been political from the very beginning of his career as a playwright and to have taken part in the war performing gruesome tasks as a medical orderly. From this comment and from those of fairly reliable contemporaries such as Zuckmayer, Bronnen, and Hans Otto Münsterer, we can be reasonably sure that from 1918 to about 1925-26, Brecht's interest in politics was quite slight.

12. Inasmuch as the parallels with Shaw are striking and Brecht himself expressed fervent admiration for this socialist-polemicist-playwright, it is surprising that only one critic has, so far, studied the relationship between the plays and theater theories of these two men.

13. As I seek to show in Chapter Six and elsewhere in this study, the ties between Germany and Russia were, in the theater, particularly strong at this time. Brecht's personal friendship with the Soviet Minister of Culture, Lunacharski, and with the leading Soviet dramatist, Tretiakov (himself a close friend of Meyerhold) leaves no doubt that Brecht and Piscator were fully aware of the tornado of brilliantly inventive theater that swept the Soviet Union from the time of the revolution up to Zhdanov's clamp-down in the early 1930s on all experimentation in the arts.

14. Important notes on how this movement relates to Brecht are to be found in Piscator's *Das politische Theater;* Willett's *Eight Aspects;* and in Helge Hultberg's *Die ästhetischen Anschauungen Bertolt Brechts* (Copenhagen, 1962). See particularly Chapter Two of Hultberg's book where he discusses the close relationship of the early Brecht to the theories of the Dadaists. We also know, incidentally, that Brecht owned Viktor Erlich's *Russian Formalism. History—Doctrine* (Gravenhage, 1955). The reader should be warned, however, that the mere presence of a book in Brecht's library was no assurance that he had actually read it. He had, furthermore, a peculiar aversion to scholarly works of all kinds.

15. "Vielleicht ist die Kunst überhaupt zu Ende." George Grosz, *Ein kleines Ja und ein groszes Nein* (Hamburg, 1955), p. 130.

16. Piscator, *Das politische Theater,* p. 37.

17. ibid.

18. ibid. "In den Dienst der Politik."

19. "Sollten wir nicht die Ästhetik liquidieren?" GW, XV, 126.

20. Willett *(Eight Aspects,* p. 171) notes that the term was used by Arnolt Bronnen (a close friend of Brecht from late 1921 on) in 1922, by Piscator and Paquet in 1924, and by Brecht, for the first time, in 1926 when he began, according to E. Hauptmann, his study of the Communist "classics." It is of some historical interest to note that the term "an Epic-Drama" had been used in England as early as 1909 by Thomas Hardy as the subtitle of *The Dynasts.* A significant difference, of course, between Hardy's work and that of Brecht, Bronnen, and Piscator, is that Hardy did not expect to see *The Dynasts* actually staged.

21. "Es handelt sich hier nicht um eine Genre-Bezeichnung, 'episch' bedeutet einfach das Politisch-Dokumentarische, die Tendenz, das Anti-Künstlerische." Helge Hultberg, *Die ästhetischen Anschauungen,* p. 55.

22. Lania writes that Paquet "Ganz bewusst auf jede künstlerische Gestaltung verzichtet, sich darauf beschränkt, die nackten Tatsachen für sich sprechen zu lassen." Given in Piscator, p. 61.

23. Döblin: "Paquet hat den Anarchistenaufstand in Chicago bewusst so dramatisiert, dass das entstehende Gebilde auf einer Zwischenstufe zwischen Erzählung und Drama verblieb." Given in Piscator, p. 62.

24. Herbert Ihering saw a close connection at this time between the development of the Russian semi-documentary film and the creation of "epic plays," plays containing: "Ein epischer Stoff von

gigantischen Ausmassen." ("Epic materials of gigantic proportions.")
It is also interesting that Ihering connects here, in almost an English
sense, the epic with the gigantic.

    Cited in Piscator, p. 204. See also the description of the effect
of *Potemkin* in the opening pages of Vol. II of Feuchtwanger's
novel, *Erfolg.*

25. Piscator, p. 37.
26. See in this connection, Reinhold Grimm's "Naturalismus und
episches Drama," in Grimm's book of essays (by various hands),
Episches Theater (Köln-Berlin, 1966).
27. Note however also that Brecht acknowledges that the Expressionists
had been of value to him. See GW, XV, 292.
28. "Die Naturalisten (Ibsen, Hauptmann) suchten die neuen Stoffe der
neuen Romane auf die Bühne zu bringen und fanden keine andere
Form dafür als eben die dieser Romane: eine epische." GW, XV,
151.
29. "Als ihnen (Ibsen, Hauptmann) nun sofort vorgeworfen wurde, sie
seien undramatisch, liessen sie mit der Form sofort auch die Stoffe
wieder fallen, und der Vorstoss kam ins Stocken, anscheinend der
Vorstoss in neue Stoffgebiete, in Wirklichkeit eher der Vorstoss in
die epische Form." ibid.
30. "Wie muss also unsere grosse Form sein? Episch. Sie muss berichten.
Sie muss nicht glauben, dass man sich einfühlen kann in unsere Welt,
sie muss es auch nicht wollen. Die Stoffe sind ungeheuerlich, unsere
Dramatik muss dies berücksichtigen." GW, XV, 186.
31. "Die alte Form des Dramas ermöglicht es nicht, die Welt so
darzustellen, wie wir sie heute sehen. Der für uns typische Ablauf
eines Menschenschicksals kann in der jetzigen dramatischen Form
nicht gezeigt werden." GW, XV, 173.
32. ibid. "Die Kämpfe um den Weizen und so weiter sind nicht auf
unseren Bühnen zu finden." Brecht conveniently ignores here the
fact that these battles were in fact regularly fought on the stages of
Meyerhold, Tretiakov, and Piscator. For a more detailed examination
of Soviet experiments on these lines, please see Chapter Six below.
33. "Das Petroleum sträubt sich gegen die fünf Akte. . . . Haben wir uns
in den Stoffen einigermassen orientiert, können wir zu den
Beziehungen übergehen, die heute ungeheuer kompliziert sind und
nur durch *Form* vereinfacht werden können." GW, XV, 197-98.
34. "Diese Form aber kann nur durch eine völlige Änderung der
Zwecksetzung der Kunst erlangt werden. Erst der neue Zweck macht
die neue Kunst. Der neue Zweck heisst: Pädagogik." ibid.

35. Mordecai Gorelik reports that Brecht made the remark, "I am the Einstein of the new stage form," in a conversation with him in 1935 when Brecht visited New York to supervise the staging of his adaptation of Gorki's *Mother*. Mordecai Gorelik, "Brecht," in *Theater Arts* (New York), March, 1967. Eric Bentley has told me that he cannot believe that Brecht meant the remark to be taken seriously. Mr. Gorelik, however, has told me (1970) that not only does he believe that the remark was meant seriously but that he still fully believes that what Brecht said then is actually true.

36. "Zumindest seit zwei Menschenaltern befindet sich das ernsthafte europäische Theater in einer Epoche der Experimente." GW, XV, 285.

37. Ulrich Weisstein, "From the Dramatic Novel to the Epic Theater: A Study of the Contemporary Background of Brecht's Theory and Practice," GR, XXXVIII, 3 (1963), p. 271. I would, however, suggest that Professor Weisstein's argument would gain additional force if he were to follow "Piscator's" ideas back to their Russian sources. This work has been begun by Marjorie Hoover in her essay, "V.E. Meyerhold: A Russian Predecessor of Avant-Garde Theater," in CL, XVII (1965), 234-250.

38. Um zeigen zu können, was ich sehe
    Lese ich nach die Darstellungen anderer Völker und anderer
        Zeitalter.
    Ein paar Stücke habe ich nachgeschrieben, genau
    Prüfend die jeweilige Technik und mir einprägend
    Das, was mir zustatten kommt.
    Ich studierte die Darstellungen der grossen Feudalen
    Durch die Engländer, reicher Figuren
    Denen die Welt dazu dient, sich gross zu entfalten.
    Ich studierte die moralisierenden Spanier
    Die Inder, Meister der schönen Empfindungen
    Und die Chinesen, welche die Familien darstellen
    Und die bunten Schicksale in den Städten.
    GW, IX, 790. The list, obviously, is far from complete. There is no mention, for instance, of the Japanese drama here.

39. For the two poles of interpretation of Brecht's reaction to Shakespeare, see (for the negative view) Helge Hultberg's "Bert Brecht und Shakespeare," *Orbis litterarum*, XIV (1959), 89-104, and (for the positive view) R.B. Parker, "Dramaturgy in Shakespeare and Brecht," *University of Toronto Quarterly*, XXXII (1963), 229-46.

40. "Die Bemühungen [um Klassikeraufführungen] sind von mir aufgegeben worden." GW, XV, 181.
41. "Die Klassik diente dem Erlebertum. Der Nutzen der Klassiker ist zu gering. Sie zeigen nicht die Welt, sondern sich selber. Persönlichkeiten für den Schaukasten. Worte in der Art von Schmuckgegenständen. Kleiner Horizont, bürgerlich. Alles mit Mass und *nach* Mass." ibid.
42. "Schön, wenn die Inhalte der Klassik also doch letzten Endes nicht benutzbar waren, warum hielten Sie sich nicht an die Form?" ibid.
43. "Die Form unserer Klassiker ist nicht klassisch. Zu frühe Stabilisierung, Prinzip der Ruhe und Abgeklärtheit." ibid.
44. "Die alte Form des Dramas ermöglicht es nicht, die Welt so darzustellen, wie wir sie heute sehen." GW, XV, 173.
45. "Um zur grossen Handlung zu kommen, sollten wir die Bauart der Klassiker studieren, besonders die Shakespeares. Shakespeare verwendet oft die ganze Substanz eines neueren Stücks in einer einzigen Szene, und nichts Wesentliches bleibt weg." GW, XVI, 938.
46. "In primitiven Rezensionen wird sie oft als die Bilder-Bogentechnik bezeichnet, als erscheine da eben nur ein Bild nach dem andern, ohne dass die Handlung zusammengerafft und die Spannung gesteuert wird. Das ist natürlich eine dumme Verkennung der grossen Bauart unserer Klassiker, der Bauart der elisabethanischen Stückeschreiber. Die Handlung (Fabel) dieser Stücke ist reich, aber die einzelnen Situationen und Vorgänge, so bildhaft sie sein mögen, sind keineswegs nur miteinander verknüpft, sondern sie bedingen sich. Jede Szene, lang oder kurz, treibt die Handlung weiter. Es gibt hier Atmosphäre, aber es ist nicht die des Milieus: es gibt auch hier Spannung, aber es ist nicht ein Katz-und-Maus-Spiel mit dem Zuschauer." ibid.

Chapter 2

1. "... im ganzen ist es ein gutes Stück nach dem Modell der aristotelischen Dramatik." Bernhard Reich, "München, 1923," p. 253, in *Bertolt Brecht, "Leben Eduards des Zweiten von England," Vorlage, Texte und Materialien,* ed. Reinhold Grimm (Frankfurt am Main, 1968).
2. "Das 'epische Theater' keimt schon im *Eduard.*" ibid.
3. For support of the contention that the early Brecht was largely apolitical in his outlook, see GW, SVI, 588; Arnolt Bronnen, *Tage mit Bertolt Brecht* (Munich, Vienna, Basel, 1960), p. 154; and Carl Zuckmayer's notes on the Brecht of this period in the autobiography, *Als wär's ein Stück von mir* (Frankfurt, 1966), p. 375 ff.
4. The adjudicator for the prize in 1922 was Herbert Ihering, who was thereafter Brecht's most ardent supporter. In giving the prize to Brecht, Ihering raved: "Seit langem hat es in Deutschland keinen Dichter gegeben, der so voraussetzungslos die tragischen Notwendigkeiten hatte: die Verknupftheit der Schicksale, die Einwirkung der Menschen." ("For a long time, there has not been a poet in Germany who has had, without reservation, the necessary elements of tragedy: interlocking destinies and the influence of men upon one another.") *Kritik,* October 5, 1922. The general tone of this article reveals, incidentally, how profoundly moved Ihering was by the language of the early Brecht. Ihering's use of the word "tragedy" should not escape our attention here, as it is a word which will later become anathema to Brecht.
5. Comment made in Ihering's review of the premiere and reprinted in his book, *Von Reinhardt bis Brecht: Eine Auswahl der Theaterkritiken 1909-1932* (Hamburg, 1967), p. 131. See also in this connection Ulrich Weisstein's important article, "The First Version of Brecht/Feuchtwanger's *Leben Eduards des Zweiten von England* and its Relation to the Standard Text," in *JEGP,* LXIX, no. 2 (April, 1970), 193-210. Professor Weisstein shows conclusively in this article that there is no real reason to regard the *Stücke* and the *Gesammelte Werke* version of *Eduard II* as definitive. This means that we do not know exactly what text was played in Munich in 1924; in fact, that particular text may no longer even exist. For the general problem of editing Brecht's work, see Gerhard Seidel's dissertation, "Studien zur Edition poetischer Werke von Bertolt Brecht" (Greifswald, 1966). A one-volume printed version of this

important work has now appeared under the title: *Die Funktions-
und Gegenstandsbedingtheit der Edition: Untersucht an poetischen
Werken Bertolt Brechts* (East Berlin, 1970).

6. Thomas Dekker, *Guls Horne-Booke,* first published in 1609. Dekker
presents a vivid picture of an audience frequently capable of action
sure to undermine the players and the play. Most modern critics
(including as knowledgeable a man as Sir Edmund Chambers) feel
that the Elizabethan theaters were in fact noisy and the behavior of
the audiences was not at all decorous. Alfred Harbage, however, in
his *Shakespeare's Audience,* says that he feels that "the boisterous-
ness at the Globe has been overestimated." Eric Bentley has told me
that he agrees with Harbage's position; I do not.

7. Phyllis Hartnoll, ed., *The Oxford Companion to the Theatre,* 2nd
ed. (Oxford, 1957), pp. 218-219.

8. Thomas Marc Parrott and Robert Hamilton Ball in their *Short View
of Elizabethan Drama* (New York, 1943) note approvingly: "This
was a stage that cried out for the narrative method," p. 61.

9. R.B. Parker, "Dramaturgy in Shakespeare and Brecht," *University of
Toronto Quarterly,* XXXII (1963). It might be argued against
Parker's view, however, that the scale and range of the Elizabethan
repertory demanded crudely delineated role playing. This is definitely not what Brecht was after at any stage of his career as a
director. See note 10 below.

10. Bernard Beckerman, *Shakespeare at the Globe: 1599-1609* (New
York, 1966), notes for instance: "In the three-year period from June
5, 1594, to July 28, 1597, a leading actor of the Lord Admiral's
company, such as Edward Alleyn or Thomas Downton, had to
secure and retain command of about seventy-one different roles, of
which number fifty-two or fifty-three were newly learned." p. 9.

11. R.B. Parker, p. 233. Though I can agree with Parker that the *effect*
of the Elizabethan repertory in performance may have been what
Brecht called for in his theories, it was sought in Brecht's theater by
quite different means. See notes 9 and 10 above. Where the
Elizabethan actor worked with a large number of texts and often
had to prepare a hot item overnight (see Hamlet's instructions to the
wandering players), Brecht's actors enjoyed the longest and most
carefully worked out rehearsal periods available to any actors in the
modern theater. Furthermore, Parker simply unquestioningly
accepts as fact Brecht's theory that his actors will remain separate
from their roles. In fact, as I shall repeatedly show, there is grave

doubt that the distance between actor and role, and role and spectator actually obtained in Brecht's theater. By the end of the rehearsal period (sometimes extending to as many as eight months and, in the case of *Eduard II,* beginning probably in October 1923 and ending in mid-March 1924) the actor or actress in Brecht's theater often seems to me to be as involved in his or her role as any Stanislavsky-trained actor in the Moscow Art Theater.

12.   Shakespeare in *Hamlet,* II, ii, is obviously aware of another V-effect in his plays, that of boys playing women's roles. He makes something of it quite openly when he has Hamlet turn to one of the visiting boy actors and say: "O, old friend! Why, thy face is valanced since I saw thee last; com'st thou to beard me in Denmark? What, my young lady and mistress! By'r Lady, your ladyship is nearer to heaven than when I saw you last, by the altitude of a chopine. Pray God, your voice, like a piece of uncurrent gold, be not cracked within the ring." Numerous other examples both from Shakespeare and from other Elizabethan and Jacobean playwrights might be given to show that the practice of using boys in female roles was thoroughly self-conscious in this period. Of some historical interest perhaps is the fact that Brecht did cast a woman as the Young Eduard in his 1924 production.

13.   "Wie irdisch, unheilig und zauberlos dies alles vor sich ging." Brecht, GW, XVI, 587.

14.   "Im Theater sitzen schon Frauen, aber die Frauenrollen werden noch von Knaben gespielt. Da es keine Prospekte gibt, übernimmt der Dichter die Aufgabe, Landschaft zu malen. Der Bühnenraum hat keinerlei Bestimmtheit, er kann eine ganze Heide sein. In *Richard III* (V, 3) trittzwischen zwei Heerlagern mit Richards und Richmonds Zelten, für beide sichtbar und hörbar, im Traum der beiden ein Geist auf, der sich an beide wendet." Notably, the Dramaturg concludes his description with the exclamation: "Ein Theater voll von V-Effekten!" GW, XVI, 586.

15.   A list of major criticism on this play is given in Reinhold Grimm's Suhrkamp volume: *Eduard-Materialien,* pp. 268-269. Besides Grimm's own work, the most important pieces of criticism on *Eduard II* are: R. Beckley, "Adaptation as a Feature of Brecht's Dramatic Technique," *German/Life and Letters,* XV (1961-62), 274 ff.; V. Dreimanis Melngailis, "*Leben Eduards des Zweiten von England:* Bertolt Brecht's Adaptation of Marlowe's *Edward II.*" Diss., Harvard, 1967; L.J. Laboulle, "A Note on Bertolt Brecht's

Adaptation of Marlowe's *Edward II*," *Modern Language Review,* LIV (1959), 214 ff.; Eric Bentley's preface to his own English translation (Grove Press, 1966); several comments made by Eric Bentley in personal letters to me; my own dissertation, University of Southern California, 1967; H.W. Grüninger, "Brecht and Marlowe," *Comparative Literature,* XXI, (Summer 1969); and the above mentioned article of Ulrich Weisstein in *JEGP,* LXIX, no. 2 (April 1970), 193-210. The latter article carefully considers not only how the play was rehearsed but also points out the major differences between the "canonic" text (the one I examine) and another version (also published in 1924) in *Der neue Merkur.* We simply do not know, as Weisstein acknowledges, how much of the canonic or of the *Merkur* text was actually played. Brecht altered the text (as Bernhard Reich notes) almost daily.

16. Eduard Kopetzki, Diss., Vienna, 1949. Mr. Kopetzki's work is otherwise remarkable for the fact that he is (to my knowledge) the first critic to wonder openly whether the term "episch" does in fact fit many of Brecht's major plays. Kopetzki argues that the term "episches Theater" gradually evolved during the production period surrounding Brecht's mounting of *Eduard II.* Kopetzki then sees the period of the "teaching plays" as marking "the highpoint of epic theater." Thereafter, in his view, we have "The falling graphic curve of the epic theater." I agree, in the main, with this point of view.

17. Grimm reprints the otherwise rare Heymel text in his *Materialien-Eduard* volume.

18. Perhaps the best evidence of this contention is the simple fact of the frequency with which this *German* play has been translated into English, the language of Brecht's "source" play.

19. "Wir wollten eine Aufführung ermöglichen, die mit der Shakespeare-tradition der deutschen Bühnen brechen sollte, jenem gipsig monumentalen Stil, der den Spiessbürgern so teuer ist." GW, XVII, 951. Note however that Jessner was doing exactly this in Berlin several years before. See Ch. 1, p. 12.

20. Brecht placed "ein Königsdrama in Hinterhof." Cited, with no source given, in Jean Tailleur, "Brecht und das elisabethanische Drama." Diss., Université de Paris, 1959, p. 36. "Garbage dump" is my own deliberately coarse rendition of the German term, "Hinterhof."

21. The king "kann ebenso ein starker böser Mann wie ein schwacher guter sein." GW, XV, 195.

22. Christopher Marlowe, *Edward the Second,* IV, v.

23. Was von ihm bleibt, sind halbgegessne
    Küchenreste und ein löcheriges Strickbett. Brecht, GW, I, 248.
24. Marlowe, *Edward II,* V, v.
25. Die Grub, drin sie mich halten, ist die Senkgrub
    Und über mich her, seit sieben Stunden, fällt
    Der Kot Londons. Doch sein Abwasser härtet
    Meine Gliedmassen. Sie sind schon wie Holz
    Der Zeder. Geruch des Abfalls macht mich noch
    Masslos vor Grösse. Gutes Geräusch der Trommel
    Lässt wachen den Geschwächten, dass ihn nicht
    Anlangt sein Tod in Ohnmacht, sondern im
    Wachen. GW, I, 289.
26. Marlowe, *Edward II,* IV, vi.
27. Brecht's version begins:
    Komm, Spencer! Baldock, komm! Setz dich zu mir!
    Mach die Probe jetzt auf deine Philosophie
    Die du aus Plato sogst und Aristoteles
    An den Ammenbrüsten hochberühmter Weisheit.

    The passage ends:

    Ach, Spencer
    Da Worte roh sind, nur trennen Herz von Herz
    Und Verständigung uns nicht geschenkt ist
    In solcher Taubheit bleibt nur körperlich Berühren
    Zwischen den Männern. Doch auch dieses ist
    Sehr wenig und alles ist eitel. Brecht, GW, I, 252.
28. Marlowe, *Edward II,* V, vi.
29. See Reinhold Grimm, *Brecht und die Weltliteratur* (Nürnberg,
    1961), pp. 31-32.
30. 's ist, Knabe, die schlumpichte Fortuna treibts
    Ein Rad. 's treibt dich mit nach aufwärts.
    Aufwärts and aufwärts. Du hältst fest. Aufwärts.
    Da kommt ein Punkt, der höchste. Von dem siehst du
    s' ist keine Leiter, 's treibt dich nach unten.
    Weil's eben rund ist. Wer dies gesehn hat, fällt er
    Knabe, oder lässt er sich fallen? Die Frage
    Ist spasshaft. Schmeck sie! GW, I, 294-295.
31. Mit offnen Knien und geschloss'nen Augen
    Schnappend nach allem, seid Ihr unersättlich Anna. GW, I, 267.
32. She laughs "ob die Leere der Welt."
33. Marlowe, *Edward II,* I, iv.

34. Brecht, *Stücke,* II, 32.
35. Major German critics such as Spielhagen, Petsch, Kayser, von Wilpert, and Pongs all seem to agree on defining the epic mode as "erzählende Kunst." The only really significant "German" exception to this is the Hungarian Marxist Lukács, who happens to write mainly in German. Lukács comes closer to the English definition when he insists on "breadth and fullness" being integral parts of the epic mode. Surprisingly and confusingly, other German critics on the one hand define the *Epik* as "erzählende Kunst" (narrative art) and thus force themselves to include short forms such as the novella and the short story, while on the other hand they too seem to recognize that "breadth and fullness" do indeed seem part of the epic poetic mode. How one then reconciles breadth and fullness as hallmarks of epic with the brevity and abstractness of many a novella and short story (defined in German terms as "epics") I do not know.
36. For the traffic accident model for epic acting, see the glossary. Brecht's version of the famous "street scene" is to be found in GW, XVI, 546-558. An English translation of the essay is available in Willett, *Brecht on Theatre,* pp. 121-129.
37. There is no evidence, however, that Brecht ever seriously used this technique in performance.
38. It is interesting that even Aristotle says of many of the tragedies of his time: "But with the other [the context makes clear that by 'other' Aristotle means playwrights other than Sophocles] tragedians, the choral songs do not more belong to that fable, than to any other tragedy, on which account the chorus sing detached pieces, inserted at pleasure." Beckley's translation.
39. Even if these placards were not used in the Elizabethan theater, as some critics now maintain, it is quite clear that Brecht could have taken the idea from the kinds of performances given at fairs during his youth. Also, we know that Valentin used such placards in his Munich beer hall appearances.
40. Note that in many of the plays of the Elizabethans, a prologue (or chorus) specifically spells out the time and place of the dramatic action.
41. Helge Hultberg erroneously maintains in his book, *Die ästhetischen Anschauungen Bertolt Brechts* (Copenhagen, 1962), that Brecht never used the term "episches Drama," but always used the term "episches Theater." Grimm, in his review of the book, *Zeitschrift für deutsche Philologie,* LXXXIV (Sonderheft), 90-111, points out

(p.97): "Gerade in jener Unterredung mit Sternberg, Hardt und Ihering, auf die Hultberg so grossen Wert legt, gebraucht Brecht wiederholt die Form 'episches Drama.' " ("Precisely in that conversation with Sternberg, Hardt and Ihering that Hultberg deems so important, Brecht uses the term 'epic drama' repeatedly.")

42. "Für Grösse musste ein anderer Begriff gesetzt werden. Sie, lieber Brecht, gingen da voran. Sie setzten für Grösse: Distanz. Das ist Ihre theatergeschichtliche Tat. Dieser Dreh- und Wendepunkt war Ihre Aufführung von *Leben Eduards II. von England* in München." Comment made in a conversation with Brecht. GW, XV, 181.

43. "Sie (Brecht) nahmen dem Schauspieler die Gemütlichkeit, die sich temperamentvoll anbiedert. Sie forderten Rechenschaft über die Vorgänge. Sie verlangten einfache Gesten, Sie zwangen zu klarem, kühlem Sprechen. Keine Gefühlsmogelei wurde geduldet. Das ergab den objektiven, den epischen Stil." ibid.

44. Bernhard Reich, "Erinnerungen den jungen Brecht," originally appeared in *Sinn und Form, 2. Brecht-Sonderheft.* I have taken the material from the reprinted and slightly shorter version given in Grimm's *Eduard-Materialien* volume. "Die Darsteller der Soldaten, die den Favoriten des Königs zu hängen hatten, machten zuerst ein paar Gesten, die eine willige Phantasie dafür hätte deuten können. Jeder deutsche Regisseur wäre weitergegangen. Brecht unterbrach und verlangte, die Akteure sollten es richtig machen: Schlinge knüpfen, das Seil am Querbalken befestigen. Achselzuckend versuchten die Schauspieler, irgendwie den unerwarteten Anordnungen des Regisseurs nachzukommen. Brecht unterbrach wieder, forderte grimmig und unentwegt, das Hängen zu wiederholen, und stellte die Aufgabe, Gaveston virtuos zu hängen; das Publikum solle sich mit Vergnügen ansehen, wie man den Burschen aufknüpft. Brecht repetierte dies geduldig und ernsthaft." p. 255.

45. ibid.

46. Cited from the reprint of the original *Kritik* article (see note four above) found in *Erinnerungen an Brecht*, ed. Hubert Witt (Leipzig, 1966), p. 33: "Diese Sprache fühlt man auf der Zunge, am Gaumen, im Ohr, im Rückgrat. Sie lässt Zwischenglieder weg und reisst Perspektiven auf. Sie ist brutal sinnlich und melancholisch zart. Gemeinheit ist in ihr und abgründige Trauer. Grimmiger Witz und klagende Lyrik."

47. ibid. "Beim ersten Worte seiner Dramen weiss man: Tragödie hat begonnen." This is not the only time in this essay that Ihering refers to Brecht's ability to write tragedy (see note 4 above).

48. ibid. Ihering notes that one must really listen to Brecht sing his own verses "um den aufpeitschenden Rhythmus seiner Sätze zu fühlen."
49. Carl Zuckmayer. *Als wär's ein Stück von mir,* p. 375: "Sein Gesang war rauh und schneidend, manchmal bänkelsängerisch krud, mit unverkennbar augsburgischem Sprachklang, manchmal fast schön, schwebend ohne Gefühlsvibration, und in jeder Silbe, in jedem halben Ton ganz klar und deutlich."
50. ibid. "Wenn er zur Laute griff, verstummte das Geschwirr der Gespräche." "Alles hockte um ihn her, wie in einen magischen Bann geschlagen."
51. Marieluise Fleisser, "Aus der Augustenstrasse," in *50 Jahre Schauspielhaus, 25 Jahre Kammerspiele im Schauspielhaus* (Munich, 1951), p. 52 ff. Reprinted in Grimm's *Eduard-Materialien,* pp. 264-266, and in *Caspar Neher,* ed. Gottfried von Einem and Siegfried Melchinger (Velber near Hannover, 1966), p. 180. My quotation is from the Neher volume as the version given there is somewhat more circumstantial than that given in Grimm: "Es war balladeskes Theater. Brecht führte selber Regie, er gebrauchte verblüffend einfache, dabei sinnfällige Mittel, die leise an den Nerven sägten."
52. ibid. "Geisterhaft steht mir die hohe Pappkulisse der Londoner Häuser mit den vielen kleinen Fensterläden vor Augen, plötzlich fliegen alle Läden auf, um aus jedem Fenster einen sprechenden Kopf freizugeben, und alle diese Köpfe stossen miteinander eine Art Gebet aus, das mehr Anklage ist als Klage und wie bei einer Litanei von oftmaligen Bittfüruns unterbrochen wird, dieses Bittfüruns aber ist keine Bitte um Erbarmen, vielmehr ein hastiges angreiferisches Flüstern, das einem mit eiskalter Drohung an die Nerven geht, und jedermann spürt, dies wird nicht weniger als eine Revolution, und nach dem letzten gespenstischen Bittfüruns fliegen mit einem einzigen Klapp die Fensterläden wieder zu."
53. This particular stage device is so close to the kind of thing that Meyerhold was doing regularly at this time with his Constructivist acrobatics that one must wonder if Brecht thought this up independently or whether he had already heard of Meyerhold's work.
54. Cited in *Neher,* p. 181. Originally appeared in Rudolf Frank's autobiography, *Spielzeit meines Lebens* (Heidelberg, 1960), pp. 264-273: "In diesem englischen Heer, das schmutzverkrustete Stahlhelme trug, lebte nicht nur die Notzeit von 1550—alle Armeen des europäischen Weltkrieges waren in ihm enthalten."

55. GW, XV, 176-184.

56. The essay first appeared in 1957 in the Second Brecht Issue of the East German journal, *Sinn und Form.* The essay is reprinted in a shortened form in Grimm, *Eduard-Materialien.*

57. See Willett, *Eight Aspects,* p. 169. According to Willett, Bronnen first used the term in 1922 or 1923. Bronnen became a friend of Brecht in 1921-22. The term does not, however, appear in Brecht's writing before 1926. By this time, we know, the term had become very fashionable in avant-garde theater circles in Berlin.

58. GW, XV, 132. "Das Wesentliche am epischen Theater ist es vielleicht, dass es nicht so sehr an das Gefühl, sondern mehr an die Ratio des Zuschauers appelliert. Nicht miterleben soll der Zuschauer, sondern sich auseinandersetzen." Brecht then adds, however: "Dabei wäre es ganz und gar unrichtig, diesem Theater das Gefühl absprechen zu wollen."

59. Eric Bentley uses the phrase in the preface to his *Seven Plays by Bertolt Brecht,* p. xxvii.

60. Emil Staiger, *Grundbegriffe der Poetik,* 4th ed. (Zurich, 1959), p. 235.

61. Julius Petersen, "Zur Lehre der Dichtungsgattungen," in *Festschrift für A. Sauer* (Stuttgart, 1925).

62. Wolfgang Kayser, *Das sprachliche Kunstwerk* (Bern, 1948).

63. Peter Szondi, *Theorie des modernen Dramas* (Frankfurt, 1956).

64. Plato, *Great Dialogues of Plato,* trans. W.H.D. Rouse (New York, 1956), p. 13.

65. ibid.

66. We might mention in this connection that Aristotle can be blamed in some measure here for erroneously claiming in the *Poetics* that the drama is non-narrative in form.

67. Willi Flemming, *Epik und Dramatik* (Munich, 1955).

Chapter 3

1. "In der Form beruht das Werk, wie übrigens sehr wenige neuere Werke, auf der Bau- und Ausdrucksweise des nationalen deutschen Theaters (von Goethes *Götz* bis zu Büchners *Woyzeck*)." Brecht, GW, XVII, 1081. This comment is rendered aesthetically and politically unreliable because of certain political overtones not present in the text of the *Gesammelte Werke* but present in the full text of this statement in the Brecht Archive. The note is taken from Mappe (portfolio) 238, p. 18. The full portfolio text, not yet cleared for publication, consists of a letter to a very high official in the East German government. The letter begs that the play *The Mother* not be taken out of the Berliner Ensemble repertoire, despite charges of "Formalism" and of similarity to the then discredited Russian Agitprop theater. Brecht's intercession with Pankow seems to have worked. The play was taken on tour to Poland shortly after the letter was written. Brecht's argument that his play was simply the same in style and structure as plays that had already been endorsed as acceptable in East Germany, plays such as *Götz* and *Woyzeck*, is, though it contains some real aesthetic truth, a deliberate political ploy. In the same letter, Brecht is also most careful to point out that he had had the play endorsed by Gorki himself in the 1930s. As Gorki's work had been accepted by Stalin, the fact that Gorki had "authorized" Brecht's play was an almost certain way to get even Pankow, with its rigidly Stalinistic "aesthetic," to endorse the play.

2. "Das Stück *Die Mutter,* im Stil der Lehrstücke geschrieben, aber Schauspieler erfordernd, ist ein Stück antimetaphysischer, materialistischer, *nichtaristotelischer Dramatik.* Diese bedient sich der *hingebenden Einfühlung* des Zuschauers keineswegs so unbedenklich wie die aristotelische und steht auch zu gewissen psychischen Wirkungen, wie etwa der Katharsis, wesentlich anders" (Brecht's italics). GW, XVII, 1036. The clear implication of this statement, of course, is that identification is in fact to be expected with the mother.

3. Maxim Gorki's novel was first published in 1907. A German translation by Adolf Hess was first published in 1923 and was then reprinted in 1927 and 1929. Numerous word-for-word parallels between Hess's workmanlike translation and the stage adaptation done by Stark and Weisenborn indicate that they worked from the translation rather than from the original.

4. Piscator, p. 37. The same connection obtains also in Brecht's theater. Volker Klotz says flatly: "Für Brecht selbst ist episches Theater und Marxismus nicht zu trennen." ("For Brecht himself, epic theater and Marxism cannot be separated.") *Bertolt Brecht: Versuch über das Werk* (Bad Homburg, 1957), p. 128. Willett extends this change from Saul to Paul to include many of the prominent Dadaists. See Willett, *Eight Aspects,* p. 109.

5. First printed in "Notizen über Brechts Arbeit 1926," *Sinn und Form II,* pp. 241-243. The notes are reprinted in *Erinnerungen an Brecht,* ed. Hubert Witt (Leipzig, 1966), pp. 49-52.

6. "Diese Dinge sind nicht dramatisch in unserem Sinn, und wenn man sie 'umdichtet,' dann sind sie nicht mehr wahr, und das Drama ist überhaupt keine solche Sache mehr, und wenn man sieht, dass unsere heutige Welt nicht mehr ins Drama passt, dann passt das Drama eben nicht mehr in die Welt." ibid. It is clear that Brecht was so attached to the theater that he never seriously considered switching to a new medium, one which might have been able to encompass the kind of materials he wanted to deal with. The film suggests itself as a rather obvious alternative, particularly as it was being used at precisely this time and with the most telling propaganda effect by the Soviets. For a discussion of Brecht's strained relationship with the film medium, please see my article, "Feuchtwanger, Brecht, and the Epic Media: The Novel and the Film," in *Lion Feuchtwanger: The Man, His Ideas and His Work,* ed. John Spalek, University of Southern California Series in Comparative Literature, 1972.

7. "Im Verlaufe dieser Studien stellte Brecht seine Theorie des 'epischen Dramas' auf." ibid.

8. In a highly biased note in his *Bert Brecht* (Berlin, 1958), Willy Haas notes: "Der Fanatismus des Konvertiten hatte ihn ergriffen. . ." ("The fanaticism of the convert had taken hold of him."), p. 76.

9. The closest Brecht comes to calling this a "didactic play" is where he notes that it is "written in the style of the didactic plays." GW, XVII, 1036.

10. As noted above, the didactic plays represent for Kopetzki the peak of Brecht's epic theater practice. That the play *The Mother* should be seen as an example of the epic style is argued by Herbert Ihering. He notes: "Ein Roman, also eine epische Dichtung lag dem Drama zugrunde. Mit zwei Mitarbeitern, mit Günther Weisenborn und Slatan Dudow ging Brecht ans Schreiben. Wurde es sein erstes

episches Drama?" ("A novel, an epic work of literature, formed the basis of the drama. Brecht began to write with two collaborators, Günther Weisenborn and Slatan Dudow. Would it become his first epic drama?") If we grant that the concluding question requires a positive answer, then Ihering creates an interesting historical problem. If *Die Mutter* was Brecht's first "epic drama," then what label should be pinned on earlier plays such as *Das Badener Lehrstück, Die heilige Johanna,* and *Die Ausnahme und die Regel?* Herbert Ihering, *Bertolt Brecht und das Theater* (Berlin, 1959), p. 20.

11. For a selection of reviews of German, Danish, and the New York production of the play, see Brecht, GW, XVII. The reader should, however, beware as the selection is tendentious. Various alternate views of the play were available to the compilers of material included in the *Gesammelte Werke* in BBA 404 and BBA 618.

12. For a good discussion of the more important differences between the 1933 *Versuche* and the later *Stücke* text, see: Daniel Frey, "La Mere de Gorki à Bertolt Brecht à travers trente ans d'historie," *Études de Lettres,* Bulletin de la Faculté des Lettres de l'université de Lausanne, Serie II, Tome 6, No. 2 (Avril-Juin 1963), 125-151. Unfortunately M. Frey seems wholly unaware of the Berliner Ensemble acting version of the text.

13. The Berliner Ensemble acting version is available in BBA 1572 and BBA 195. The latter is Brecht's own directing text. The Ensemble version of *Die Mutter,* edited by Joachim Tenschert, is now available (1970) through the Henschel Verlag, East Berlin.

14. For a very confusing (if you do not know the Ensemble version) discussion of the role by Brecht himself, see "Der Volksschauspieler Ernst Busch," in *Theaterarbeit: Sechs Aufführungen des Berliner Ensembles,* Herausgeber: Berliner Ensemble und Helene Weigel (Berlin und Frankfurt am Main, 1961). Here Brecht discussed the Lapkin role and its importance in some detail, but completely neglected to mention the fact that no such role existed at that time in any published version of the text.

15. This information was given to me in a series of personal interviews with Elisabeth Hauptmann in East Berlin in 1966-67. E. Hauptmann said specifically: "When we got Busch to play the worker, Brecht took care to make sure that his lines, his part, fitted the great actor Busch."

16. See comments of the actor Ernst Kahler, who played in both the Berlin production of the play and the Leipzig production that

immediately preceded it, found in *Theaterarbeit,* pp. 149-150. One might note, however, a curious justification of Busch's being given many of Pawel's lines. Ernst Busch had played Pawel in Brecht's 1930-32 production.

17. A typescript of this version is contained in BBA portfolio 441.

18. Though it might be argued that Brecht's decision to end his play in 1917, rather than with the abortive 1905 revolt that Gorki ends with, is an epic device, this argument presents more epic problems than it solves. Much of the extension is achieved simply by making Pawel's death come later. This is, of course, simply a change of date, not one of structure. Furthermore, by then having a scene where Pelegea Wlassowa opposes World War I and is beaten up for her pains, Brecht ensures his audience's sympathy for her. Finally, by having the play end with the successful 1917 revolution he provides himself with a magnificent and politically effective "curtain." This curtain asks directly for the audience's support for a cause that has already been successful elsewhere. Surely Gorki's muted ending in 1905 has less "dramatic tension," less chance of involving an audience directly than Brecht's rousing, good old-fashioned finale.

19. Comment found in BBA 195/03. Same remark was made in the original *Versuche* text of 1933.

20. "Fast schäme ich mich, meinen Sohn diese Suppe hinzustellen. Aber ich kann kein Fett mehr hineintun, nicht einen halben Löffel voll." GW, II, 825. E. Hauptmann told me that the idea of narrative exposition at the beginning of this play was her own and was derived from Japanese plays read not, as has usually been supposed, in Waley's translations, but in the German translations of the Sinologist, D. Richard Wilhelm. "His yellow books," said Miss Hauptmann, "were in all our libraries."

It has also been suggested that this mode of direct audience address might have been derived from German sources. Heinrich Henel and Reinhold Grimm have both suggested Medieval and Jesuit sources for the device. Or, as they have also pointed out, Brecht really did not need to look further than Goethe's *Faust* and "Mephistos unvergessliche Ad spectatores am Ende vieler Szenen." Heinrich Henel, "Szenisches und panoramisches Theater," in *Episches Theater,* ed. Reinhold Grimm (Köln-Berlin, 1966), p. 390. Inasmuch as Shakespeare has become virtually a German cultural institution, we might point out that the device is found in Shakespeare's plays extremely often and that Brecht could have derived it easily enough from there. See also Max Spalter, *Brecht's Tradition* (Baltimore, 1967).

21. A recording of the Ensemble with Ernst Busch and Helene Weigel is available through Eterna (East German label) 11006-10. For the effect of Weigel (the actress cited by Brecht over and over again as the model of "epic" acting) in the role, either listen to the above recording or read the following reviews. These reviews were not printed by Brecht but are of particular interest as they note that Brecht spelled out the theory of epic theater, and the effect it was supposed to have to his early and late audiences through the medium of his program notes. One critic notes: "Im Programmheft wird das Publikum darüber aufgeklärt, was mit dem epischen Theater eigentlich los ist, dass es nicht Suggestion, sondern Argument ist, nicht Wachstum sondern Montage, nicht Gefühl, sondern Ratio." ("The program explains to the public what the epic theater is all about. That it is not suggestion but argument, not growth but montage, not emotion but reason.") I have not seen the original of this comment. This paraphrase of the original program note appeared in the *Deutsche Tageszeitung*, Jan. 18, 1932, and was signed with the initials H.K. Another reviewer observed of the same 1932 production: "Namentlich Helene Weigel als die Mutter, der die bösen Kapitalisten immer eine Kopeke vorenthalten, die ihr gerade fehlt, wuchs über den kommunistischer Leitartikel zu einem Menschen von Fleisch und Blut." ("Namely, Helene Weigel as the mother, from whom the evil capitalists always withhold precisely that one kopeck that she needs, grows beyond the Communist editorial to a human being of flesh and blood.") *Velhagen und Klassings Monatshefte*, Jan., 1932, anon. review found in BBA 404/26. In a review of Helene Weigel in the 1951 production we find: "Hier müssen wir aber wenigstens erwähnen, dass Helene Weigel—ausser in sparsamen und wohl erwogenen Momenten—nicht neben der Rolle steht, sondern völlig in ihr aufgeht." ("Here we must at least mention that Helene Weigel—aside from sparingly used and well-considered moments—does not stand alongside the role but is completely absorbed in it.") *Tägliche Rundschau*, Berlin, Jan. 14, 1951. Review found in BBA 618/83. For some reason these particular reviews are not among the several dozen reprinted in the *Gesammelte Werke*.

22. Cited by Bjørn Ekmann in *Gesellschaft und Gewissen: Die sozialen und moralischen Anschauungen Bertolt Brechts und ihre Bedeutung für seine Dichtung* (Copenhagen, 1969), p. 189.

23. Brecht speaks of "Die eingeschüchterte, gläubige, gebannte Menge." GW, XVI, 675.

24. In a general comment on the "epic actor" and the "epic spectator," D.I. Grossvogel notes: "The noh actor, who comes before this spectator as simply another man, does so in order that, as he changes into an actor, he may lead the spectator into that other reality beyond the footlights; it is an oriental courtesy." Grossvogel then goes on to ask: "When Brecht uses the device, is his statement of separation sufficient to subvert it?" *Four Playwrights and a Postscript* (New York, 1962), p. 32. Answering the question himself, Grossvogel adds: "Even when the stage is turned by the playwright into a conscious statement of its own irreality, it is doubtful whether it effects the sort of spectator 'disengagement' that Brecht desires." Occasionally Brecht himself seems fully aware of this. His notes of the effect of Mei Lan-Fang's performances in Moscow in 1935 are one clear example of this. Another is the note (*Schriften zum Theater,* VI, 213): "Wenn der Schauspieler den Zuschauer rühren will, muss er nicht einfach selber gerührt sein." ("If the actor wishes to move his audience, it is not enough for him to simply be moved himself.") The statement is nothing, of course, but a paraphrase of Diderot's *Paradoxe sur le comedien.*

25. Specifically, of the 110 pages of the play in the *Stücke* edition, twenty-two take place in Wlassowa's room and forty-one in the apartment of the teacher who befriends her. Only some thirty-four pages of text are played "outdoors."

26. "Wer niedergeschlagen wird, der erhebe sich!
Wer verloren ist, kämpfe!
Wer seine Lage erkannt hat, wie soll der aufzuhalten sein?
Denn die Besiegten von heute sind die Sieger von Morgen
Und aus niemals wird: heute noch."
Brecht, GW, II, 895.

27. "Die Nützlichkeit aristotelischer Wirkungen sollte nicht geleugnet werden; man bestätigt sie, wenn man ihre Grenzen zeigt. Ist eine bestimmte gesellschaftliche Situation sehr reif, so kann durch Werke obiger Art eine praktische Aktion ausgelöst werden. Solch ein Stück ist der Funke, der das Pulverfass entzündet." GW, XV, 249. Apparently the West Berlin Senate in 1970 felt much the same way. The budget of the Theater am Halleschenüfer was reduced in 1970 largely because the theater had the temerity to play *The Mother* and the Berlin Senate was dismayed at the possible incendiary effect of the play.

28. Georg Lukács, "Grundlagen der Scheidung von Epik und Dramatik," in *Aufbau,* Heft 11/12, 1955. A thorough search of the Brecht Archive (1970) has failed to turn up a copy of the essay with Brecht's marginalia. We do, however, know that it would be most unlikely that Brecht would have failed to read this essay by his old enemy. Published in as prominent an East German journal as *Aufbau*, it would have come to Brecht's attention immediately.

29. "Tragödie und grosse Epik erheben... beide den Anspruch auf die Gestaltung der Totalität des Lebensprozesses." Lukács, "Grundlagen," p. 978.

30. "Es fehlt der ganze Lebensumkreis der Beziehung von Eltern und Kindern, es fehlen die materielle Grundlage der Familie, ihr Wachsen, ihr Niedergang usw. Man vergleiche nur dieses Drama mit den grossen Familiengemälden, die in epischer Weise die Problematik der Familie gestalten, mit den *Buddenbrooks* von Thomas Mann, mit dem *Werk der Artamonows* von Gorki. Welche Breite und Fülle hier der realen Lebensumstände der Familie, welche Verallgemeinerung dort auf die rein menschlichmoralischen, willensmässigen, in kollidierende Handlung umsetzbaren Eigenschaften der Menschheit! Ja, man muss die aussergewöhnliche Kunst der dramatischen Verallgemeinerung Shakespeares gerade darin bewundern, dass er die ältere Generation der Familie nur durch Lear und Gloster verkörpert. Hätte er—was ein epischer Dichter unbedingt hätte tun müssen— entweder Lear oder Gloster oder beiden eine Frau mitgeben, so hätte er entweder die Konzentration auf die Kollision abschwächen müssen (wenn der Konflikt mit den Kindern einen Konflikt mit den Eltern herbeigeführt hätte), oder die Darstellung der Frau hätte nur als abschwächendes Echo des Mannes wirken können. Es ist für die verdünnte Luft der dramatischen Verallgemeinerung charakteristisch, dass auf den Zuschauer diese Tragödie notwendig als ein erschütterndes Bild wirkt und etwa die Frage nach den fehlenden Frauen überhaupt nicht auftaucht." Lukács, "Grundlagen," pp. 980-981.

31. Aristotle (in Beckley's translation) has: "The epic, however, differs from tragedy in the length of the composition, and in the metre... But it is the peculiarity of the epic to possess abundantly the power of extending its magnitude, for tragedy is not capable of imitating many actions that are performed at the same time, but that part only which is represented in the scene, and acted by the players."

Aristotle is obviously defining his terms in order to have them fit at least the epics of Homer and the tragedies of Sophocles. Where Aristotle himself, however, does come close to talking about "epic drama" is when he notes: "Now, I call that tragedy an epic system, which consists of many fables." Many plays of Shakespeare would, according to this definition, qualify as "epic systems." Of Brecht's major plays, however, only the *Caucasian Chalk Circle* would seem to fit this description.

32. That is, *both* the closed (Aristotelian or Sophoclean) and the open or panoramic form (as used by Marlowe, Shakespeare, Goethe, and sometimes by Brecht).

33. See note 27 above.

34. Eric Bentley draws our attention to this fact in the preface to his *Seven Plays,* pp. xxx-xxxi.

35. Esslin, *Brecht,* p. 50. Those attending the 1970 Brecht Symposium in Milwaukee experienced much the same phenomenon. Because of a power failure, the didactic play, *The Measures Taken,* performed by Theater X, was moved after opening night out of the theater into the vestibule. The play was then performed in two different very bare locations and with no lighting effects. The effect of the performances held under these conditions was not distinguishable from that of the premiere performance given in the theater with full stage effects. We might remember Aristotle's note in Part VI of the *Poetics:* "For the power of Tragedy, we may be sure, is felt even apart from representation and actors."

Chapter 4

1. The full German text reads: "Da es sich weniger darum handelte, dass sich eine neue Dramaturgie, mehr darum, dass sich eine neue Spielweise an einem antiken Stück versuche, kann die neue Bearbeitung nicht in der üblichen Weise den Theatern zur freien Gestaltung übergeben werden." GW, XVII, 1214.

2. Inasmuch as several productions in this period were done in languages other than German, Brecht's usual role (if he was asked to help with the production at all) was that of consultant—often as thoroughly disgruntled consultant. It is significant that virtually no play done in translation in the exile period was a popular success. In America, though he shuttled steadily back and forth from his California home to New York, he never was able to get established in the American theater capital. It is possible that he might have established himself after the war (*Galileo,* for instance, had some success on Broadway) had he not been driven out of the country by HUAC. For the effect on Brecht of having no theater of his own for many years, see Eisler, *Fragen Sie mehr über Brecht,* p. 234.

3. With the contents of the desk drawer on microfilm, Brecht left the United States immediately after his "cooperative" appearance before HUAC.

4. Beginning in 1968, Joachim Tenschert has edited and published editions of six Berliner Ensemble versions of Brecht's plays.

5. Brecht wrote in his diary: "Ohne das Ausprobieren durch eine Aufführung kann kein Stück fertiggestellt werden." *Materialien-Sezuan,* p. 16.

6. After fifteen years of wandering, Brecht and Weigel knew that their first Berlin production would have to be enough of a success to induce the East Berlin authorities to offer them a theater of their own.

7. GW, XV, 181.

8. One wonders, for instance, why Brecht did not choose a play by Euripides, a man whose pacifist stance is so clear. Surely the iconoclastic Euripides, with his ironic commentaries on the heroes of his contemporaries, is far closer to Brecht than the urbane Sophocles?

9. See *Neher,* p. 208. See also *Materialien-Antigone,* p. 114.

10. The best close study of the relationship of Brecht's text to that of Hölderlin is that of Hans-Joachim Bunge, "Antigone-modell 1948 von Bertolt Brecht und Caspar Neher. Zur Praxis und Theorie des

epischen (dialektischen) Theaters Bertolt Brechts." diss. (Greifswald, 1957). Note in Bunge's title the substitution of dialectic for epic. Bunge was very close to Brecht at the time "dialectic theater" was seriously proposed as a better formulation than "epic theater." See also Peter Witzmann, *Antike Tradition im Werk Bertolt Brechts* (Berlin, 1964), pp. 75-100.

11. See note 1 above.

12. "Beim *Sophokles* bildet die *Antigone-Kreon*-Begebenheit das Nachspiel eines siegreichen Kriegs: Der Tyrann (das ist einfach der Herrscher) rechnet ab mit persönlichen Feinden, die ihm den Sieg erschwert haben, stösst dabei auf einen menschlichen Brauch und erfährt den Zerfall seiner Familie." *Materialien-Antigone*, p. 116.

13. It is possible that Brecht drew this totally pacifistic view of Kreon from a 1917 treatment of the Antigone theme by Walter Hasenclever. For other source materials used by Brecht in his adaptation, see Grimm's brief but excellent analysis in *Brecht und die Weltliteratur,* pp. 38-40.

14. The 1948 prologue demanded that the audience see parallels between the Greece of Antigone and Kreon, and the Berlin of 1945. Later, obviously worried that such specificality might very quickly date the play, Brecht wrote a new prologue. The rest of the play, however, remained substantially unchanged.

15. Friedrich Hölderlin, *Werke,* ausgewählt und mit einem Vorwort versehen von Fritz Usinger (Hamburg, n.d.), p. 429.

16. GW, VI, 2286.

17. "Der Krieg Thebens mit Argos ist realistisch dargestellt." *Materialien-Antigone*, p. 119.

18. "Das Ziel sind die Erzgruben von Argos." ibid.

19. Witzmann, *Antike Tradition,* p. 85.

20. Hat der hinstürzende Flüchtling
Die Dirzäischen Bäche gequert, aufatmend
Sieht er Thebe, die Siebentorige, stehn, da greift
Den vom Blut des Bruders Besprengten Kreon, der hinten
Einpeitscht alle sie in die Schlacht, und zerstückt ihn.
GW, VI, 2280.

21. So fällt jetzt Thebe.
Und fallen soll es, soll's mit mir, und es soll aus sein
Und für die Geier da. So will ich's dann.
GW, VI, 2327.

22. Though later Brecht was to specifically reject Antigone/von Stauffenberg parallels, all his denials are not enough to discount the text of the play itself. In the text the parallels are plain and indisputable.

23. Brecht also rejects attempts to view Antigone as a wholly moral being. Perhaps he was as influenced here by Anouilh's interpretation of her character as by Marxist doctrine. Again Brecht's external argument says one thing and his play another.

24. Euch beweine ich, Lebende
    Was ihr sehen werdet
    Wenn mein Auge schon voll des Staubs ist!
    GW, VI, 2311.

25. Wandte sich um und ging, weiten Schrittes, als führe sie Ihren
        Wächter an.
    GW, VI, 2312.

26. Despite Brecht's comments (see note 22 above), Antigone obviously exits as an extremely sympathetic character. Very little has been done within the text itself to cut off audience sympathy for her.

27. Aber auch die hat einst
    Gegessen vom Brot, das in dunklem Fels
    Gebacken war. ibid.

28. In der Unglück bergenden
    Türme Schatten: sass sie gemach, bis
    Was von des Labdakus Häusern tödlich ausging
    Tödlich zurückkam. ibid.

29. Der grossnamige Sieg ist aber gekommen,
    Der wagenreichen günstig, der Thebe,
    Und nach dem Kriege hier,
    Macht die Vergessenheit aus.
    Hölderlin, *Werke,* p. 427.

30. ibid.

31. GW, VI, 2284.

32. Herr, ein schön Bild von gar Gewaltigem malst du.
    Und, überliefert, wird's der Stadt gefallen
    Wenn klug vermischt mit einem andern: Wägen
    Herauf die Gassen fahrend, voll mit Eignen! ibid.

33. GW, VI, 2289-91.

34. Sophocles, *Three Tragedies,* trans. H.D.F. Kitto (London, 1962), p. 13.

35.   GW, VI, 2289.
36.   The German text reads:
      Wie dem Stier
      Beugt er dem Mitmensch den Nacken, aber der Mitmensch
      Reisst das Gekröse ihm aus.   ibid.
37.   . . . aber die Mauer
      Setzt er ums Eigene, und die Mauer
      Niedergerissen muss sie sein!   ibid.
38.   The Berlin Wall, we should recall, was not built until after Brecht's death. The line did not, therefore, carry then the burden which it does now.
39.   See particularly note 20 above.
40.   Frank Jones, "Tragedy with a Purpose: Bertolt Brecht's *Antigone*," *TDR,* II, no. 1 (November 1957), p. 43.
41.   One wonders, however, whether plays with a specific and limited political purpose do not in fact almost always tend to become melodramas. Inasmuch, therefore, as "epic" is, in the early theory, a synonym for "political," perhaps the epic theater always ran that risk. The productions of Piscator might serve to illustrate the general hypothesis.
42.   GW, XVII, 1214.
43.   GW, XVI, 661-63.
44.   "Wiederrufen wir also, wohl zum allegemeinen Bedauern, unsere Absicht, aus dem Reich des Wohlgefälligen zu emigrieren, und bekunden wir, zu noch allgemeinerem Bedauern, nunmehr die Absicht uns in diesem Reich niederzulassen." ibid.
45.   GW, XVI, 664.
46.   ibid.
47.   "Und die Fabel ist nach Aristoteles—und wir denken da gleich—die Seele des Dramas." ibid. I believe that John Willett might be in error here when he renders "Fabel" as "narrative."
48.   GW, XIV, 698.
49.   Brecht might have found the basic idea for this (if not in Aristotle) in Goethe's *Noten und Abhandlungen zum besseren Verständnis des Westöstlichen Diwans.* In the *Noten* Goethe points out that both Greek drama and French neoclassical drama are mixtures of the three major genres as he understands classical genre division. He is very conscious also, of course, of the epic element in many of his own plays. For a good discussion of Goethe's general awareness of this whole problem area, see Marianne Kesting, "Zur Struktur des

modernen Dramas," in *Episches Theater,* ed. Reinhold Grimm (Köln/Berlin, 1966), pp. 304-307.

50. "Die hellenische Dramaturgie versucht durch gewisse Verfremdungen, besonders durch die Einschnitte für die Chöre, etwas von der Freiheit der Kalkulation zu retten, die Schiller nicht weiss, wie sicherzustellen." GW, XVII, 1213-14.

51. "So wie der Chor in die Sprache Leben bringt, so bringt er Ruhe in die Handlung—aber die schöne und hohe Ruhe, die der Charakter eines edeln Kunstwerkes sein muss. Denn das Gemüt des Zuschauers soll auch in der heftigsten Passion seine Freiheit behalten; es soll kein Raub der Eindrücke sein, sondern sich immer klar und heiter von den Rührungen scheiden, die es erleidet. Was das gemeine Urteil an dem Chor zu tadeln pflegt, dass er die Täuschung aufhebe, dass er die Gewalt der Affekte breche, das gereicht ihm zu seiner höchsten Empfehlung; denn eben diese blinde Gewalt der Affekte ist es, die der wahre Künstler vermeidet, diese Täuschung ist es, die er zu erregen verschmäht. Wenn die Schläge, womit die Tragödie unser Herz trifft, ohne Unterbrechung aufeinanderfolgten, so würde das Leiden über die Tätigkeit siegen. Wir würden uns mit dem Stoffe vermengen und nicht mehr über demselben schweben. Dadurch, dass der Chor die Teile auseinanderhält und zwischen die Passionen mit seiner beruhigenden Betrachtung tritt, gibt er uns unser Freiheit zurück, die im Sturm der Affekte verlorengehen würde." Friedrich Schiller, "Über den Gebrauch des Chors in der Tragödie." First printed as an introduction to Schiller's *Braut von Messina.*

52. For a list of reviews, see *Materialien-Antigone,* pp. 143-147.

Chapter 5

1. W. H. Sokel, "Brecht's Split Characters and his Sense of the Tragic," in *Brecht: A Collection of Critical Essays,* ed. Peter Demetz (Englewood Cliffs, New Jersey, 1962), p. 133.
2. F. N. Mennemeier, "Mother Courage and Her Children," in Demetz, p. 139.
3. It should be noted, however, that although Brecht relied very heavily on many details of the Zürich production, he was fundamentally opposed to the reaction that that production had called forth. The press, almost unanimously, saw Mother Courage as a Niobe figure. In order to try to undercut any such response, for his own production Brecht tried to cut any and all lines in the text that might tend to make Courage a sympathetic figure.
4. Brecht's relationship with the East German government was, to say the very least, an exceedingly complicated affair. Some details of the relationship are updated and corrected in the new paperback German edition of Esslin's book, *Brecht, das Paradox des politischen Dichters* (Munich, 1970).
5. For a list of the major tours of the Ensemble before Brecht's death and immediately thereafter, see the handsome Berliner Ensemble volume, *Theaterarbeit.*
6. Brecht's view (probably derived from either sporting events or from the Elizabethan or Greek stage) was not always rigorously adhered to in Brecht's lifetime. There are now signs that theory on this point has hardened into dogma at the Ensemble.
7. The play was then kept on the program for several hundred performances. However, the Ensemble then and now would (and does) withdraw a play periodically and put it back into rehearsal. The advantages of the method are obvious. The Ensemble avoids thereby the mechanical or zombie quality that afflicts those Broadway productions that are blessed (cursed) with very long runs.
8. Brecht does, however, also draw slightly on the nineteenth-century Swedish work, *Lotta Svärd* by Johan Ludvig Runeberg (in the formulation of one critic, "The Swedish Tennyson"). However, as the same critic notes, the romantic acceptance of the heroism of war on the part of Lotta Svärd is completely alien to Brecht's Courage. For a discussion of the Swedish text and of the genesis of the German play in Sweden, see Roland Huntford, "Brecht in the North," in *Industria International,* Stockholm, 1963. This obscure article contains a great deal of useful information. Of particular interest is the claim of the Swedish actress Naima Wifstrand that the

role of the "dumb" Kattrin was created for Helene Weigel, to enable her to play a major role in a country where she had no command of the language. Unfortunately this ingenious plan was never carried out as Brecht had no opportunity to produce *Mother Courage* in Sweden.

9. Brecht obviously intended here that the audience "piece out" this simple setting with their own thoughts. He says at one time, rather obviously echoing the chorus that introduces Shakespeare's *Henry V:* "Das Publikum gewöhnt sich schnell daran, dass die Dekorationen in schöner Weise das Wesentliche einer Gegend oder eines Raums zeigen. Es ergänzt durch die Phantasie unsere Andeutungen die ja realistischer Natur sind und nicht etwa Symbole oder subjektive Gestaltungen von Malern. Der nackte Rundhorizont der 'Courage'- Aufführung wird dem Publikum zum Himmel, ohne dass es vergisst, im Theater zu sein." ("The audience quickly gets used to elegant settings showing only the essential features of a landscape or a room. Our imagination completes our intimations, which are, after all, of a realistic nature, and not simply the symbols or the subjective creations of a scene painter. The naked circular backdrop that forms the horizon in the *Courage* production becomes the sky to the audience but without their ever forgetting that they are in a theater.") Brecht, GW, XVI, 917. At another point in the same period Brecht writes: "Palm [the Ensemble costumer] weiss, dass historische Treue nicht genügt, den Geist eines Zeitalters heraufzubeschwören. Auch hier muss eine Auswahl und Überhöhung erfolgen, eine Typisierung." ("Palm knows that historical accuracy is not enough to conjure up the spirit of an age. Even here one must select, exaggerate, and typify.") Brecht, GW, XVI, 768.

10. "Nackte, aller Konvention, aller herkömmlichen Moralbegriffe entkleidete Sprache." Hans Mayer, *Bertolt Brecht und die Tradition* (Pfüllingen, 1961), p. 81. For an excellent discussion of Brecht's language in this play as it relates particularly to animal imagery, please see Walter Boeddinghaus's "Bestie Mensch in Brechts *Mutter Courage,"Acta Germanica*, ii, 1968. 81-88.

11. I am reminded particularly of the short tale, "Wenn die Haifische Menschen wären," from the *Geschichten vom Herrn Keuner*, and of Jenny's song from the *Threepenny Opera.*

12. "Weg ist er, wie die Laus unterm Kratzen." Brecht, GW, IV, 1349.

13. "Ich hab hier mein Vertrauen in die Menschheit verloren." ibid.

14. "Die Menschheit schiesst ins Kraut im Frieden. Mit Mensch und Vieh wird herumgesaut, als wärs gar nix." ibid.

15. "Wie viele junge Leut und gute Gäul diese Stadt da vorn hat, weiss kein Mensch, es ist niemals gezählt worden." ibid.

16. The actual model of the wagon was taken over from Teo Otto's magnificent designs for the 1941 production of the play in Zürich. Brecht himself said of the wagon and its obvious symbolic function: "Der Wagen wird sich während der Historie mehrmals ändern. Er wird voller und weniger voll mit Waren behängt, die Blache wird beschmutzter oder reinlicher, die Schrift des Firmenbretts ver-blasster und dann wieder neu gemalt sein, je nach gutem oder schlechtem Geschäftsgang. Nun, zu Beginn ist er voll behängt und frisch bespannt." ("The wagon goes through several changes during the play. There are fewer or more wares hanging from it, the cover becomes cleaner or dirtier, the writing on its business sign fades or is newly painted, all depending on good or bad business. Now, at the beginning, it is loaded down with wares and the wagon has a fresh cover on it.") Brecht, *Schriften,* VI, 61. Volker Klotz sees the wagon as "der stete Handlungsort" ("the unified place of action"), *Bertolt Brecht* (Darmstadt, 1957). I believe that Klotz may mean here (as my translation suggests) that this constitutes a radical renaissance of the "unity of place." Viewed thus, might we not see Courage as carrying her house snail-like upon her back? If the wagon does help to link the individual scenes (supposedly played in different places but actually all before the same backdrop), then we are back to an almost neoclassical rigor in the relation of individual scenes to one another.

      The major thing that these particulars underline is the importance of the turntable stage to Brecht, not only in *Mother Courage,* but in the exile plays in general. The turntable stage is second only to the wagon in drawing the constituent parts of the play together. It is used as symbolically as the wagon when it is frequently turned against Courage's line of "progress" in the play. For one production Brecht insisted on taking a twelve-ton "port-able" revolving stage to Paris for the few performances of the play to be given there. Here, as always, Brecht's pursuit of "simple effects" often involved expenditures beyond the capacity of many a commercial theater.

17. For a complete photographic record of all major scenes in the play in Brecht's production of it, see his *Couragemodell 1949* (Berlin, 1961), and the filmed version of the play.

18.   Ihr Hauptleut, lasst die Trommel ruhen
    Und lasst eur Fussvolk halten an:
    Mutter Courage, die kommt mit Schuhen
    In denens besser laufen kann.
    Mit seinen Läusen und Getieren
    Bagage, Kanone und Gespann —
    Soll es euch in die Schlacht marschieren
    So will es gute Schuhe han.
       Das Frühjahr kommt. Wach auf, du Christ!
       Der Schnee schmilzt weg. Die Toten ruhn.
       Und was noch nicht gestorben ist
       Das macht sich auf die Socken nun.
    Ihr Hauptleut, eure Leut marschieren
    Euch ohne Wurst nicht in den Tod.
    Lasst die Courage sie erst kurieren
    Mit Wein von Leibs- und Geistesnot.
    Kanonen auf die leeren Mägen
    Ihr Hauptleut, das ist nicht gesund.
    Doch sind sie satt, habt meinen Segen
    Und führt sie in den Höllenschlund.
    Brecht, GW, IV, 1350-51. Additional verses of the song are scattered throughout the play and form yet another leitmotif linking the "episodes" together. For further verses see scenes 7, 8 and 12.
       To experience the enormous emotional impact of this and the other songs of *Mother Courage,* listen to Ernst Busch and Helene Weigel on Eterna 110002-5. Of particular note is Weigel's rendition of the lullaby to the dead Kattrin.

19.   See the complete photographic record of this in the *Couragemodell.*

20.   "Ich seh, die Burschen sind wie die Birken gewachsen, runde Brustkästen, stämmige Haxen: warum drückt sich *das* [my italics] vom Heeresdienst, möcht ich wissen?" Brecht, GW, IV, 1354.

21.   "Ihr solltet lieber Jakob Ochs und Esau Ochs heissen, weil ihr doch den Wagen zieht. Aus dem Gespann kommt ihr wohl nie heraus." ibid.

22.   Specific and non-ironic references to Christ have been noted in this play by Albrecht Schöne, "Bertolt Brecht, Theatertheorie und dramatische Dichtung," in *Euphorion* (1958), Heft 3, pp. 272-292. Schöne sees the song of the crucified Christ (pp. 118-119 in the *Stücke*) as a direct and deliberate connection of the death of Christ with that of Schweizerkäs. This reinforces, of course, the basic image of the cross that dominated the play in Brecht's production.

23. Brecht uses fortune-telling again and in exactly the same way in his Schweyk where the owner of the inn, "The Goblet," predicts death for some SS men.

24. For the Brecht connoisseur this particular act invokes Brecht's interest in Shakespeare. Brecht contemplated at one time doing a production of *Lear* in which the king would physically tear up a map of England. *Schriften*, III, 186. For all his interest in Shakespeare, however, Brecht never did complete a Shakespearean production of his own. The famous Berliner Ensemble production of *Coriolan* was only completed after Brecht's death.

25. "Eilif, Schweizerkäs und Kattrin, so möchten wir alle zerrissen werden, wenn wir uns in 'n Krieg zu tief einlassen täten." Brecht, GW, IV, 1356.

26. "Du bist selber ein Kreuz." ibid.

27. Please see note 18 above.

28. Das Frühjahr kommt. Wach auf, du Christ!
Der Schnee schmilzt weg. Die Toten ruhn.
Und was noch nicht gestorben ist
Das macht sich auf die Socken nun.
Brecht, GW, IV, 1438.

29. A separate paper would be needed to describe fully the complex use of songs in *Mother Courage*. It is clear that they do not interrupt or fragment the story line. As Mennemeier has pointed out (Demetz, p.141), "The Song of the Wise and Good," taken over largely from the *Threepenny Opera* where it did in fact interrupt the action, occupies a much more organic position in *Mother Courage*. Joachim Müller in his essay, "Dramatisches und episches Theater" (in Grimm's *Episches Theater*), makes a similar point and notes his indebtedness to similar studies of this point by Hans Mayer and Volker Klotz. The distinguished Polish critic Andrzej Wirth also agrees with this point of view in his fine essay, "Die Funktion des Songs in *Mutter Courage und ihre Kinder*," first printed in *Sinn und Form II*. See also in this connection Eric Bentley's articles, "Epic Theater is Lyric Theater," in *The German Theater Today*, ed. Leroy R. Shaw (University of Texas Press, 1963), and "Brecht und der 'Zonk,' " in *Listen* (March-April 1964). In the latter article, Bentley goes so far as to maintain (only somewhat tongue in cheek) that it is the plays that interrupt the songs in Brecht's work.

30. I must point out that though these scenes can be removed without interrupting the play's basic plot line, they do contribute a great deal to character development.

31. Her bourgeois background is described in the vaguest terms later in the play in the "Song of the Great Capitulation." We do not know what got either Mother Courage or anyone else involved in the war in the first place. The play gives no concrete background on this whatsoever. Mennemeier remarks of this lack of background and its implications: "It seems to be not without importance that the much-maligned instigators of the catastrophe in the play never become dramatically tangible themselves. . ." In Demetz, pp. 140-141.

32. It is quite clear that Brecht does not give us "ein volles Menschen-leben" as Reinhold Grimm has claimed in his *Strukturen*, p. 24.

33. Could we add this play (and above all *Galileo*) to the following list given by Friedrich Spielhagen in his *Neue Beiträge zur Theorie und Technik der Epik und Dramatik*, Leipzig, 1898: "Überall in diesen Dramen: in *Rosmersholm, Wildente, Frau von Meere* u.s.w. eine lange Vorgeschichte, die wir durchaus kennen müssen, sollen uns diese höchst komplizierten Menschen in den höchst komplizierten Verwickelungen, in welchen der Dichter sie uns vorführt klar werden." ("Everywhere in these dramas: in *Rosmersholm, The Wild Duck, Woman from the Sea*, etc. there is a long previous history which we have to know completely if these highly complicated people in their highly complicated entanglements, in which the author presents them to us, are to become clear to us.") p. 234.

34. Angelika Hurwicz, a rather stocky and far from pretty actress, was later to play Grusche in *The Caucasian Chalk Circle*.

35. Besides playing most of Brecht's female leads (many of which were written specifically for her) Weigel was married to Brecht and managed the fortunes of the Berliner Ensemble until her death in 1971.

36. Ernst Busch was Brecht's favorite male lead and was best known in Germany as a powerful singer of political cabaret songs.

37. See note 3 above. In each rewriting of the play Brecht had attempted to make Courage less "sympatisch," less of a Niobe figure. In an earlier version of scene 5 for instance, Mother Courage herself donates and tears up some officers' shirts for use as bandages. Also, in earlier versions, she urges Kattrin (in the same scene) to rescue an orphaned baby. Both these humanistic touches are deliberately cut in the last version.

38. "Unwillkürlich krampft sich das Herz des Zuschauers zusammen, wenn er sieht, wie hoffnungslos der Planwagen gealtert und heruntergekommen ist und in welche furchtbare Ruine sich die einst so energische, aktive und nicht auf den Kopf gefallene Frau

verwandelt hat, die trotzdem die Ursachen der furchtbaren Not, die über sie hereingebrochen ist, nicht begreift: Die Szene wird zu einem schrecklichen Symbol für das tragische Schicksal eines ganzen Volkes." Boris Sachawa, "Stärken und Schwächen des Brecht-Theater," in *Kunst und Literatur* (5), 1957, p. 1369.

39. George Steiner, *The Death of Tragedy* (New York, 1961), p. 348.

40. "Eine der bühnenwirksamsten Szenen Brechts findet sich im 11. Bild der *Mutter Courage,* wo die stumme Kattrin auf dem Dach der Bauernhütte die Trommel schlägt, um die Kinder der schlafenden Stadt Halle vor einem nächtlichen Überfall zu retten–bis die Kugelbüchse sie trifft und ihre letzten Schläge abgelöst werden von den Kanonen der erwachenden Verteidiger. Wenn irgendwo, dann wird Brechts Verfremdungstendenz hier selbst verfremdet, wird die kritische Distanzhaltung des rauchend beobachtenden Theaterbesucher hier überwältigt." Schöne, p. 290.

41. Eric Bentley, ed., *Seven Plays by Bertolt Brecht* (New York, 1961).

42. "Zuschauer mögen sich mit der stummen Kattrin in dieser Szene identifizieren; sie mögen sich einfühlen in dieses Wesen und freudig spüren, dass in ihnen selbst solche Kräfte vorhanden sind." *Schriften,* VI, 131.

43. Steiner, *Death of Tragedy,* pp. 353-354.

44. *Schriften,* VI, 161. "Der Erfolg des Stücks, das heisst der Eindruck, den das Stück machte, war zweifellos gross. Leute zeigten auf der Strasse auf die Weigel und sagten: 'Die Courage!' Aber ich glaube nicht und glaubte damals nicht, dass Berlin–und all andern Städte, die das Stück sahen–das Stück begriffen." How painful must have been this identification of Weigel with the role of Mother Courage to the theorist Brecht! That she "became" (in a direct Stanislavskian sense) the role is attested to by a comment of the Hollywood director Wanamaker. He notes that the performance was "indistinguishable from that of a superb Stanislavsky trained actress." Cited in Willett, *Eight Aspects,* p. 185.

45. "Es lohnt sich, auf den "unmittelbaren Eindruck" des anscheinend einmaligen, aktualen Schreckensvorgangs zu verzichten, *um tiefere Schreckensstrata zu erreichen* wo das oftmalige, immer wiederkehrende Unglück die Menschen schon zu einer Zeremonisierung der Abwehrgebärden gezwungen hat–die ihnen freilich doch niemals die aktuale Angst ersparen kann. Sie muss in der Darstellung die Zeremonie durchdringen." *Schriften,* VI, 133-134. My italics.

46. "Es ist nicht der Fall—wiewohl es mitunter vorgebracht wurde,—dass episches Theater, das übrigens—wie ebenfalls mitunter vorgebracht— nicht etwa einfach undramatisches Theater ist, den Kampfruf 'hie Vernunft—hie Emotion' (Gefühl) erschallen lässt. Es verzichtet in keiner Weise auf Emotionen. Schon gar nicht auf das Gerechtigkeits- gefühl, den Freiheitsdrang und den gerechten Zorn: es verzichtet so wenig darauf, dass es sich sogar nicht auf ihr Vorhandensein verlässt, sondern sie zu verstärken oder zu schaffen sucht. Die 'kritische Haltung,' in die es sein Publikum zu bringen trachtet, kann ihm nicht leidenschaftlich genug sein." *Schriften,* GW, XVII, 1144. Statement made (very defensively) in a conversation with the East German dramatist Friedrich Wolf.

47. "Das Wesentliche epischen Theater ist es vielleicht, dass es nicht so sehr an das Gefühl sondern mehr an die Ratio des Zuschauers appelliert, nicht miterleben soll der Zuschauer, sondern sich auseinandersetzen." GW, XV, 132.

48. "Dabei wäre es ganz und gar unrichtig, diesem Theater das Gefühl absprechen zu wollen." ibid.

49. The about face is as complete and as devious as that of Goethe with reference to Shakespeare. Compare the Goethe of the "Rede zum Shakespeare-Tag," with the older man who wrote "Shakespeare und kein Ende."

50. The phrase is the subtitle of Brecht's play.

51. Reinhold Grimm, Bertolt Brecht: *Die Struktur seines Werkes* (Nürnberg, 1959), p. 81. For an excellent discussion of this whole topic area, see the whole of Chapter IX of this book. See also Kaspar Königshof's article, "Über den Einfluss des Epischen in der Dramatik," *Sinn und Form* (7), 1955, 578-591. Despite its xeno- phobic conclusion, the article makes some good points.

52. Bentley in *Seven Plays,* p. xlv, notes: "As for *Mother Courage,* it might well have been suggested by the first part of the *Wallenstein* trilogy." It is a commonplace of criticism that Schiller's *Wallenstein* is modelled on Shakespeare's panoramic history plays. To my knowledge, Bentley was one of the first (1946) to note the Brecht-Shakespeare connection and observed in an article, "What is Epic Theatre?" *Accent,* VI, No. 2 (Winter, 1946), p. 112: "The Greeks and the French use long Epic narrations. Shakespeare's open structure is copied by all his imitators from Goethe to Hugo. Brecht's Epic procedure is this open structure."

53. Reinhold Grimm in "Vom Novum Organum zum Kleinen Organon," in *Das Ärgernis Brecht,* ed. Willy Jäggi and Hans Ösch, p. 52, writes: "Kurzum: die verfremdende Dramenstruktur ist nichts anderes als die sogenannte 'offene' Form des Dramas, die seit Jahrhunderten gleich berechtigt neben dem 'geschlossenen,' klassisch-klassizistischen Kunstdrama existiert—ob die Ästhetik das nun wahrhaben will oder nicht." ("In short, the 'alienating' dramatic construct is nothing else but the so-called 'open' classic or classical art drama. This is so whether Aesthetics wishes to grant it or not.") See also note 51 above.

54. Volker Klotz, *Bertolt Brecht,* p. 57 has: "Brecht knüpft in seinem dramatischen Aufbau an die 'offene' Form der Elisabethaner, der Stürmer und Dränger, Grabbes und Büchners an." ("In the way in which he builds his dramas, Brecht is joined with the 'open' form of the Elizabethans, the dramatists of the Storm and Stress movement, and with the work of Grabbe and of Büchner.")

55. R.B. Parker notes: "That Elizabethan plays, and particularly Shakespeare's history plays, had a great influence on 'epic' drama is by now a commonplace of Brecht criticism; but no one seems to have worked out exactly how close the two dramaturgies are." Comment made in "Dramaturgy in Shakespeare and Brecht," *University of Toronto Quarterly,* XXXII (1963), p. 229.

56. Max Spalter, *Brecht's Tradition* (Baltimore, 1967). Essentially a pedestrian and incomplete restatement of the points made by Klotz in 1957. See note 43 above. See my review of the book in *MLJ,* LIII, No. 4 (April 1969), pp. 280-81.

57. "Die Bezeichnung *Chronik* entspricht gattungsmässig etwa der Bezeichnung *History* in der elisabethanischen Dramatik." GW, XVII, 1143.

58. See note 7 above.

59. "Formal bedeutet ihm heute das epische Element, was es jedem grossen Dramatiker bedeutet hat: ein rhythmisches Prinzip. *Mutter Courage* enthält nicht mehr epische Bestandteile als eine Shakespearesche Historie." Paul Rilla, *Essays* (Berlin, 1955), p. 440.

60. Echoing Brecht, Grimm notes that "eine solche Welt nicht mehr ins alte Drama passt." Reinhold Grimm, *Strukturen: Essays zur deutschen Literatur* (Göttingen, 1963), p. 25.

61. "Kurzum: die verfremdende Dramenstruktur ist nichts anderes als die sogenannte 'offene' Form des Dramas. . ." Reinhold Grimm, "Vom Novum Organum," in *Das Ärgernis Brecht,* p. 52.

62. Brecht himself was obviously aware of the connection. See footnote 47, Chapter 1 above.

Chapter 6

1. "So witzig und lebendig der Dialog in dem tyrannisierten Prag geführt wird, so wenig ist doch aus der Szenenfolge ein bleibendes Stück geworden." Carl Niessen, *Brecht auf der Bühne* (Cologne, 1959), p. 52.

2. Ernst Josef Aufricht's response to the play is typical. Aufricht (who also spent the war years in exile, some of them in America) claims that he asked Brecht and Weill to do *Schweyk* as a musical for Broadway. Because Aufricht-Brecht-Weill had been the winning combination for the *Threepenny Opera,* Aufricht had very little trouble lining up backing for the production. However, when Brecht delivered the finished play Aufricht found it unacceptable. He noted: "Brecht hatte seitenlang Dialoge aus den Büchern von Schwejk abgeschrieben. . ." ("Brecht had taken pages of dialogue at a time from the Schweyk volumes. . .") *Erzähle damit du dein Recht erweist* (Berlin, 1966), p. 256. Aufricht also suggests that Kurt Weill concurred with this negative judgment and refused to write the music for the piece. The whole project fell through after this and another work of Brecht's went into the desk drawer. Despite the initial response to the play (a response that still pervades most Brecht criticism), there has been some positive writing on the play. See Pavel Petr, *Haseks "Schwejk" in Deutschland* (Berlin, 1963); Vladimir Rus, "Brecht's *Schweyk im zweiten Weltkrieg* and Hasek's *Good Soldier Schweik,*" diss. New York University, 1963; Hans Mayer, *Bertolt Brecht und die Tradition* (Munich, 1965); Harold Lenz, "Idee und Bild des Friedens im Bertolt Brecht," in *Der Friede, Idee und Verwirklichung: Festschrift für Adolf Leschnitzer* (Heidelberg, 1961), pp. 281-289; Daniel Frey, "Études brechtiennes Schweyk," in *Études de Lettres* (University of Lausanne), IX (1966), 125-148, where Frey specifically connects the kindness of the "idiot" Schweyk with the humanity of Brecht's "dumb" Kattrin; and John Fuegi with Charles Hoffmann, "Brecht, Schweyk, and Commune-ism," in the *Festschrift für Detlev W. Schumann* (Munich, 1970), pp. 337-349. See also Brecht's diary notes on the play in *Spectaculum III* (1960). Alternate endings to the play and other variants on the published text are available in BBA 512 and BBA 1986.

3. Brecht's diary entry for June 24, 1943 reads: "im grossen den *schweyk* beendet. ein gegenstück zur mutter courage." "Tage-

buchnotizen zum Schweyk," in *Spectaculum III*, p. 337. As is usual with Brecht in his diaries and in his private correspondence, he writes or types almost everything in lower case letters.

4. See notes 2 and 3 above.

5. Brecht's actual contribution to the "Piscator" production is somewhat in doubt. In *Das politische Theater*, Piscator deals with the play as though it were definitely put together by a team of writers and other artists (himself and Brecht among them). Brecht himself, however, claimed (GW, XVI, 598) to have written the whole thing. Yet Sternberg speaks of going with Brecht to see "Piscator's Schwejk." *Der Dichter und die Ratio* (Göttingen, 1963), p. 13. Sternberg also notes that at exactly this time Brecht came to him with a plan for a very different *Schweik* than the version then playing on Piscator's stage.

6. See, for instance, Martin Esslin, *Brecht, The Man and His Work* (U.S. paperback edition of *Brecht, A Choice of Evils*), p. 47 et passim.

7. For a detailed description of the scope and thrust of Piscator's work in this period (the late 1920s), see either Piscator's *Das politische Theater,* or John Gassner's "Varieties of Epic Theater in Modern Drama," *Comparative Literature Studies,* Special Advance Issue, June, 1963. The text of the 1927-28 Piscator production of *Schwejk* is available in its entirety and with notes on the various "endings" tried and rejected by Piscator in BBA 511.

8. Almost all of Piscator's "plays" of this period were not only political in content, they openly demanded revolution.

9. As noted above (note 5), opinions vary on the part played by Brecht in preparing the Piscator text.

10. The Viennese film version of the original novel is largely apolitical and retains the "popular" elements in Hasek's novel that Piscator did not want to include.

11. "Teile des Romanes auf die Bühne zu bringen," Gasbarra in *Das politische Theater,* p. 184.

12. Gassner, "Varieties of Epic Theater," p. 27.

13. ibid.

14. ibid.

15. See Brecht, GW, XVI, 596-598, and GW, XVI, 283-285.

16. "Das Theater des Piscator besorgte den Anschauungsunterricht. Hier konnte man sehen, wie die Revolution von 18 gescheitert war, wie die Kämpfe um Märkte und Rohstoffe Kriege hervorriefen, wie die Kriege vermittels unwilliger Völker geführt wurden, wie siegreiche Revolutionen gemacht wurden." GW, XVI, 595.

17. "Überblickt man die Stoffe der erzählenden und vorführenden Künste, so erblickt man die grossen Gegenstände Krieg, Geld, Öl, Eisenbahnen, Parlament, Lohnarbeit, Boden verhältnismässig selten, meist als dekorativen Hintergrund oder Anlass von Meditationen." *Schriften zum Theater,* III, 132.

18. See for instance Piscator's attack on Brecht's play, *Trommeln in der Nacht (Drums in the Night)* as given in Brecht's *Schriften zum Theater,* II, 292-317. Piscator's basic objection to the play (an objection which can be extended to almost all of Brecht's plays) is that Brecht has simply written a drama of the individual (Kragler) rather than a documentary on why a revolution failed. Piscator suggested a massive rewriting job that would have utilized tables of statistics and the liberal use of documentary film. Brecht then, as he would always do later, rejected the suggestion of extending the play in this way. No play of Brecht is really dependent on the use of film. Years later in fact he would refer to film (previously seen as virtually indispensable for treating "the big subjects" on the stage of the "epic theater") as a "betriebsfremder Mittel." In his later years Brecht seems to have realized how substantially he had retreated from a broad treatment of the "big subjects." In his notes on *Arturo Ui* for instance he notes ruefully that he had found it technically impossible to present the whole nexus of events that brought Hitler to power. The only way he saw to manage subjects of this complexity was to resort to the ancient device of the highly schematized parable. See *Schriften zum Theater,* IV, 176-177. Technically, Brecht consistently retreated from the frankly revolutionary (aesthetic and political), genuinely "epic" productions of Piscator.

19. Sternberg, pp. 13-14.

20. ibid.

21. "Unter dem riesigen Zimmer, in dem Ludendorff an seinen Karten regiert und die deutschen Divisionen hin- und herschiebt, befindet sich ein grosser kellerartiger Raum, der mit Soldaten gefüllt ist; und wenn man näher hinsieht, ähneln sie alle in irgendeiner Form dem Schweyk. Und die Schweyks werden in Bewegung gesetzt. Sie wehren sich nicht direkt, aber sie kommen nicht oder nicht rechtzeitig an. Es gibt Zwischenfälle. Immer mehr und immer vielseitigere Zwischenfälle, die sie hindern; sie brauchen mehr Zeit, sie verschwinden. Es gibt nirgendwo einen aktiven Widerstand; es gibt nicht einmal im Gespräch eine Opposition, die direkt gegen den

Krieg gerichtet wäre: sie folgen allen Befehlen, sie respektieren ihre Vorgesetzten, sie setzen sich, wenn sie die Marschorder bekommen, in Bewegung. Aber niemals erreichen sie in der Zeit, die Ludendorff oben an der Karte bestimmt, ihren Bestimmungsort, und niemals erreichen sie ihn vollzählig." Sternberg, p. 14. One of the crucial differences in the later treatment will be the reduction of the "epic" number of soldiers, all in some way resembling Schweyk, to the single figure of Schweyk himself. Brecht's whole thesis (developed in the play) that it is the Schweyks (collectively) who defeated Hitler is predicated on there being a great number of little men all consciously resisting. In fact, historically, it would seem far more likely that most of the little men did actually reach Stalingrad and did their damndest to take the city. What Brecht does in his play is to retain the dream of hordes of Schweyks from the sketch given by Sternberg above and assumes that this dream then pervades the play itself. In fact it does not. The "epic" dream has been replaced by another "drama of the individual." In the process, a finely wrought work of art has displaced a political commentary of far grander proportions.

22. See, for instance, Esslin, *Brecht, The Man and His Work*, p. 308.
23. Esslin, p. 35.
24. ibid.
25. Jaroslav Hašek, *Osudy dobrého vojáka Švejka*, (Prague, 1953), II, 74-75. It is interesting to note that the novel still is almost instantly sold out in Czechoslovakia whenever the authorities allow a new edition to be printed. When I was in Prague in 1966 no bookstore in the whole city could sell me a copy. Clearly the original Schweik is not considered a good model to be followed in a Socialist state. Note also that the one kind act in the original Czech novel is not carried over to the "Piscator" version. Piscator was, in fact, very hostile to the Schweik figure in many ways and presented him largely as a negative example. This was one of the reasons why the collective had such difficulty in finding a suitable ending for their presentation. Hasek's Schweik was, as they saw, completely indestructible, but the far-left team of collaborators felt that he ought to be killed off because of his asocial cooperation with what (in Marxist terms) was clearly his class enemy. In one ending, therefore, the team had Schweik blown up by a hand grenade. Somehow, however, this was not really satisfactory as an ending and another scene was written (and played once) in which Schweik, after being blown up, appears

with other victims of the war (mangled beyond description and recognition) before the throne of God. Here Schweik continues his fight with the "authorities of the higher regions" (Piscator, p. 187). So terrible was the scene in production that Piscator felt that it overburdened the play. The idea of the scene was to live on, however, in the scene of the cripples at the coronation in *The Threepenny Opera* the same year and in the final scene of Brecht's 1943 adaptation.

26. "Der Vojta is gemein zu die Dienstmädchen, sie is schon die dritte seit Lichtmess und will schon weg, her ich, weil die Nachbarn sie triezen, weil sie bei einem Herrn is, wo ein Quisling is. Da is es ihr gleich, wenn sie ohne Hund heimkommt, sie muss nur nix dafir können." GW, V, 1947.

27. "Melde gehorsamst, ich kann alles aufklärn. Das Packerl gehert niemand hier. Ich weiss es, weil ich es selber hinlegt hab." ibid., 1964.

28. "Der kommt nicht lebend davon." ibid.

29. "Meinen besten Freund hab ich so hineingerissn, dass er mir womeglich heit nacht erschossen wird, wenn nicht, kann er von Glick sagn, und es passiert ihm morgen frih." ibid.

30. "Gestern Nacht von N.Y. zurück, erzähle Steff einiges von dem Schweyk-plan. Er sagt sogleich, der original schweyk wurde sich um balouns schwierigkeiten kaum kümmern, ihm eher zum eintritt in die deutsche armee zuraten. . ." *Spectaculum III,* p. 337.

31. "Jedoch beschliesse ich auf der stelle, diese unpolitische haltung schweyks widerspruchlich in die kleine fabel (RETTUNG DES FRESSERS BALOUN) einzubauen." ibid.

32. Niessen, p. 52.

33. "Das Zentrum des Bühnenbaus bildet die Wirtschaft 'Zum Kelch' in Prag. . . Im dritten Akt erscheint dem Schweyk in Gedanken und Traum nur noch ein Teil des 'Kelch,' sein Stammtisch. Die Anabasis dieses Aktes bewegt sich im Kreis um den 'Kelch' Rest. . ." GW, V, 1995.

34. "Sie ist das Wunschbild des armen kleinen Menschen, dem schon in der *Dreigroschenopers* Brecht das Motto dichtete: 'Erst kommt das Fressen, dann die Moral.' " Lenz, p. 286.

35. In contrast, in Hasek's novel Schweik looks forward to the end of the war and the fights he will get involved in at the inn. In Hasek, it should be remembered, the inn is nowhere near as important in terms of plot or of metaphysics as it is in Brecht.

36. The relationship of these sentiments to the other major plays of the same period is too obvious to be missed. Clearest of all, of course, are the echoes of Galileo and Mother Courage. Both these characters feel that in a good world heroism would not be needed.

37. Brecht himself called for the use of puppets in the production. Almost certainly the original idea, however, stems from the "Piscator" *Schweyk*. Felix Gasbarra notes in his new edition of Piscator's *Das politische Theater* (p. 184), that Piscator toyed for a long while with the idea of having several figures in the 1927-28 production appear as marionettes or puppets.

38. Alternate endings to *Schweyk* (the Hasek novel and the Piscator production, of course, remained essentially unfinished), are available in BBA 512.

39. "Da haben Sie Ihr Pilsner. . . Hier ist keine Politik. Ich bin Gewerbetreibende, wenn jemand kommt und sich ein Bier bestellt, schenk ichs ihm ein, aber damit hörts auf." GW, V, 1917.

40. Komm und setz dich, lieber Gast
Setz dich uns zu Tische . . .

. . . .
Referenzen brauchst du nicht
Ehre bringt nur Schaden
Hast eine Nase im Gesicht
Und wirst schon geladen.

Sollst ein bissel freundlich sein
Witz und Auftrumpf brauchst du kein'
Iss dein' Käs und trink dein Bier
Und du bist willkommen hier
Und die 80 Heller.

Einmal schaun wir früh hinaus
Obs gut Wetter werde
Und da wurd ein gastlich Haus
Aus der Menschenerde.

Jeder wird als Mensch gesehn
Keinen wird man übergehn
Ham ein Dach gegn Schnee und Wind
Weil wir arg verfroren sind
Auch mit 80 Heller!
GW, V, 1987-88. Aptly, the song is first sung as Schweyk is in danger of dying from exposure in the snows of Russia. He is

awakened by the song as it comes to him in his dreams. This helps to underscore the fairylike quality of the song's sentiments with its sudden switch: "one day the world was changed." No explanation is given as to how this came about.

41. Am Grunde der Moldau wandern die Steine
    Es liegen drei Kaiser begraben in Prag.
    Das Grosse bleibt gross nicht und klein nicht das Kleine.
    Die Nacht hat zwölf Stunden, dann kommt schon der Tag.

    Es wechseln die Zeiten. Die riesigen Pläne
    Der Mächtigen kommen am Ende zum Halt.
    Und gehn sie einher auch wie blütige Hähne
    Es wechseln die Zeiten, da hilft kein Gewalt.
    Brecht, GW, V, 1968. The composition of this song gave Brecht considerable trouble. He notes in his diary: "es fehlt noch das moldaulied. merkwürdigerweise kann ich es nicht schreiben." ("The 'Moldau Song' still has to be completed. remarkably, I can't write it.") *Spectaculum III*, p. 338. Perhaps Brecht realized how fatalistic the song really is. Certainly his friend Eisler saw this when he came to compose the Schweyk music. See the special Hanns Eisler issue of *Sinn und Form* (p. 272) for Eisler's views on this song.

42. "Der Krieg dauert nicht ewig, so wenig wie der Friedn. . ." GW, V, 1990.

43. *Pauken und Trompeten (Drums and Trumpets)* is an adaptation of Farquhar's, *The Recruiting Officer*. Actually, however, it is not at all certain that these later plays were really written by Brecht.

44. ". . . Ich bin ein Schwein, und das Schwein geht heim." GW, I, 123.

45. Schweyk says of his own behavior toward Brettschneider: "In solchen Zeiten muss man sich unterwerfen. Es ist Übungssache. Ich hab ihm die Hand geleckt." ("In such times one must subjugate oneself. It's all a matter of practice. I licked his hand.") GW, V, 1938.

46. "Verlangens nicht zu viel von sich. Es ist schon viel, wenn man überhaupt da is heutzutag. Da is man leicht so bescheftigt mit Ieberleben, dass man zu nix anderm kommt." ibid., 145. Here, as elsewhere, I have not attempted in the text to translate dialect forms.

47. "Wenn du im Kreig ieberleben willst, halt dich eng an die andern und das Iebliche, keine Extratouren, sondern kuschn, solang bis du beissen kannst." ibid., 1990.

48. "Ich sag: mir sin mit schuld." GW, V, 1945.
49. See note 21 above. The ways in which Schweyk does in fact hinder the Nazi war effort are actually minor. Surely Schweyk considerably overstates his own role in Hitler's defeat when he responds to Hitler's claim that it is "forces of nature" that are responsible for his defeat: "Ja, ich her, der Winter und der Bolschewik." We can only agree with seeing Schweyk as a "force of nature" if we are willing to generalize completely from him and see him as the embodiment of all "little men" pressed unwillingly into the service of the mighty. However, one ideological difficulty with this point of view is that there should then be Schweyks in the Soviet forces also. Unless, of course, we can believe that Schweyks and Socialism cannot co-exist. If there are no Schweyks in the Soviet forces, then what future does the character have in the Soviet state? If there are Schweyks then they could as easily bring about the defeat of the Soviets as the Czech Schweyk can defeat Hitler. Actually Schweyk is far too fully developed as an individual character for us to believe that either army is made up of similar figures. He is not, therefore, "a force of nature," and his contribution as an individual was so statistically minor that it cannot be placed on the same level as the Russian winter and the entire Bolshevik fighting force. This extension of Schweyk by Brecht is another example in the play of wishful thinking.
50. That Schweyk is aware of his guilt is made even plainer in the unpublished versions of the text.
51. See, however, notes 49 and 50 above.
52. Schweyk would "nicht aktiv an einer kommenden sozialistischen Revolution teilnehmen." Petr, p. 168.
53. Frederic Ewen, *Bertolt Brecht: His Life, His Art, and His Times* (New York, 1967); Dieter Schmidt, *"Baal" und der junge Brecht* (Stuttgart, 1966).
54. Lenz, Mayer, and Ralph Ley have drawn this specific parallel. See Mayer's chapter, "Brecht und die Humanität," in his *Anmerkungen zu Brecht;* Ralph Ley, "The Marxist Ethos of Bertolt Brecht and its Relation to Existentialism," diss. Rutgers, 1963; and the Lenz article mentioned above in note 2. Each writer (but particulary Mayer) recognizes the special nature of Brecht's humanism. It is from Mayer that I draw the formulation, "shabby" or "grubby" humanism, used in the title of this chapter.
55. *Three Who Made a Revolution* (New York, 1964), p. 35.

56. Sternberg, p. 12.
57. "man kann nicht sagen: in dem arbeiterstaat russland herrscht die freiheit. aber man kann sagen: dort herrscht die befreiung." BBA 73/03.

Chapter 7

1. Ronald Gray, *Bertolt Brecht* (New York, 1961), p. 76.
2. Karl Heinz Schmidt, "Zur Gestaltung antagonistischer Konflikte bei Brecht und Kaiser," in *Materialien zu Brechts "Der Gute Mensch von Sezuan,"* ed. Werner Hecht (Frankfurt am Main, 1968), p. 111: "Im Stück wird der Grundkonflikt auf epische Weise durch verschiedene Entwicklungsetappen und Ebenen geführt." Startlingly enough, Schmidt argues in this same essay for a view of Brecht as a "Socialist Realist."
3. For a highly tendentious examination of Brecht's moral views, see Bjørn Ekmann, *Gesellschaft und Gewissen: die sozialen und moralischen Anschauungen Bertolt Brechts und ihre Bedeutung für seine Dichtung* (Copenhagen, 1969).
4. See particularly Peachum in *The Threepenny Opera* and also Brecht's *Me Ti: The Book of Changes* (or, an alternate translation, "The Book of Ins and Outs"), and *The Keuner Stories.*
5. E. Hauptmann has told me that she believes Brecht must have seen *Christophe Colombe* performed in Berlin.
6. For an excellent discussion of the striking parallels between the work of Brecht and Claudel in this period, see the 1968 revised edition of Willett, *Eight Aspects,* p. 117.
7. See Eisenstein's *Film Form and Film Sense,* ed. and trans. Jay Leyda (New York, 1957). It is through his work with both Meyerhold and Tretiakov that Eisenstein first decides to move from the theater to the cinema. See particularly the effect on Eisenstein of Japanese art as he discusses the subject in Chapter Two of *Film Form.* A clear borrowing from the Kabuki in Eisenstein's work is the "Fiery Furnace" playlet in his film, *Ivan the Terrible.*
8. Tretiakov was murdered in 1937 after having been "tried" on a trumped-up charge of being a Japanese spy. He and Meyerhold (murdered in February, 1940) were partially rehabilitated in 1967-68 with the reappearance (in small editions) of some of the plays of Tretiakov and some of the theoretical writings of Meyerhold. In the preface to the handsome Soviet volume, *Meetings with Meyerhold* (a book of reminiscences by friends and acquaintances), published in Moscow in 1967, it is frankly admitted that Meyerhold was illegally arrested and executed. It is almost impossible to overestimate the importance of the lives and the deaths of these two men to Bertolt Brecht. Tretiakov was, for several years, Brecht's main supporter and only translator in Russia. In turn, Brecht did an adaptation of Tretiakov's play, *I Want a Child,* a play

denounced by Stalin's henchman Zhdanov in the 1930s as a "formalist aberration." It is probably Brecht's identification with Meyerhold and Tretiakov and his very realistic fear of sharing their fate that was the major factor in his decision not to spend the war years in the Soviet Union. Upon hearing the news of Tretiakov's execution, Brecht wrote:

> My teacher
> The great, the friendly
> Has been shot, by a people's court condemned.
> As a spy. His name is damned.
> His books are destroyed. Conversation concerning him
> Is made suspect and is silenced.
> What if he is innocent?

Title of the German original, "Ist das Volk unfehlbar?" Poem now available in GW, IX, 741-743. For unpublished materials on this topic please see BBA 477 and BBA 1396.

9. Eugene Vakhtangov is a curious case in the history of Soviet attacks on so-called "Formalism" in the arts. Perhaps because he had the good sense to die in 1922, well before Zhdanov was established as watchdog for the arts, Vakhtangov's work has remained acceptable in the Soviet Union all through even the bleakest periods of socialist realism. Vakhtangov has become, therefore, for Soviet artists and even for Brecht, a kind of stalking horse. For years, Soviet artists who wanted to explore other paths than those of the Moscow Art Theater, yet did not particularly welcome the fate of Meyerhold and Tretiakov, would mutter the name of Vakhtangov to ward off the evil spirits of socialist realism. This simple fact of political-aesthetic history may help to explain Brecht's hierarchy of values with reference to Soviet artists. Brecht (GW, XV, 385-86) carefully sets up the following table designed to show the progressive qualities of three Soviet artists. Stanislavsky is placed first; then, as a bridge, comes Vakhtangov; and third is Meyerhold. The order is politically determined and is precisely the reverse of Brecht's own scale of values. The example may serve to show how precise a knowledge of background politics must obtain in order to read any but the simplest of Brecht's writings on theater.

10. Brecht planned to ask Okhlopkov, Eisenstein, and Tretiakov to become members of a "Society for Theatrical Science" that he thought of forming in 1937. Stanislavsky, still alive at the time, whereas Tretiakov may already have been dead, is not listed as a potential member. See Schriften zum Theater, III, 331.

11. Willett, *Eight Aspects,* pp. 176-179.
12. For the importance of the Soviets and the complete obscurity of Brecht in America in the mid-1930s, see Lee Simonson's introduction to Norris Houghton's *Moscow Rehearsals: An Account of Methods of Production in the Soviet Theater* (New York, 1936), and Harold Clurman's *The Fervent Years.* Neither Clurman nor Simonson even bothers to mention Brecht.
13. The quotation is taken from p. 39 of Edward Braun's book of translations of some of Meyerhold's major writings on theater, *Meyerhold on Theatre* (New York, 1969).
14. *Meyerhold on Theatre,* p. 54.
15. ibid., p. 63.
16. ibid., pp. 56, 65.
17. Nikolai A. Gorchakov, *The Theater in Soviet Russia* (New York, 1957), p. 208.
18. It is of some importance to note that Tretiakov who, as noted above, knew intimately the work of both Brecht and Meyerhold, seems to have been more impressed with Meyerhold's productions than with those of Brecht. Tretiakov commented on Brecht's 1931 production of *A Man's a Man*: "The performance produced a tremendous impression on me, second only to Meyerhold's *Rogonosetz*." Willett, *Eight Aspects,* p. 148. Tretiakov might, of course, have changed his rating, had he been able to see some of Brecht's Berliner Ensemble productions of the big exile plays.
19. *Schriften zum Theater,* I, 252.
20. See Willett, *Eight Aspects,* p. 178.
21. The full comment runs as follows: "Die Figur im Smoking ist fast ganz verschwunden. Vielleicht sähe man sie überhaupt nicht mehr, wenn man nicht so gut von ihr Bescheid wüsste, wenn sie nicht so berühmt wäre, mindestens vom Stillen Meer bis zum Ural." GW, XV, 427.
22. See Willett, *Eight Aspects,* pp. 185-86.
23. Houghton, *Moscow Rehearsals,* p. 152.
24. A basic bibliography of Far Eastern theater is given in the *Oxford Companion to the Theater.* For a detailed picture of Chinese staging and an analysis of the numerous similarities between Elizabethan and Chinese staging, please see either A.E. Zucker's *The Chinese Theater* (Boston and London, 1925), or L.C. Arlington's *The Chinese Drama* (New York, 1966). Surely the best place to see the influence of the Chinese theater on Brecht's work is the play, *The Horatians and the Curatians,* written in Svendborg in 1934 but not produced at all until 1958.

25. At one point Brecht notes (the comment was probably made circa 1936): "Die Verwerfung der Einfühlung kommt nicht von einer Verwerfung der Emotionen und führt nicht zu einer solchen. Es ist geradezu eine Aufgabe der nichtaristotelischen Dramatik, nach-zuweisen, dass die These der Vulgärästhetik, Emotionen könnten nur auf dem Weg der Einfühlung ausgelöst werden, falsch ist." ("The rejection of identification does not come from a rejection of emotions and does not lead to it. It is a particular task of non-Aristotelian dramaturgy to demonstrate that the vulgar aesthetic thesis that emotions can only be called forth through identification is false.") GW, XV, 242. As is often the case in Brecht's critical writings, he has here set up a straw man in order promptly to knock him down. There is, of course, an extremely rich history of writing on the art of the actor that makes the point that Brecht belligerently makes here. I am reminded particularly of Diderot, Coquelin, Salvini, Marinetti (who incidentally met Meyerhold in Moscow in 1914), Maeterlinck, the German theorist Georg Fuchs (frequently cited by Meyerhold in his early critical writings), Max Reinhardt, and Gordon Craig. In German writing before Fuchs (very early twentieth-century) we find explicit examinations of this problem in E.T.A. Hoffmann, in Tieck's *Dramatic Leaflets,* and in Schopen-hauer and Nietzsche. Even had Brecht not been familiar with this long and distinguished tradition when he wrote the above, he had had at least one practical demonstration of the truth of his thesis. When Brecht's "Clown Show" had been staged at the Baden-Baden festival in the 1920s and the grotesquely padded clown was sawed up with a patently false gigantic saw, people in the audience had fainted!

26. For specific notes on this version, see: *Materialien-Sezuan.*

27. It is of some historical interest to note that Brecht himself was the earliest model for one of the three gods. After Brecht and his friends Bronnen and Döblin were treated rather haughtily at a theater festival to which they had been invited in Dresden in 1926, Brecht wrote a satirical ballad on a city's failure to recognize the arrival of three visiting gods.

28. *Materialien-Sezuan,* p. 11: "Es ist Scharadenarbeit, schon der Umkleide- und Umschminkakte wegen."

29. We know that Brecht worked closely with Besson and that he saw the finished work.

30. A separate essay will have to be written on the connections, some sincere, some parodistic, between *Sezuan* and *Faust.*

31. This is, of course, generally true of Brecht. Tretiakov saw at once, for instance, that Brecht's locale for his version of *The Mother* was really Berlin and not Russia. Very much the same can be said for Galileo's "Italy" and the "Greece" of Brecht's *Antigone.*

32. There is a province of Sezuan but no such town. As usual, Brecht's geography is extremely unreliable.

33. It is also worth noting that the play opens in almost exactly the same way as does Sophocles' *Agamemnon,* where the watchman on the roof tells us his troubles, says why he is looking for a signal, and then actually sees the signal at the end of his brief and very necessary expository speech.

34. If Wang is actually smart, as he sometimes appears to be in the play, then he would, of course, have tried earlier to find suitable lodgings.

35. If we are willing to grant Shen Te's hypothesis, what then should we think of Mother Courage? She also does "evil" for the sake of her children. She too is a "tiger" in defense of her young.

36. "Dringt nicht wenigstens dieses Stück in tragische Bezirke vor?" Reinhold Grimm, "Zwischen Tragik und Ideologie," in *Das Ärgernis Brecht,* ed. Willy Jäggi and Hans Osch (Basel and Stuttgart, 1961), p. 111.

37. The role of Sun in the play is nicely underscored by the role of rain.

38. See in *Materialien-Sezuan,* pp. 95-100, "Fragment einer Fabelerzählung," "Zeitungsbericht." In the first of these the story of the Good Person of Sezuan is cast in biblical language. In the second, the tale sounds as if it were taken from a regular German newspaper.

39. Most late medieval plays are, of course, built on this pattern. Often a dumb show precedes the dramatic action itself.

40. "Freilich würde ich glücklich sein, die Gebote halten zu können der Kindesliebe und der Wahrhaftigkeit. Nicht begehren meines Nächsten Haus, wäre mir eine Freude, und einem Mann anhängen in Treue, wäre mir angenehm. Auch ich möchte aus keinem meinen Nutzen ziehen und den Hilflosen nicht berauben. Aber wie soll ich dies alles? Selbst wenn ich einige Gebote nicht halte, kann ich kaum durchkommen." Brecht, GW, IV, 1497.

41. ibid. p. 1490.

42. ibid. p. 1498.

43. Brecht's awareness of this is underlined by a question asked by the first god: "Machten die sieben guten Könige Geschäfte?" ("Did the seven good kings involve themselves in businss deals?")

44.   Edward M. Berckman, "The Function of Hope in Brecht's Pre-Revolutionary Theater," in *Brecht Heute/Brecht Today*, Vol. 1, pp. 11-26. We may also note, for instance, the frequency of use of the numbers three and four in the didactic plays and in Brecht's operas. *The Beggar's Opera* becomes the *Dreigroschenoper*. Four lumberjacks and a character by the name of Trinity Moses appear in *Mahagonny*. In *Das Badener Lehrstück vom Einverständnis* there are three mechanics and three clowns. In both *Die Massnahme* and *Mann ist Mann*, tragedy turns about the relationship of a quartet to a missing comrade. *Mutter Courage* and *Die Horatier und die Kuriatier* both turn significantly upon the number three.

45.   Would it be an accident that the theme of the song (we shall all disappear like smoke) happens to fit rather neatly with the story of a tobacconist whose goods "go up in smoke." It just happens that the song is sung as Shen Te's unwelcome guests are helping themselves to her meager stock.

46.   This is true of almost all Brecht's plays of this period. One wonders, therefore, if Ekkehard Schall was correct in the Ensemble production in presenting the songs of Sun as "operetta numbers." See *Materialien-Sezuan*, p. 147.

47.   The parallels here with the Greek chorus are, of course, striking.

48.   "Da das Stück sehr lang ist, will ich es doch mit Poetischem versehen, einigen Versen und Liedern. Es mag leichter und kurzweiliger werden dadurch, wenn es schon nicht kürzer werden kann." *Materialien-Sezuan*, p. 15. The Greeks and the Elizabethans, of course, provided the same rhythmical changes of pace and for the same reasons.

49.   Kaum war da eine windgeschützte Stelle
Kam des ganzen winterlichen Himmels
Zerzaustes Gevögel geflogen und
Raufte um den Platz, und der hungrige Fuchs durchbiss
Die dünne Wand, und der einbeinige Wolf
Stiess den kleinen Essnapf um.
GW, IV, 1529.

50.   Oh, ihr Unglücklichen!
Euerm Bruder wird Gewalt angetan, und ihr kneift die Augen zu!
Der Getroffene schreit laut auf, und ihr schweigt?
Der Gewalttätige geht herum und wählt sein Opfer
Und ihr sagt: uns verschont er, denn wir zeigen kein Missfallen.
Was ist das für eine Stadt, was seid ihr für Menschen!
ibid. p. 1536.

51. Ich will mit dem gehen, den ich liebe.
    Ich will nicht ausrechnen, was es kostet.
    Ich will nicht nachdenken, ob es gut ist.
    Ich will nicht wissen, ob er mich liebt.
    Ich will mit ihm gehen, den ich liebe.
    ibid. p. 1552.
52. Warum
    Ist auf die Bosheit ein Preis gesetzt und warum erwarten den Guten
    So harte Strafen?
    ibid. p. 1604.
53. Ronald Gray, *Bertolt Brecht*, p. 76.
54. One gets the definite impression that the time span encompassed by
    Brecht's play is determined more by simple biology than by the
    tenets of "epic theater."
55. For a description of certain other, rather complicated stylistic
    parallels, see Sartre's fine essay, "Brecht et les Classiques," in *World
    Theatre*, Paris, VII (Spring 1958).
56. Brecht was fully aware of the need for dramatic condensation. He
    notes in his diary in July 1939: "My notes on the playing times for
    the scenes showed terrible delays. Five-hour plays are not too long
    for a three-hour workday, particularly if the plays are epic, i.e., not
    too much of a strain [on the spectator]. However, at present two and
    a half hours are enough." *Materialien-Sezuan*, p. 11.
57. "Überlickt man die Stoffe der erzählenden und vorführenden
    Künste, so erblickt man die grossen Gegenstände Krieg, Geld, Öl,
    Eisenbahnen, Parlament, Lohnarbeit, Boden verhältnismässig selten,
    meist als dekorativen Hintergrund oder Anlass von Meditationen."
    Schriften zum Theater, III, 132.
58. "Die Zersetzung der menschlichen Beziehungen durch die bare
    Zahlung wird in einem kleinen, überschaubaren Bereich persönlicher
    Bekanntschaften vorgeführt. Es ist eine vorindustrielle, höchstens
    frühindustrielle Welt." Henning Rischbieter, *Brecht* (Velber bei
    Hannover, 1966), Vol. II, 38.

Chapter 8

1. "Am stärksten ist die Episierung des Theaters im *Kreidekreis* entwickelt." "Dramatisches, episches und dialektisches Theater," in *Episches Theater,* ed. Reinhold Grimm, p. 183.
2. "Was wir zu tun haben, ist: die Statisten durch gute Schauspieler ersetzen. Ein guter Schauspieler ist gleich einem Bataillon Statisten. Das heisst, er ist mehr." *Materialien zu Brechts "Der kaukasische Kreidekreis,"* ed. Werner Hecht (Frankfurt am Main, 1966), p. 20.
3. Parts of the argument presented in this chapter have been presented in my article, *"The Caucasian Chalk Circle* in Performance," *Brecht Heute/Brecht Today,* Vol. 1, pp. 137-149. See also *Brecht inszeniert "Der kaukasische Kreidekreis,"* text by Angelika Hurwicz (Grusche in Brecht's production), photos by Gerda Goedhart (Velber bei Hannover, 1964). The Berliner Ensemble stage text of the play was edited by Joachim Tenschert and published by the Henschelverlag (East Berlin) in 1968.
4. See *Materialien-Kreidekreis,* p. 31. Unfortunately no explanation is given as to why the play was not produced on Broadway. We may guess that the sheer size of the cast may have made the play seem to backers to be prohibitively expensive. This, at least, is the reason that Brecht himself gives for *Galileo's* closing on Broadway after a brief but reasonably well attended run. Apparently the costs were such that the play simply did not permit a big enough return on the investment to satisfy the play's backers.
5. A prologue spelling out the purpose of a play was, of course, an essential part of many medieval and even some Elizabethan plays. In fact, from its prologue to its closing "progress," Brecht's play is remarkably similar in many particulars to the kind of structure we associate with the late medieval stage.
6. Brecht attributes the play to Li Hsing-tao. Klabund (pseudonym for Alfred Henschke, the husband of the one of Brecht's leading actresses) published an adaptation of the original Chinese play in 1925. Max Reinhardt produced the play in the same year that he invited Brecht to Berlin to work as a dramaturg.
7. It should be stressed that in the Klabund and the Chinese versions the "good" mother is also the "real" or "biological" mother of the child. Brecht's change provides yet another comment by him on the questionable nature of the mother instinct. It is interesting that very often in Brecht's plays it is only those who are not "real" mothers

that have a "good" mother instinct. Kattrin, the sucker, it might be argued, is a better "mother" than Mother Courage. Grusche, in turn, is obviously a better mother than the child's "real" mother. Likewise, we might remember than Shen Te begins to call more and more frequently for Shui Ta when she discovers that she is to become a "real" mother.

8.   Again one is tempted to compare Brecht's rather conservative use of Chinese conventions with those used widely in Soviet productions in the 1920s and 1930s. See particularly Houghton's full description of Okhlopkov's production of *Aristocrats* as discussed above in Chapter 7.

9.   Actually, of course, even the Moscow Art Theater now sometimes uses somewhat stylized sets and increases the tempo of some of its productions by mounting several sets at once on its small turntable stage. Also, two further things should be pointed out about Stanislavsky and what we understand by Stanislavskianism. Meyerhold himself was very close to Stanislavsky at the beginning and at the end of the "Formalist's" career. Indeed it is said in the Soviet Union that Stanislavsky, shortly before his death, told Yury Bakhrushin (his deputy at the Opera Studio): "Take care of Meyerhold; he is my sole heir in the theatre—here or anywhere else" (found in Braun's *Meyerhold on Theatre,* p. 251). We tend in the West to see the two men as polar opposites and to take Soviet artists much too literally when they say that they subscribe to the theories of Stanislavsky. Let me illustrate this contention with a brief personal anecdote. In the spring of 1966 I saw some splendidly stylized, obviously non-naturalistic theater in Moscow. Before viewing the production, I was assured by the director of the theater that I was about to see a Stanislavskian production. Afterwards, as I emerged somewhat dazed, the director turned to me once again and said: "You see, I told you it would be a Stanislavskian production." Quite obviously, some Soviet artists have, in the interest of being left alone, kept the hallowed name but have radically changed the game.

10.   Again it must be stressed that both in milieu and in construction this play is only slightly "Oriental." Much of the dramaturgy could have been taken straight from Shakespeare. I think particularly here of the way in which Shakespeare handles the crossing of the English Channel in the Henry cycle. There we are told explicitly that we must "piece out the setting with our thoughts." For a good, concise examination of some basic similarities between the physical theater

and the plays of Shakespeare's period and the theater of the Chinese, please see L.C. Arlington's book, *The Chinese Drama* (New York, 1966), pp. 27-29.

11. Volker Klotz in *Materialien-Kreidekreis,* p. 141.

12. A wholly unexplored area of criticism of Brecht's aesthetic theory is the primary level of the relationship of Brecht's actor to his role. Even if the reporter or narrator of the accident that forms the core of the famous "Street Scene" does simply report and does not become, in a Stanislavskian sense, either the victim or the driver of the delinquent vehicle, no one, to my knowledge, has asked the question of whether the narrator himself may be presumed to have seen the accident and therefore reports on it as himself. If the narrator does appear as himself then we may presume that he mediates between us (those who did not see the accident) and those who were too personally involved to be able to give any kind of objective report. It is worth reminding the reader that there are few situations filled with greater tension ("Spannung") than a street corner where an accident has just taken place.

13. Those who only read English and are relying on Eric Bentley's "revised English version" of the play in the Grove Press edition may be puzzled here. Bentley divides his version into five sections where Brecht's *Collected Works* text has six. Azdak first appears in Scene *Four* of Mr. Bentley's version.

14. Busch may be heard by the American listener on the Stinson Record (SLP 52) singing songs of the Lincoln and International Brigades. Very few people can deliver a political song with quite Busch's verve.

15. In other words, the actors *become* the members of the Kolkhos. The players then undergo a further change when these "real" collective farmers "become" actors in an ancient play. Please see note 13 above.

16. Scenes 1-3 in Bentley's English version.

17. Angelika Hurwicz, *Brecht inszeniert* (pages unnumbered), photos by Gerda Goedhart.

18. "Das Kind ist, um die Kälte in der Geschirrkammer anzudeuten, in eine Decke gehüllt. Aber auch, um für den Zuschauer den Übergang vom Säugling zum grösseren Kinde nicht zu krass zu machen." ibid. One should also mention here that the biological fact of the growth of the child (as with Shen Te's unborn child in *Sezuan*) would considerably hinder any chronological rearrangement of scenes for large sections of the *Chalk Circle.*

19. "Brecht verzichtete auf die Gestaltung des 'interessanten' Dilemmas der Grusche. Ihm war interessanter die dramaturgische Verknüpfung mit der späteren Gerichtsszene, wo Grusche das Kind mit allem Nachdruck für sich beanspruchen wird." ibid.

20. "Die Scheibe wurde gegenläufig zur Marschrichtung der Grusche in Bewegung gesetzt, sie lief darauf fort, blieb aber immer in Bühnenausschnitt. Ihr entgegen kamen die einzelnen Stationen ihrer Flucht, die Scheibe hielt an, solange die jeweilige Szene spielte, dann wurde die Scheibe wieder in Bewegung gesetzt, und während Grusche weiterwanderte, fuhr die jeweilige Station weg. Das hintere Drittel der Bühne war durch eine 'Fahne' abgedeckt, die nicht ganz so breit war wie die Scheibe an dieser Stelle. Hinter dieser Fahne wurden, vom Publikum aus nicht sichtbar, die Dekorationsteile aufgesetzt und an der Fahne vorbei nach vorn gefahren. Ebenso verschwanden sie hinter der Fahne und wurden hinter dieser Abdeckung von der Scheibe heruntergenommen. Auf diese Art konnte die lange, ereignisreiche Flucht ohne Unterbrechung gezeigt werden. Die Notwendigkeit, in Sekundenschnelle die Dekorationsteile von der Scheibe herunterzunehmen und gleichzeitig neu aufzusetzen, ergab, dass alle Dekorationsteile aus leichtem Kaschee hergestellt wurden." Karl von Appen, "Über das Bühnenbild," in *Materialien-Kreidekreis,* p. 99.

21. See, however, note 9 above.

22. For the relationship of Brecht to the various composers who worked with him at different times please see Hans Bunge's volume of conversations with Hanns Eisler, *Fragen Sie mehr über Brecht* (Munich, 1970), and Willett, *Eight Aspects,* pp. 125-142.

23. "Für den zweiten Akt (*Flucht in die nördlichen Gebirge*) bräuchte das Theater eine treibende Musik, die den sehr epischen Akt zusammenhält." *Materialien-Kreidekreis,* p. 22. Brecht's concluding note on the same music, "sie sollte aber dünn und delikat sein," fits very nicely stylistically with the delicate "Chinese brush work" of the scenes painted on the backdrop.

24. In exile in Hollywood Brecht became a personal friend of Chaplin, his particular favorite of the silent American screen.

25. See Chapter 7 and Norris Houghton's notes on Okhlopkov's extraordinarily stylized and almost obtrusively "Chinese" production of Pogodin's play, *Aristocrats.*

26. The scene is reminiscent in many ways of *Eduard II* where Brecht had soldiers run at breakneck speed across planks placed high above the stage.

27. "Wenn die sie zu fassen kriegen, machen sie Hackfleisch aus ihr."
    GW, V, 2042.
28. Other Berliner Ensemble productions which would be almost
    unplayable without the turntable stage include *Coriolan* and
    Schweyk.
29. Wer wird den Fall entscheiden, wem wird das Kind zuerteilt?
    Wer wird der Richter sein, ein guter, ein schlechter?
    Die Stadt brannte. Auf dem Richterstuhl sass der Azdak.
    GW, V, 2065.
30. "Häufig werden die Songs als 'V-Effekte' interpretiert. Sie unter-
    brechen den Dialog, folglich, so wird geschlossen, haben sie auch das
    Spiel zu unterbrechen. Aber Brecht wünschte zum Beispiel bei der
    Wiederbegegnung Grusches mit ihrem Verlobten, dass die Schau-
    spieler den Text der Sänger mit feinstem mimischen Ausdruck
    begleiteten. Misstrauen, Vorwurf, Enttäuschung sollten sich auf den
    Gesichtern spiegeln. Der Song als poetische Auslegung des Schwei-
    gens. An der gleichen Stelle sollte auch der Sänger, der die
    vorwurfsvollen Gedanken Simon Chachawas ausdrückt, nicht
    unbeteiligt, erzählend singen wie sonst, sondern zornig, anklagend.
    Dieser Augenblick ist keinem Stilprinzip unterzuordnen, er ist
    einfach ein poetischer, auf sich selbst beruhender künstlerisch
    schöner Augenblick. . ." *Materialien-Kreidekreis*, p. 63.
31. "Nun geschiet es im Drama, dass bei der Erhebung des Azdak zum
    Richter die Panzerreiter ihn mit der Purpurrobe des gehängten
    Vorgängers bekleiden; sie setzen ihm einen umgestülpten Flaschen-
    korb aufs Haupt und sprechen: 'Schaut, was für ein Richter!' "
    Albrecht Schöne, "Theatertheorie und dramatische Dichtung,"
    Euphorion, LII, No. 3 (1958), 294.
32. ibid. p. 295.
33. Und so brach er die Gesetze wie ein Brot, dass es sie letze
    Bracht das Volk ans Ufer auf des Rechtes Wrack.
    Brecht, GW, V, 2086. I have included here two lines of the German
    poem rather than the one line of my English translation in order that
    the reader may get some idea of the driving rhythms of some of the
    verse of this play. This is verse that sweeps along, that allows no time
    for sober thought. The two lines above are then followed by:
    Und die Niedren und Gemeinen hatten endlich, endlich einen
    Den die leere Hand bestochen, den Azdak.
    We might ask ourselves if this is verse that is designed to set us apart
    from the action to make us distance ourselves from the "good-bad

judge Azdak"? Again, as with *Sezuan,* I would suggest that such verse is profoundly moving, marvelously seductive, and not at all conducive to making "the calmly smoking spectator check the reckoning."

34. "Ich bitt dich auf den Knien um Erbarmen, geh jetzt nicht weg, der Speichel rinnt mir heraus. Ich hab Todesfurcht." GW, V, 2089.

35. "Sie verleiht der Szene einen Zuwachs an Wirkungsgewalt, der dramatischen Figur eine Überzeugungskraft, welche die Distanzhaltung des rauchend beobachtenden Zuschauers überwinden." Schöne, p. 295.

36. Ronald Gray, *Bertolt Brecht* (New York, 1961), p. 110.

37. "Es ist verständlich, wenn im weitgehend katholischen Krakau die Liebe Grusches zu dem Kind an die Marien-Legende erinnert." *Materialien-Kreidekreis,* p. 117. Professor Grimm, in the article "Bertolt Brecht," in *Deutsche Dichter der Moderne: Ihr Leben und Werk,* ed. Benno von Wiese (Frankfurt, 1969), notes the fact that Grusche stopping behind to help the abandoned child, despite the considerable danger to herself, reminds us of the story of the Good Samaritan. Listen for a moment to the way in which the child (through the medium of the singer) wins Grusche's heart:
Wisse, Frau, wer einen Hilferuf nicht hört
Sondern vorbeigeht, verstörten Ohrs: nie mehr
Wird der hören den leisen Ruf des Liebsten noch
Im Morgengrauen die Amsel oder den wohligen
Seufzer der erschöpften Weinpflücker beim Angelus.
We, no more than Grusche, can fail to respond to such a plea.

38. Heinz Politzer, "How Epic is Brecht's Epic Theater," *Modern Language Quarterly,* XXIII (1962), 108.

39. David J. Grossvogel, *Four Playwrights and a Postscript* (New York, 1962), p. 33.

40. "Rollen wie der Azdak und die Grusche können in unserer Zeit nicht durch Regiearbeit gestaltet werden. Nicht weniger als fünf Jahre am Berliner Ensemble waren nötig, der ausserordentlichen Angelika Hurwicz die Voraussetzungen zu geben. Und das ganze Leben Buschs, von der Kindheit im proletarischen Hamburg über die Kämpfe in der Weimarer Republik und im spanischen Bürgerkrieg zu bitteren Erfahrungen nach 45 war nötig, diesen Azdak hervorzubringen" (February 7, 1954). *Materialien-Kreidekreis,* p. 34.

41. Angelika Hurwicz, *Brecht inszeniert* (pages unnumbered).

42. Rudolf Frank, "Brecht von Anfang," in *Das Ärgernis Brecht,* p. 43.

43. "Um für das Pariser Gastspiel die Aufführung in Höchstform zu bringen, sind Striche im Text gemacht und ist das Tempo beschleunigt worden. Die Tempobeschleunigung dient ja nicht nur der Kürzung, sondern mehr noch der Belebung der Aufführung. Die Mehrzahl der Szenen und Figuren *gewinnt* durch das Tempo." GW, XVII, 1208.

Chapter 9

1. Walter Weideli, *The Art of Bertolt Brecht* (New York, 1963), p. 109.
2. "Das dichterisch vollendetste Werk Brechts dürfte *Leben des Galilei* sein. Ein Höhepunkt des episch-dialektischen Theaters, das auf dieser Hochstufe wieder zu einem geschlossenen dramatischen Theater wird, ohne die verfremdende Distanz zu verlieren." In Grimm, *Episches Theater,* p. 184.
3. "*Leben des Galilei* ist technisch ein grosser Rückschritt, wie *Frau Carrars Gewehre* allzu opportunistisch." My citation is from Schumacher's massive and excellent volume on *Galileo, Drama und Geschichte, Bertolt Brechts "Leben des Galilei" und anderer Stücke* (Berlin, 1965), p. 245. The comment is also to be found in the essay, "Form und Einfühlung," in the West German edition of *Materialien-Galilei,* edited by Werner Hecht. Curiously, this essay was not then reprinted in the East German edition of the same work. That Helene Weigel (and, by extension, Werner Hecht) did not like Schumacher's approach to the play we may assume from Schumacher's refreshingly frank contribution (pp. 68-75) to the volume, *Helene Weigel zum 70. Geburtstag* (Berlin, 1970), ed. Werner Hecht. The omission of Schumacher's stimulating essay from the East German *Materialien* should alert us to a particular editing stance of Hecht's that leaves something to be desired. What we most desire, of course, is to have the *Collected Works* supplemented with a reasonably full edition of Brecht's diaries, his "Work Books," and his letters. To bend over backwards in trying to be fair to both Werner Hecht and to Helene Weigel, I must point out that the publication of the materials most Brecht scholars are itching to see is a massively complex undertaking. Both Frau Weigel and Herr Hecht have assured me recently (October, 1970) that they want nothing more than to get these materials into proper order for full publication. While we wait for these vital supplementary materials, we must simply remember that the texts of many of the *Schriften zum Theater* are not contextually complete and our reading of them will almost certainly be modified as soon as these materials are properly placed in a full personal and political context.
4. See again Schumacher's *Drama und Geschichte.* This volume is as yet the only source for Brecht's own "Work Book" commentaries on *Galileo.* In his contribution to the volume, *Helene Weigel zum 70. Geburtstag,* however, Schumacher does note that he was only allowed to use about half the quotes from the "Work Books" which he considered directly relevant to his theme.

5. See *Materialien-Galilei,* the stage version of the play, edited by Joachim Tenschert (published in East Berlin in 1970), and the *Model Book* for *Galileo: Aufbau einer Rolle-Galilei* (Berlin, 1956). The latter volume is bound in three parts: one has the text of the play (not the stage version!), one is devoted to Laughton as Galileo, and the third is devoted to Busch in the same role.

6. For Brecht's own notes on the fate of *Galileo* in the two 1947 American productions with Laughton, please see *Materialien-Galilei,* p. 77.

7. One example of such condensation is Brecht's combining of two original characters (Doppone the student and Ludovico the suitor) in the one character of Ludovico, student and suitor. Some critics have felt that this combination is not really at all well worked out. See in this connection Otto M. Sorensen, "Brecht's *Galileo:* Its Development from Ideational into Ideological Theater," *Modern Drama,* XI, No. 4 (February, 1969), 416-417. Other noteworthy examples of condensation in the final version are the dropping of two whole scenes (the plague scene and the crossing of the frontier) and the concentration of the *Discorsi* scene by reducing the number of times Galileo tries to smuggle out his secret writings.

8. For a relatively unbiased and clear introduction to the historical Galileo, see Stillman Drake's translation of some of Galileo's major writings, *Discoveries and Opinions of Galileo* (New York, 1957). For an interpretation of the role played by Galileo in the development of modern physics, please see I. Bernard Cohen, *The Birth of a New Physics* (New York, 1960). It is of particular importance to note that in Professor Cohen's view, Galileo was in fact a true Catholic trying desperately to reconcile "separate secular and theological cosmologies" (p. 129). This is the Galileo that the American dramatist Barry Stavis presents in his fine play *Lamp at Midnight*, which ran on Broadway at the same time that Brecht's *Life of Galileo* had its brief run there. Because Brecht has deliberately twisted history to make Galileo violently anti-Catholic and a proto-Marxist, Mr. Stavis has told me in a conversation that he considers Brecht's play to be a "vulgarization of history." There is much to be said for this point of view.

9. See Schumacher, *Drama und Geschichte,* for a discussion of the relationship of the Stavis play to historical fact.

10. We know from contemporary accounts that Charles Laughton, despite the prudishness of Brecht's text, was able to insert some sexuality into his playing of the part.

11. See note 8 above. According to Cohen, Galileo's life up until his mid-forties is of little importance to the history of modern science.

12. Yet, of course, the problems of the coexistence of science and of dogma have persisted well into the twentieth century. The case of Lysenko in the Soviet Union and that of Snopes in the United States happen to be the best know examples. We know further that the question of Marxism as itself an inflexible dogma had the greatest personal interest to Brecht. For years he had been the heretic Formalist facing the Socialist Realist East German and Soviet aesthetic "popes."

13. Schumacher, for instance, notes: "Wenn das Wesen des Dramas im Konflikt besteht, dieser von bestehenden Gegensätzen nicht zu trennen ist, erweist sich das Antithetische als ursprüngliches konstitutives Element des Dramatischen. *Leben des Galilei* ist als Ganzes wie in seinen Teilen antithetisch struktuiert. . ." ("If conflict is an essential feature of the drama, and if conflict is predicated on the presence of opposites, then it would appear that the antithetical itself constitutes the primary element of the drama. *The Life of Galileo* is, both as a whole and in its constituent parts, constructed antithetically.") Schumacher, *Drama und Geschichte,* p. 295.

14. One has heard so much of Brecht's opposition to Schiller that it may seem farfetched to wonder if there is not considerably more than an echo of Schiller's *Don Carlos* in Brecht's treatment of Galileo. We know that Brecht himself said that the thirteenth scene of the play had a great deal in common with Schiller. See note 46 below. We might remember here the comment of the twenty-two-year-old Brecht: "Ich habe *Don Carlos,* weiss Gott, je und je geliebt," ("God knows I have loved and loved *Don Carlos.*") Brecht, GW, XV, p. 9. Again Brecht seems to have swung through a full critical circle. He loves Schiller, then loathes Schiller, and then returns to pay Schiller the ultimate compliment (for Brecht) of borrowing something (without an ironic twist) from the German bourgeois classic.

15. "Die einzigen Schwierigkeiten bereitete die letzte Szene. Ahnlich wie in der *Johanna* brauchte ich am Schluss einen Kunstgriff, um auf jeden Fall dem Zuschauer den nötigen Abstand zu sichern. Selbst der unbedenklich sich Einfühlende muss zumindest jetzt, auf dem Weg der Einfühlung selber in den Galilei, den V-Effekt verspüren. Bei streng epischer Darstellung kommt eine Einfühlung erlaubter Art zustande." Cited by Schumacher, *Materialien-Galilei,* p. 153. Original found in BBA 275/12.

16. See Schumacher, *Drama und Geschichte*, p. 252 et passim.

17. *"Leben des Galilei* ist technisch ein grosser Rückschritt, wie *Frau Carrars Gewehre* allzu opportunistisch. Man müsste das Stück vollständig neu schreiben, wenn man diese 'Brise, die von neuen Küsten kommt,' diese rosige Morgenröte der Wissenschaft haben will." Original source BBA 275/14. Schumacher *Materialien-Galilei*, p. 153, and in Schumacher, *Drama und Geschichte*, p. 245.

18. "Alles mehr direkt, ohne die Interieurs, die 'Atmosphäre,' die Einfühlung. Und alles auf planetarische Demonstration abgestellt. Die Einteilung könnte bleiben, die Charakteristik des Galilei ebenfalls, aber die Arbeit, die lustige Arbeit, könnte nur in einem Praktikum gemacht werden, im Kontakt mit einer Bühne." ibid.

19. "Im *Galilei* mit seinen Interieurs und Stimmungen wirkt die dem epischen Theater entnommen Bauart der Szenen merkwürdig theatralisch." ibid.

20. "Im Formalen verteidige ich dieses Stück nicht besonders kräftig." BBA 976/33. Cited in Schumacher, *Drama und Geschichte*, p. 284, and in *Materialien-Galilei*, p. 154.

21. Käthe Rülicke in *Materialien-Galilei*, p. 94.

22. See note 7 above.

23. Given in Schumacher, *Drama und Geschichte*, p. 284.

24. "Symmetrie gehört zum Wesen der Komposition des klassizistischen Dramas." ibid. "Die Symmetrien in *Leben des Galilei* unterstreichen als dramaturgische Strukturelemente den gleichsam 'konservativen' Charakter des Stückes."

25. ibid.

26. See the general comments of the actors at the Ensemble in *Sinn und Form II* and Käthe Rülicke's specific observation: "Überflüssig für den, der Brechts Proben sah, aber vielleicht nicht allgemein überflüssig der Hinweis: auf Brechts Proben wurde niemals theoretisiert." ("Redundant for those who saw Brecht's rehearsals, but perhaps not generally redundant is the note: there was never any theorizing at Brecht's rehearsals.") *Materialien-Galilei*, p. 108.

27. For the projections used in the American productions please see *Aufbau einer Rolle-Galilei-Laughton*.

28. Please see Käthe Rülicke's full report on the rehearsals in *Materialien-Galilei*, pp. 91-152.

29. ibid., p. 105: "The *Life of Galileo* is, it is true, with reference to the time at which it takes place, a historical play, but what it has to say is in no way simply historical but rather, contemporary." See also in

this connection Brecht's comment on Galileo's admonition to Andrea: "Careful as you go through Germany with the truth under your coat!" Brecht told the actors: "It is dangerous to appear in Germany with the truth under your jacket; over and over again that has been so since the Peasants' War. One must be careful when one tells the truth." *Materialien-Galilei,* p. 96. Could we then apply the latter comment back to Galileo and to Galileo's failure to tell the truth before the Inquisition? The parallels here and elsewhere in the play between Galileo and Brecht himself are very striking indeed. An essay exploring some aspects of this similarity is Guy Stern's "The Plight of the Exile: A Hidden Theme in Brecht's *Galileo Galilei,"* *Brecht Heute/Brecht Today,* Vol. I, (Frankfurt am Main, 1971), pp. 110-116. See also J.H. Wulbern's essay in the same volume.

30. See Käthe Rülicke, *Materialien-Galilei,* p. 109.

31. See the line: "Federzoni, wir mögen noch eine Zeit erleben, wo wir uns nicht mehr wie Verbrecher umzublicken haben, wenn wir sagen, zwei mal zwei ist vier." ("Federzoni, we may ourselves still experience a time when we don't have to look over our shoulders like criminals when we say: two times two is four.") GW, III, 1306.

32. See the anecdote, "Verfremdungseffekte," in *Geschichten vom Herrn B.,* ed. André Müller and Gerd Semmer (Frankfurt am Main, 1967), p. 79.

33. See Hanns Eisler on the topic in *Fragen Sie mehr über Brecht,* transcript of conversations between Eisler and Hans Bunge (Munich, 1970), p. 213. This book and Sternberg's *Der Dichter und die Ratio* are two of the most sensitive and sensible accounts I know of that deal with Brecht as a human being rather than a mythological figure.

34. See Eisler, Schumacher, and Rülicke.

35. Rülicke, *Materialien-Galilei,* p. 121 reports: "Hätte er [Brecht] in den bisherigen Proben den 'Lumpen' aufgebaut, so holte er jetzt die positiven Seiten der Figur heraus."

36. "Busch bereitete sich auf die Rolle des Galilei gründlich vor. Er las Bücher über klassische und moderne Astronomie und Physik und bewies Brecht und mir natürlich sofort, dass wir von Astronomie überhaupt keine Ahnung hätten." Eisler in the foreword to *Aufbau einer Rolle-Galilei-Busch,* p. 11.

37. "In diesen Diskussionen, und das zeigt den guten Instinkt Buschs, nahm er bereits die dozierende Haltung Galileis an, und es wurde ihm zur natürlichsten Sache von der Welt, über Astronomie zu debattieren und Termini der Physik und Astronomie gehörten nun zu seiner Alltagssprache." ibid.

38. "Ein Freund, der damals in Rom war, erzählte mir: 'Ich sah eine Büste und dachte mir, das ist doch dort Ernst Busch. Wie kommt seine Büste hierher? Schon jetzt? Als ich näher trat, sah ich, es war die Büste Galileis.' " ibid.

39. Charles R. Lyons, *Bertolt Brecht: The Despair and the Polemic* (Carbondale, 1968), p. 120.

40. ibid.

41. GW, III, 1329.

42. ibid.

43. "Sie werden ihn umbringen. Die *Discorsi* werden nicht zu Ende geschrieben." ibid., p. 1325. The first sentence here reminds us of Baloun's comment on Schweyk, who has just been led off to the torture chambers of the S.S. This is, of course, only one of the more subtle hints in this play that point us back to another of Brecht's shabby humanists.

44. The note in Brecht's directing text reads: "Erschüttert, er kann kaum sprechen," *Materialien-Galilei*, p. 147.

45. GW, III, 1342.

46. "Schall, das sind Schillersche Sätze, grosses Pathos! " *Materialien-Galilei*, p. 137. "Sprechen Sie mit grossem Schillerschem Pathos, Schall, spielen Sie Don Carlos." ibid., p. 142. See also Hanns Bunge's extremely insightful remark: "Also der einzige Schiller-Schüler ist eigentlich Brecht." *Fragen Sie mehr über Brecht,* p. 253. See also note 14 above.

47. "Das muss aber kolossal wirken, wie die H-Bombe!" *Materialien-Galilei*, p. 141.

48. "Was sehe ich nun während dieser geistigen Auseinandersetzungen überdies auf der Bühne? Einen Mann, der am Fernrohr seine Sehkraft geschwächt hat und nun beim Arbeiten im Mondlicht—weil er illegal eine Abschrift seines für die Menschheit nützlichen Werks herstellt—fast erblindet ist. Das wird nicht gesprochen, sondern gezeigt. Ich sehe weiter einen Mann, einen dem 'Laster' des Denkens und Arbeitens, das ihm 'wie Krätze anhaftet,' verfallenen Mann, in immer noch gefährdeter Situation von einer widerwärtig dummen Tochter als Spionin seiner Feinde belauert. Und diesen Mann soll ich hassen? Verurteilen? Mögen mich noch so viele Kommentare dazu auffordern—ich kann es nicht!" Fritz Erpenbeck, *Aus dem Theaterleben* (Berlin, 1959), p. 333.

49. The responses of the Paris critics are given in Grossvogel, *Four Playwrights,* p. 40. See also *Théâtre Populaire,* May 24, 1957.

50. "Als Brecht das Galilei-Stück schrieb, nahm er bereits eine wesentlich dialektischere Stellung zum Problem der Einfühlung und der Auslösung von Gefühlen durch Bühnenvorgänge ein als in den Anmerkungen zu den vor 1933 entstandenen Stücken." *Materialien-Galilei*, p. 161.

51. "Einerseits kommt nämlich der *Einfühlungsakt* auch unter Verwertung rationeller Elemente vor, andererseits kann der V-Effekt auch rein gefühlsmässig gesetzt werden." ibid., pp. 162-63.

52. "Wenn ich nach demjenigen urteilen soll, was ich in der Englischen Schaubühne gelesen habe, so sind ihre Schauspiele mehr Nachahmungen der Personen, als Nachahmungen einer gewissen Handlung. Man sucht eine Anzahl von Personen aus, die in ihrem Leben eine Verbindung miteinander gehabt haben. Wenn man sie nun von ihren wichtigsten Begebenheiten soviel reden lassen als genug ist, eine Anzahl Zuschauer einige Stunden lang zu unterhalten, und wenn man zu einem merkwürdigen Punkte order zu dem Ausgange ihres Lebens gekommen ist, so höret man auf." J.E. Schlegel, in *Meisterwerke deutscher Literaturkritik,* ed. Hans Mayer (Stuttgart, 1962), pp. 107-108.

53. This particular formulation of Lessing's objectives is taken from Werner P. Friederich's *German Literature* (New York, 1948), p. 68.

ILLUSTRATIONS

1. Swan Theater, London 1596.

2. Close view of an Elizabethan stage, 1692.

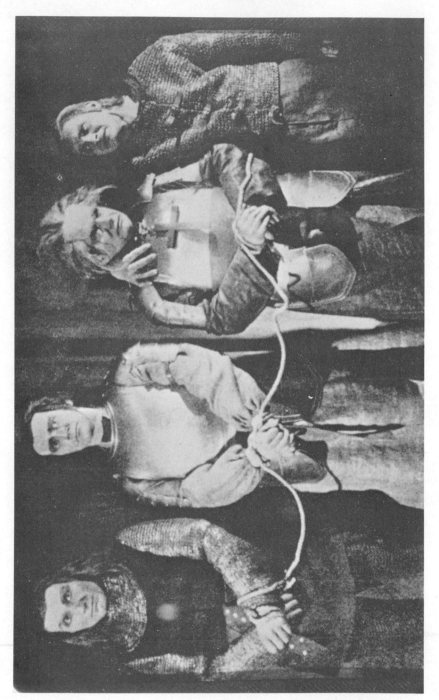

3.   Erwin Faber as Eduard (far right) with the captured peers. Munich 1924.

4. Caspar Neher's sketch of London Town for Brecht's production of *Eduard II*. Munich 1924.

5. The stage realization of Neher's sketch (fig. 4). The ballad seller with "chorus." Munich 1924.

6. Erwin Faber (right) as Eduard in the dungeon scene. "I wanted to upset the plaster monument style." Munich 1924.

Lob des Kommunismus

7. Title projection accompanying the song "In Praise of Communism." Set by Caspar Neher. Brecht's 1951 production of *The Mother* at the Deutsches Theater, Berlin.

8. Caspar Neher's sketch for Scene One of Brecht's 1951 production of *The Mother*. Berlin.

9. The stage realization of Neher's design for the teacher's apartment. Mrs. Wlassowa (Helene Weigel) gets up from her sick bed to distribute Communist leaflets. Berlin 1951.

10. Neher sketch for the factory scene in *The Mother*. Berlin 1951.

11. The stage realization of Neher's design for the factory scene (see fig. 10). Berlin 1951.

12. Wlassowa visits her son Pawel in prison. Berlin 1951.

13. Closer view of scene given in fig. 9. Helene Weigel as the ill but indefatigable fighter for the revolution. Berlin 1951.

14. The flag that is "most dangerous for all those who exploit and rule by force, the inexorable flag." Scene Five. Berlin 1951.

15. The standard-bearer of fig. 14 having been shot, Wlassowa picks up the "dangerous flag." Scene Five. Berlin 1951.

16. Neher's sketch for the prologue for Brecht's adaptation of *Antigone*. Chur 1948.

17. The stage realization of Neher's sketch for the prologue. Chur 1948.

18. Antigone (Helene Weigel)
    supported by her retainers as
    the death sentence is passed.
    Chur 1948.

19. Closeup of Helene Weigel as
    Antigone. Chur 1948.

20. Neher's sketch for the opening scene of *Antigone*. Chur 1948.

21. The stage realization of Neher's sketch for the opening scene of *Antigone*. Antigone, in full view of the full cast, prepares to bury her brother.

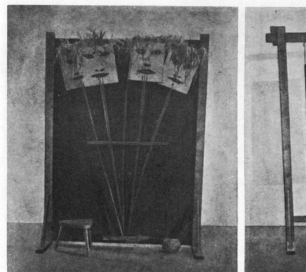

22 & 23. Rack with masks and the large gong that was used for marking points of emphasis in the play and for beating time for the choral dances. Chur 1948.

24. The masked chorus of Theban Elders. Chur 1948.

25. Kreon dances mockingly around his opponent Teiresias. Chur 1948.

26. A dying messenger reports the total destruction of the Theban armies at Argos-Stalingrad. Chur 1948.

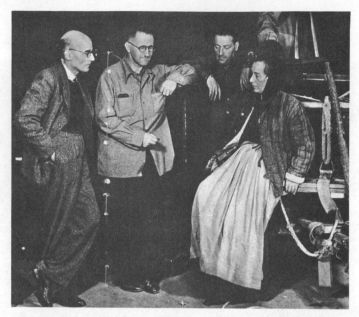

27. Brecht rehearses *Mother Courage* with three of his major artistic collaborators on the play: Erich Engel (left), Brecht, Paul Dessau the composer, and Helene Weigel. Berlin 1948.

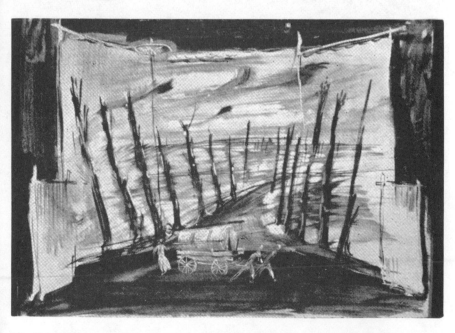

28. General scene sketch by Teo Otto for the world premiere of *Mother Courage*. Zurich 1941.

29. The opening scene of *Mother Courage* at its Berlin premiere. Directed by Engel/Brecht, music by Dessau, and sets by Teo Otto and Heinrich Kilger. Berlin, January 11, 1949.

30. Closeup of the full wagon and its happy owners. Berlin 1949.

31. Scene One. Courage (Helene Weigel) proves that her "horse" does not have foot and mouth disease. The recruiting officer begins his examination of Eilif and Schweizerkäs. Kattrin, mortally afraid of soldiers, sits hunched over on the wagon. Berlin 1949.

32. The potential cannon fodder is subjected to detailed examination. Berlin 1949.

33. Worried about the recruiter's interest in her boys, Courage tries to frighten them with the prediction of their deaths. Each person draws a black cross from the recruiter's helmet. Berlin 1949.

34. Anxious to make a sale to one of the soldiers, Courage's attention is diverted long enough for her to lose the first of her sons. Berlin 1949.

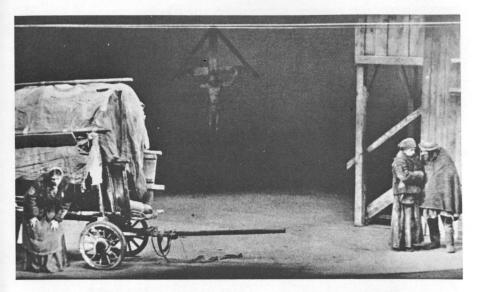

35. Kattrin, Courage's "cross" (played by Angelika Hurwicz) overhears her mother discussing with the cook (Ernst Busch) the inn at Utrecht that can only provide a living for the cook and Courage herself. Berlin 1949.

36. After placing the cook's trousers on top of her mother's skirt, Kattrin prepares to take up her bundle and leave, thus hoping to be a burden to her mother no longer. Berlin 1949.

37. Mother Courage prepares to take up her cross. Berlin 1949.

38. Completely alone, Courage begins to drag the now empty and tattered wagon from the stage. Berlin 1949.

39. As the armies of Christ sing the song with which the play opened, Courage hobbles after them, knowing no other business than that of war. Berlin 1949.

40. "The most moving scene in twentieth-century drama," the death of Kattrin. Berlin 1949.

41. The sound of silence. Courage, after refusing to recognize
     the body of her dead son. Berlin 1949.

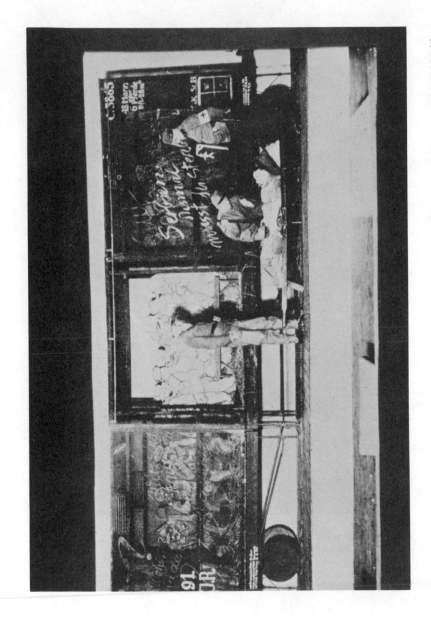

42. Dramaturgy of the moving sidewalk. A scene from Piscator's 1927-28 production of Schweik. Berlin 1927-28.

43. Schweyk (played by Martin Flörchinger) confuses the Nazi railway guard at the Prague goods depot. Berliner Ensemble production, 1962.

44.   The dog-stealing scene. Berliner Ensemble production, 1962.

45. Schweyk gives Frau Kopecka (played by Gisela May) the package of meat that she is to prepare for Baloun. Berliner Ensemble production, 1962.

46. Schweyk invites his own arrest. Berliner Ensemble production, 1962.

47. Schweyk and Ajax on their way to Stalingrad. Berliner Ensemble production, 1962.

48. Baloun (Wolfgang Lohse) complains about his appetite to Frau Kopecka and Schweyk. Meanwhile, an SS man (Stefan Lisewski) disturbs the peace of the inn.

49. The three gods with Wang the water seller in the world premiere of *The Good Person of Sezuan*. Zurich 1943.

50. The "tobacco factory" with its exploited laborers. Zurich 1943.

51. Giorgio Strehler's Milan production of *The Good Person of Sezuan*. The "evil" cousin, Shui Ta, gets off to a good start with the local police. The policeman is, rather obviously, a somewhat old-fashioned but otherwise typical Milanese cop. Milan 1958.

52. General scene sketch for a 1952 production of *The Good Person of Sezuan* in Frankfurt. Brecht attended the last weeks of rehearsal for this production.

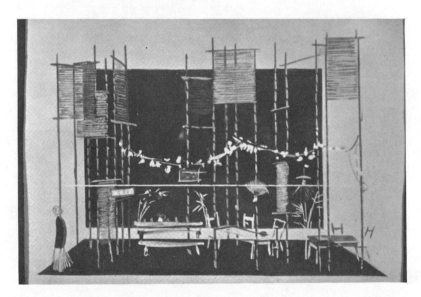

53. The basic set of fig. 52 is rearranged for the wedding scene. Frankfurt 1952.

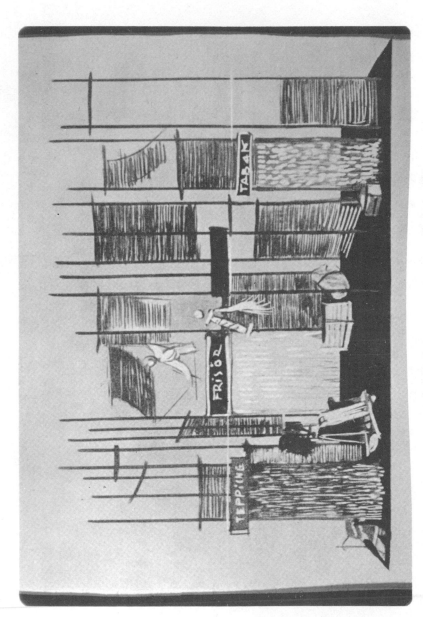

54. The street with the barber shop and Shen Te's tobacco shop. Frankfurt 1952.

55. Shen Te (Käthe Reichel) in the Berliner Ensemble production of the play. Berlin 1957.

56. Shui Ta resolves to throw out the poor family camped in Shen Te's small shop. Berlin 1957.

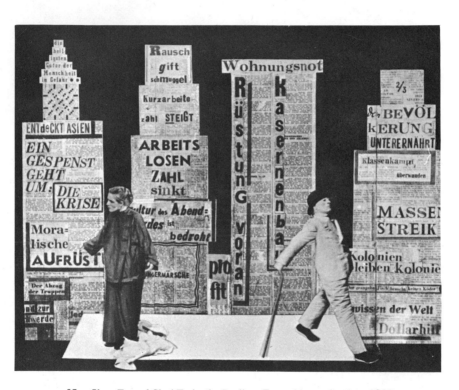

57.   Shen Te and Shui Ta in the Berliner Ensemble production. 1957.

58.   The prologue of *The Caucasian Chalk Circle*, directed by Brecht, set by Karl von Appen. Berlin 1955.

59. The singers say that which Simon and Grusche are too shy to say to one another. Note the stylized barrier of "the river" here. Berlin 1955.

60. Ernst Busch in the role of the professional singer who "directs" a production of *The Caucasian Chalk Circle*. Berlin 1955.

61. Basic scene and costume sketch by Karl von Appen for Brecht's production of *The Caucasian Chalk Circle*. Berlin 1955.

62. The stage realization of von Appen's. scene sketch. Grusche (Angelika Hurwicz) is tempted to rescue the child. Berlin 1955.

63. Grusche with the child wrapped in a blanket speaks with her brother (Erich S. Klein). Berlin 1955.

64. The tired Grusche approaches the rope bridge across the chasm. Berlin 1955.

65. The bridge over the chasm. Berlin 1955.

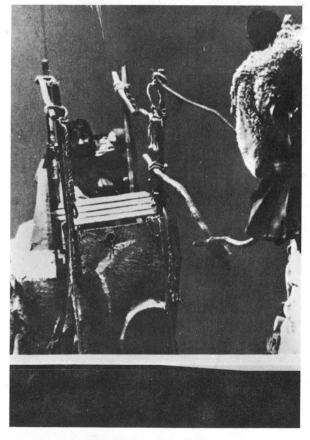

66. Grusche reaches the safe side of the bridge. The soldiers
     reach it just as it collapses into the chasm. Berlin 1955.

67. Azdak (Ernst Busch) chats with the court servant, Shauwa (Harry Gillmann). One of the soldiers who helped install Azdak as judge lowers in the background. Berlin 1955.

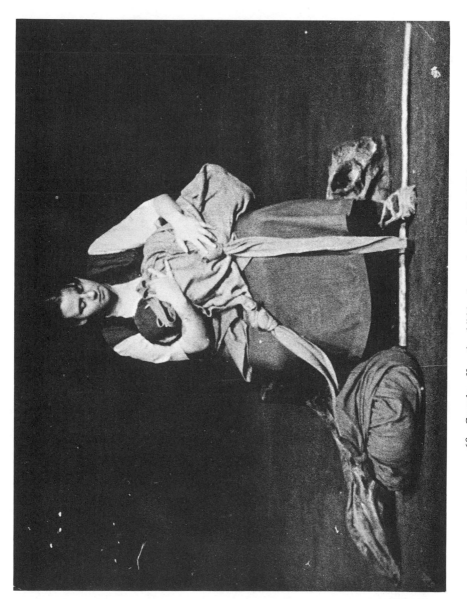

68. Grusche offers the child her barren breast. Berlin 1955.

69. Azdak deliberately antagonizes Grusche in the court scene. Berlin 1955.

71. Josef Kamper in the three-quarter mask of one of the guards, who pursues Grusche in the Northern Mountains. Berlin 1955.

70. Helene Weigel in the half-mask of the governor's wife, the biological mother of Grusche's child. Berlin 1955.

73. Wolf Kaiser in the almost full-face mask of the Fat Prince. Berlin 1955.

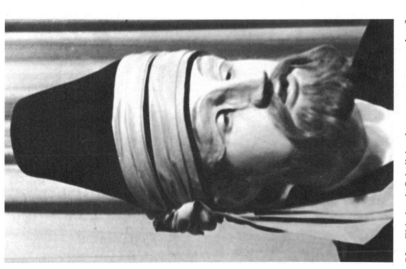

72. Ekkehard Schall in the one-quarter mask of the governor's adjutant. Berlin 1955.

74. The chalk circle test in Brecht's production. Berlin 1955.

75. The chalk circle test in Tyrone Guthrie's production of the play. Minneapolis 1965.

76. The closing "progress" in Brecht's production of *The Caucasian Chalk Circle*. Berlin 1955.

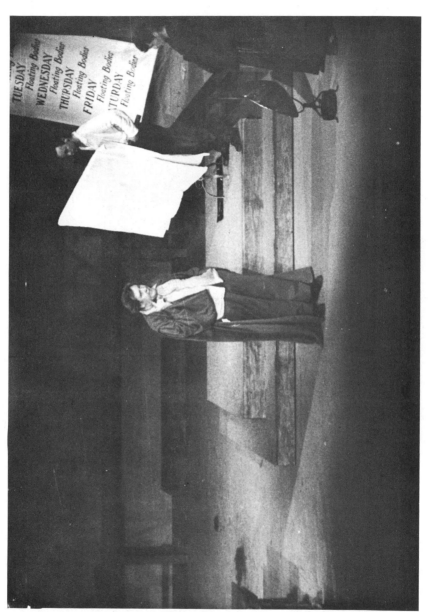

77. Charles Laughton (without beard) as Galileo. Los Angeles 1947.

78. Charles Laughton (with beard) as Galileo. Background projection: the instruments of the Inquisition. New York 1947.

79. Caspar Neher's sketch for the Berliner Ensemble production of Galileo that Brecht was rehearsing at the time of his death. Berlin 1957.

80. Neher's sketch for the showing of the telescope to the Florentine court. Berlin 1957.

81. Neher's sketch for the carnival scene. Berlin 1957.

82. Ernst Busch as Galileo in the opening scene of the play. Berlin 1957.

83. Busch as the almost blind Galileo in the final scene of the Berliner Ensemble version. 1957.

84. Busch as Galileo in the final moment of the play. He asks his daughter, "What kind of night is it?" and receives the answer, "Bright." Berlin 1957.

INDEX

References to illustrations are printed in boldface type.